ALCOHOLISM

Genetic Culpability
or
Social Irresponsibility?

The Challenge of Innovative Methods to Determine Final Outcomes

Ronald Marshall

University Press of America,® Inc.
Lanham · New York · Oxford

4720 Boston Way
Lanham, Maryland 20706

12 Hid's Copse Rd.
Cumnor Hill, Oxford OX2 9JJ

Printed in the United States of America
British Library Cataloging in Publication Information Available

Library of Congress Cataloging-in-Publication Data

ISBN 0-7618-1846-4 (cloth : alk. ppr.)
ISBN 0-7618-1847-2 (paper : alk. ppr.)

™ The paper used in this publication meets the minimum requirements of American National Standard for Information Sciences—Permanence of Paper for Printed Library Materials, ANSI Z39.48—1984

TABLE OF CONTENTS

FOREWORD

Ronald Marshall, Ph.D., of the University of The West Indies, in Trinidad, has taken on the critical issues in alcohol abuse and alcoholism—their etiology, course, prevention, and treatment.

In today's scientific and policy environment, the hope is that a genetic source for and biological solution to alcoholism will be found. But Dr. Marshall, for a number of reasons, is dubious about this likelihood. Although some studies—by Schuckit and Goodwin, among others—have identified a genetic source for the confluence of alcoholism in families, Dr. Marshall points out a number of problems with this conclusion.

For one thing, the alcoholism thought to be genetically transmitted is defined in different ways in different studies. Some researchers claim that alcoholism is genetically transmitted for severely alcoholic individuals, some claim genetic transmission occurs in specific types of alcoholics (e.g., those who are antisocially or criminally predisposed), and some claim that genetic transmission holds for broad populations of problem drinkers. But not all can be correct.

At the same time, as Dr. Marshall notes, a range of other factors have been implicated in both alcohol abuse and alcoholism. These include familial attitudes about alcohol, membership in groups where antisocial behavior is more common, beliefs and attitudes that encourage alcohol abuse, social norms that permit excessive drinking and acting out while drunk, and cultural differences in the patterns of use of alcohol.

Thus, Dr. Marshall faces the essential conflict—if individuals or societies accept that alcohol abuse or alcoholism is genetically caused, then both the society and the individual may simply give in to uncontrolled drunkenness, rather than questioning it. Yet, as Dr. Marshall shows, the evidence does not support the idea that alcoholics lose control of their drinking. Rather their beliefs that alcohol controls their actions determine how they drink, and how they act while drunk.

The genetic causality hypothesis is a major component of the disease model of alcoholism, against which Dr. Marshall also argues. He favors a model of alcoholism that gives a larger role to individual psychological factors, and social and cultural factors. It is in these areas that he seeks solutions to the costly problems of alcohol in modern societies.

Of course, even if there is a genetic strain of alcoholism, this does not account for either the broad range of problem drinkers or of problem drinking. Much of this excessive, binge drinking occurs, for example, among younger drinkers, many of whom do not display alcoholism throughout their lives (and even older persons show the ability to shift their drinking patterns with age). A large proportion of problems also occur for normal drinkers, during occasional outbursts of excessive drinking.

Under any circumstances, the solution for alcoholism, according to the disease theory, is simply for the individual to accept responsibility for his incapacity to regulate his or her drinking and to cease alcohol consumption.

It is for such reasons that Dr. Marshall takes a "responsibility" approach—one that places and accepts responsibility for rectifying problem drinking on people—both on the individual drinker and on society. These levels of dealing with alcohol abuse interact. For example, individual problem drinkers who have more social resources—and where society offers them more resources—stand a better chance to rectify their problems. If, instead of accepting this responsibility, and devoting the resources to the problem needed to make a difference in the occurrence of alcohol problems, societies look towards genetic and biological solutions, Dr. Marshall fears we will experience more, rather than fewer, alcohol problems.

There are good reasons for him to think this. When people believe that alcohol controls their actions, it is more likely to do so. And when society passes responsibility for problems to the individual drinkers' bodies, and washes its hands of a need to take action, alcohol problems are likely to multiply due to government neglect.

Rather, Dr. Marshall calls society to action in facing up to and correcting drinking problems. Societal actions that can have an impact are to teach children realistic views of alcohol, and the need and obligation to control their drinking. Laws that regulate in realistic ways the sale and distribution of alcohol have a strong role to play, although prohibition and overly restrictive regulations have a tendency to backfire. Finally, a cultural outlook that accepts the positive role alcohol has to play, while expecting and demanding that individuals can control their drinking, will show advantages over societies that either ban alcohol, or which view its misuse as an uncontrollable disease.

Stanton Peele, Ph.D., Esq.
Author, Diseasing of America
Morristown, NJ, USA

PREFACE

Writing a book on alcohol consumption became incumbent upon me when I was preparing my dissertation: *Family Composition and Alcohol Consumption: A Study of the Relationship between Different Family Units and Variations in Alcohol Consumption*. What dawned upon me was that the variance on alcohol problems was spread among so many factors that I felt it warranted further enquire on my part.

It is a fact that in the real world, the variance in alcohol consumption has to be shared among many factors, that it is better to adopt a holistic scientific approach to getting a firm grip on the study. In so doing we would be in a stronger position to understand the alcohol problem or even to beat it.

Policy-makers believe that they have to spend a mountain of resources on alcoholism, since they do not know where the true (significant) variance lies. I feel nothing is further from the truth. The fact is that one can undertake specific measures to curb the unnecessary overindulgence in alcohol consumption, by attempting to identify and analyze new variables or old ones that have not been sufficiently operationalized or explored.

The book attempts to debate whether excessive alcohol consumption is a deliberate and voluntary pastime engaged in by persons as a hobby; or serves as a temporary relief from daily problems that have become too heavy a burden; or an uncontrollable substance descending upon unsuspecting at-risk individuals. I think it is the task of the sociologist to put this argument into perspective. I am putting the issue squarely: is it genetic culpability or social irresponsibility, shared at both the individual and governmental levels?

Sociologists are generally interested in group differences. For example, they have attempted to discover why there are differences between women and men in rates of alcoholism, and why the differences vary across cultures. In general, sociologists do not try to explain why a specific individual might become an alcoholic. Instead, they are interested in explaining rates of alcohol consumption between different groups or cultures. However, this study does both: it identifies the irresponsible group from the normal group of drinkers and determines why individuals drink to the point of creating a personal and social problem.

While there are those who will argue that drinking has a symbolic significance, that is, people usually drink to something, and that this practice goes back thousands of years when victors toasted their victories over the vanquished, drinking also takes place in celebration of an achievement—a graduation, a promotion or a wedding.

Where ethnicity is concerned, studies have shown that ethnic groups drink or consume alcohol differently. For example, in a study done by Caetano (1984) Hispanics were found to have the highest rates of drinking, while Blacks were found to have the highest rate of frequent heavy drinking, whereas White males stopped drinking between the ages of twenty and thirty. Predictors of drinking were age, income, education, employment status, marital status, and religious affiliation.

In the early days, particularly during the temperance movement, intoxication was viewed as a disease (Rose and Barrett 1988). But all this has changed; there is a greater concern for the social and economic cost of alcohol consumption. So that the financial cost and the debilitating aspect of alcoholism might be a cause of concern for all. The cost of medical care, insurance premiums and business losses, prosecution and incarceration run into millions worldwide and it is mounting. As a matter of fact, many costs cannot be directly determined (Alcohol Alert 1991, p. 1).

According to Rose and Barrett, the early temperance movement saw that "intoxication was a disease" (1988, p. 130). Yet, according to the authors, those people (followers of the temperance movement) moved away from that position to one of controlling alcohol drinking itself. In this respect deviant behavior was seen not only attached to one small group, but to every one who drank.

This essay intends to scrutinize the findings of most of the scientific studies, sociological as well as non-sociological, to determine which one of the factors is the most relevant in understanding alcoholism or alcohol abuse. This will be done in two parts. First, I will look at the non-sociological, particularly the genetic, following which I will then examine the sociological. After this, the facts and the implications will be laid bare.

I have been able to go through the various arguments attributed to excessive alcohol consumption and arrive at two distinct approaches namely, the genetic approach and the sociological approach, which I think are responsible for the abuse of this substance.

The book is highly methodological and argumentative as it compares various research findings over the years and analyzes them with a view to revealing/ demonstrating their statistical significance and methodological relevance. As such it brings the reader up to date with state of the art information as regards alcoholism or heavy drinking. This is the approach I have used to debate my position on the "social irresponsibility" thesis of alcoholism.

In this respect, the book departs from a purely narrative one as the author seeks to place the majority of excessive alcohol consumption squarely within the sociological framework. The book appearing at this time is significant. There is an increase in alcohol consumption and greater varieties of the substance have become available to certain populations, namely, women, pregnant mothers, adolescents and families.

To date, very few studies have focussed on "irresponsibility" as the main reason for persons becoming alcoholics. Most of the high profile researches have concentrated on the fierce debate and illusive search (to date) for an alcoholic gene, while the plethora of indicators point to the social arena. But the social arena is so wide we might very well be saying that the cause of the disorder called alcoholism is to be found somewhere out there in the vast sea of social interactions—a daunting task for any researcher and one which makes for confusion of sorts.

The issue of social irresponsibility needs to be teased out of social interactions to determine what level or percentage of alcoholics could fall into this category. We suspect a whole lot. It is always interesting to note that the so-called chronic alcoholic or problem drinker knows how and when to drink. Some are never known publicly. Their habit is kept under cover for years. Some alcoholics are professionals; some are students aspiring to excel in their chosen fields. Some are doctors, lawyers, dentists, and top executives.

Certainly, the alcoholic is not the stereotypical person who spends the entire day drinking in a pub; who has nothing to do, no family ties or commitment, and who staggers out of a bar at the end of the day spouting expletives.

Some alcoholics display a keen sense of "responsibility." They belong to mainstream society: conservative, educated, family-oriented, and law-abiding citizens.

Remarkably, these same persons do not know when to remove themselves from a situation which facilitates their drinking and which prevents them from responding to the "stop!" signals; remarkably, these are the same persons who, under sober conditions, are able to analyze a drinking situation and respond positively. Also, it is indeed interesting that, if continued, alcohol consumption threatens an individual's life (heart disease, cirrhosis of the liver, hypertension), most of these alcoholics may respond positively and cease drinking. Why then view alcoholism as a disease? Is it an attempt to medicalize and keep on medicalizing this social problem?

This book is an attempt to answer all these questions, ranging from the disease model to the social irresponsibility model.

It is the contention of the author that irresponsibility on the part of individuals and governments is the prime reason for the high rate of "alcoholism," and that in truth and in fact, there are few alcoholics who are victims of their genetic makeup, or their psychiatric/psychological predisposition.

The challenge which remains however, is to determine the social factor/s carrying the greatest weight, or explaining the highest variance.

Ronald Marshall

CHAPTER 1

Introduction and Background to Alcoholism[1]

Introduction

Prelude to Irresponsible Behavior

The study of alcoholism, or alcohol abuse for that matter, is extremely relevant as a means of understanding, not only patterns of alcohol consumption, but uncovering some of the many issues involved in this phenomenon. For example, the present work can set off interest in other areas explained by the "irresponsibility" thesis and carve out an entirely new approach to understanding "irresponsibility" distinctly from other causal factors.

Alcohol drinking remains one of the most intractable social problems of our time and this has been brought about in part, by the ambivalence we have demonstrated over this drug. In addition, the multicausal nature of alcohol consumption has led to an everlasting challenge, in terms of identifying a substantial or reliable outcome.

Learned Behavior and Irresponsibility

The author will argue that alcoholism is learned behavior and that continued learned maladaptive tendencies may lead to irresponsible behavior. In adopting this position we naturally come up against the disease model. The question is this: if alcoholism is not a disease, then what is it? Is it a social malaise mimicking the behavioral patterns of a disease? Still, not all those who drink heavily have a disease. Again, even if one drinks heavily and consistently to develop an alcohol problem, I know of no one who would voluntarily go out of his way to fall victim to a disease.

> One of the main lines of evidence responsible for undermining disease conceptions of alcoholism is the repeated finding that individuals who have been diagnosed as suffering from this disease have been able to return to drinking in a normal, controlled fashion (Bruno et al. 1998, p. 109).

The authors went on to point out that the "loss of control" thesis, where the alcoholic drinks himself into oblivion, remains questionable: controlled laboratory studies have shown that, since the 1960s, severely dependent individuals are able to maintain considerable control of their drinking, including the amount drank, the time drunk, and the length of drinking sessions (p. 111).

The Elusive Alcohol Gene

As far as the genetic factor is concerned, Bruno et al. raised the issue of the elusive alcohol gene. They argued that "the genetic factor has never been substantiated as a primary cause of excessive drinking..."

> Certain behaviors do tend to "run in families", but this does not prove a genetic link—poor manners can run in families too. It is likely that hereditary factors can increase one's susceptibility to developing alcohol problems, but many of the "susceptible" don't become "alcoholics", and some of the unsusceptible do" (Bruno et al. 1998, p. 112).

According to the authors, behavior is one thing, disease is another, suggesting that there is a clear distinction between the two of them and that they should not be confused. They argued further that heavy drinking remains risk behavior; not a disease. This is an interesting point and is further explored in subsequent chapters in varying degrees.

The Disease Model and Increased Drinking

I will argue that the disease model, far from contributing to reduced levels of alcoholism, has contributed to the opposite—increased levels of alcohol consumption. Further, governments have been fed the illusion of the disease model by scientists and some physicians and that the Alcoholics Anonymous (AA) uses fundamental social and psychological principles to get its members to remain sober. Still, they do not advise "members ... to throw away pills" (Rychtarik et al. 2000, p.134). Again, the disease model does not explain the large number of alcoholics whose parents do not drink. But more relevant is the argument that the model has contributed to high levels of irresponsible drinking.

It is the "irresponsibility" thesis comprising a constellation of demographic, social, situational, and behavioral factors, which contributes to high levels of drinking. Such factors include race, class, ethnicity, age, group influence, depression, anxiety, and the like. At any one point in time it is these factors acting alone, but most times together, which push normal individuals who are usually in control of their natural faculties, to drink excessively.

The Disease Model versus Social Irresponsibility

Alcoholics who live under the disease model use it as a cover from social opprobrium and as an excuse to continue drinking, disguising their condition as "helpless."

"Social irresponsibility" extends to teenagers, just as adults, although they (teenagers) may be under more intense pressure to imbibe, and consequently, vary much more in terms of their drinking patterns than, their adult counterparts.

Social Self as Predictor

Alcohol by its intoxicant nature has great appeal to the young, middle-aged and old. Even those who do not drink are impressed by its magnificence of presentation and what it has come to symbolize. It is a form of companionship for the lonely and those engaged in leisure time activities. This can run the gamut from very lonely, to sometimes-lonely, to not-so-lonely, to feeling-lonely. It's a matter of how one interprets situations which act as predictors of alcohol use.

At once we realize that the presence of alcohol may not really be the problem, but what it has come to mean to different people and how these people behave in accordance with that perception.

Alcohol will remain one of the greatest (most dangerous) drugs of all times with societies having a history of ambivalence towards it. It is not simply a matter of putting alcohol in a corner or banning it, for that matter. It is how we exercise control over our behavior. It is a popular view that it is better for society to deal with alcohol problems than with hard drugs. However, hard drugs do not have "presentation" and "social acceptance" as alcohol does. Hard drugs do not have the "legitimacy" that alcohol does, and hard drugs are not caught between interest groups—"right and wrong," "individual rights" and "democracy." In addition, alcohol policies aimed at control, for example the sale of alcohol to minors, have remained "unenforced" at best. This tells us something about alcohol. It is not an ordinary drug. Its presence evokes ambivalence, excitement and expectations even indifference.

The Question of "Responsible" and "Irresponsible Behavior"

There are penalties in some countries for drunk driving and selling alcohol to minors but enforcement is not a serious issue in some countries.

The vast majority of people feel that whenever "accidents" happen it is due to someone who could not hold his/her liquor. In short, these persons knew that they could not drink (no doubt, from past experience) and therefore failed to take the necessary precaution. These individuals failed "to live up to their responsibilities" and therefore forfeited the "gains" of imbibing. This is a theme which will be occurring throughout this book: the issue of social "irresponsibility." Responsibility is a concept which has remained partially hidden in the alcohol literature. But increasingly we will have to appeal to people's sense of responsibility for their own health and the health and well being of others.

The unspoken position is drink, get high, but be "responsible." The problem is one of temptation, perception and risks. Risk behavior is increasing. What alternative routes do we have at our disposal for achieving the same feeling derived from the consumption of alcohol? This is what the individual will have to determine for himself/herself in the future.

Alcohol and Modern Society

It might very well be that modern-day society, unlike its counterpart in the past, increasingly has to contend with alienation, loss of self-esteem, lack of confidence and the want of a temporary escape. Under these circumstances, we become wary and may need to find consolation through drinking. In light of this, an international effort should be made to alter the alcohol content of alcoholic beverages. In the first instance, this would be the responsibility of governments as they attempt to alter the social and physical situation and in the second, the responsibility of individuals to take a cue from this development and *act responsibly* towards themselves and others. In this social responsibility thesis I will argue, and at the same time demonstrate, that alcoholism or alcohol abuse gets its cue from society's toleration and symbols, and that many of us have been socialized to accept that it is alright to alter one's mood and thus alter one's reality, or rather one's perception of reality. Since whatever we regard to be real is real in its consequences, it is to be noted that alcohol, which can change mood, cannot only change outlook, but can also change physiological coordination. It has an effect on both mind and body at the same time. We have also grown to understand that when a habitual drinker cannot hold his liquor, he is considered less of a man and therefore "irresponsible." We tend to look down on a man who cannot hold his liquor and maintain his composure. It's like saying it's alright to steal but do not reveal any tell-tale signs: make a clean scene.

From Temperance to Prohibition to Alcoholics Anonymous (AA) there has been an interplay of public concern and individual responsibility over the use of alcohol. This interplay has not let up. In large measure, it has grown to one of societal consensus using legislative, informative and persuasive means via conferences, the print and electronic media. The fight to control the debilitating effects of alcohol abuse has taken up steam time and time again and this may be due to the effects of governments' policies or to the nature of the drug itself. It is the only mind-altering substance for which you need not have a prescription, and some health care officials merely advise: "when taking medication do not drink."

Alcohol—A Free Radical

By and large, alcohol remains a free radical in society, inflicting damage on the young, the old, the unsuspecting, as well as those who know better. It is viewed simultaneously as a "good thing" and as a "bad thing." It is caught up in situational and perception factors. Those who go to parties expect to see alcohol in different varieties and strengths, including the all-too-present beer. In a study conducted by Rogers and Greenfield (1999) it was reported that beer was the only alcoholic beverage to predict harm to one's health, social relations, and to create dependence. Yet beers may be seen as the least dangerous of alcoholic drinks. At parties, the feeling is that a drink adds to the camaraderie and free talk; relieving inhibitions and drawing people closer together, making them "more sociable."

It is widely held that those who see alcohol as a bad thing, probably have had a bad experience with it, know someone who has had a bad experience with it, or simply are intolerant of its effects. These individuals are in the minority. The vast majority of persons, including the "occasional drinkers," imbibe carelessly.

Targeting the Non-Drinkers

It is suspected that non-drinkers are the ones on whom we must focus; those who consider that they have mastery over their drinking, but gradually developed a tolerance for the drug, sometimes without knowing that it places them into a new classification called "problem drinkers," and they eventually filter into other categories called "alcohol abusers" or "alcoholics." The vast majority of alcoholics are but a small fraction of people who cause alcohol-related problems among the population of alcohol drinkers. There are those who create problems but remain in their classification and there are those who change classifications ever so often; the point to consider is that these individuals unknowingly, by their drinking, slip through categories. Some people labeled "alcoholics" stop suddenly, for no apparent reason. Others, when they start drinking cannot stop. Other peoples' progression can be anticipated by the intensity of their drink, that is, from beer to wine to whiskey to gin.

Alcoholism—A Family Disease

Genetically, it has been proven, notwithstanding methodological concerns, that some forms of alcoholism can be attributed to inheritance. However, the real concern is "how it is transmitted." Some argue the fact that transmission is not clear should not cast doubt on the genetic argument. Others argue that the "environmental trigger" explains a vast number of alcoholic siblings who may eventually become alcoholic.

My position is that if the necessary steps are taken, we can make a significant impact on understanding alcoholism and the question of "loss of control" will be thrown out the window. To my mind, "loss of control" is a term which has come to mean different things to different people. To many people, "loss of control" means that the individual shows outward indication that he/she is affected by alcohol in terms of speech, utterances, thinking, physical coordination, drowsiness and/or any behavior considered anti-social. Yet, "loss of control" has another meaning, depending on where the drinking takes place and who is making the assessment. In a pub where drinking is heavy, those who are considered "out of control" are not so deemed by their friends, who forbid them to leave, even if they have had enough. These individuals would lose face if they left. Others "lose control," but can carry on "normally" until they reach their final destination—home. This may even entail driving under the influence of alcohol.

Ambivalence in Meanings

This ambivalence, in the "loss of control" approach, where individuals take matters into their own hands and sometimes pass "the alcoholic test," and sometimes not, militates against effective measures adopted by authorities, and may contribute to a reluctance on the part of many to enforce laws regarding drinking.

The vast body of research points to alcoholism as having many variants, but within these researches, we find that there is not only a "control" factor but a "personal responsibility" factor as well. For example, what prevents an alcoholic from making judgments prior to drinking, where once he starts, he cannot stop? Is it that his thinking processes are impaired even before he starts to drink? What preoccupation he has, if any at all? Let us suppose that when he is not drinking, he is a normal, balanced, thinking person and he has no negative preoccupation: he thinks of his wife, his children and his job, his successes, his joys and he is overly enthusiastic. We wonder whether he will start to drink, knowing from past experiences what the results will be? If he drinks in spite of those feelings, then he is totally affected not only by the alcohol, but he is tied to the habit conceptually and drinking merely reinforces the habit, making it more difficult for him to operate effectively during the non-drinking periods. It also raises the question that the alcohol habit can override any previously held socially gratifying habits or experiences. In addition, it has implications for the vast majority of problem-drinkers who might be on their way to becoming alcoholics by acquiring a habit similar, though not in intensity, to the alcoholic. And this certainly widens the net and reinforces the argument that the vast majority of alcoholics are not normally distributed throughout the population. This argument can hold for those who are genetically driven, but certainly not for those who are socially driven, or who acquire their drinking habit by social and cultural means. The effects and the demonstration of their habit go a long way in influencing special populations, particularly teenagers into drinking. Perhaps it might be a good opportunity to point out the various classification of drinkers:

Frequent heavy drinkers:	Drinks five or more drinks at a sitting, once a week or more often[2]
Frequent high maximum:	Drinks once a week or more often and drinks five or more drinks at a sitting occasionally (at least once a year)
Frequent low maximum:	Drinks once a week or more often but never drinks as many as five drinks at a sitting
Infrequent:	Drinks less than once a week but at least once a month; may or may not drink five drinks at a sitting
Occasional:	Drinks less often than once a month
Abstainer:	Has not drunk alcoholic beverages in the last six months

Adapted from R. Caetano's, Ethnicity and Drinking in Northern California – A Comparison among Whites, Blacks and Hispanics 1984, p. 33.

The author informs us that this index was built on "the information on quantity and frequency of drinking wine, beer and spirits..." (p. 33). Some researchers, on the other hand, basically identify three types of drinkers: social drinker, problem drinker and alcoholic:

Social drinker	-	drinks when the occasion warrants it
Problem drinker	-	drinks until he becomes intoxicated
Alcoholic	-	drinks till it interferes with the everyday functioning of his roles.

Genetic Culpability and Social Irresponsibility

Social irresponsibility means when governments have the resources to do better, but fail to act; when governments lack the political will but are instead influenced by status groups and economic interests in formulating alcohol policies.

Social irresponsibility also means when governments do not carry out research to establish the relationship between alcohol consumption and poor educational performance or attainment, motor vehicle accidents, liver diseases, poor productivity levels, spousal abuse, murders/suicides, family deterioration and discrimination.

Social irresponsibility can be a charge, against the developed as well as the developing countries, whether a country is full of resources or whether there is a paucity of it. It simply comes down to controlling alcohol use through policy and decision making by those charged with the responsibility of developing a healthy society.

It is difficult to measure which governments, unlike people, are more "irresponsible" than others. What we do know is that enough is not being done as evidenced by those socially incapacitated by alcohol—those who swell the ranks of the dysfunctional on a daily basis and are cast on the sidewalks of life's chances.

However, at a quick glance we can note which country has a problem with alcoholism, yet fails to pass adequate legislation, passes inadequate legislation, or is yet to pass legislation. But it is not a simple matter to measure "irresponsibility" on a country by country basis. One has to uncover a plethora of factors that militate against the best legislative efforts, not to mention a miasma of unresponsiveness both from the general (drinking) public and those who do not want to willingly give information, or reluctantly do so. This has implications for severely compromising any study whose aim is to curb alcoholism through legislative means. Still, some countries have been identified as "drinking countries."

Ensuring that Alcoholism Remains in Society

So long as alcohol remains a free agent in society, readily available to anyone brave enough to embrace it, particularly in altered personal and social circumstances, we will have moved one step closer to ensuring that alcoholism remains one of the most devastating drugs the world has known, in spite of arguments to the contrary.

Summary

Alcohol abuse continues to be a leading cause of concern in the world as a silent and devastating drug affecting many populations, sometimes under altered circumstances, but mostly under unaltered situations.

The issue of learned behavior as a precursor to irresponsible drinking remains a debatable one in the alcohol literature. Yet, it is an ever-present argument that people may drink but not "lose control."

As a result, societies may remain silent on their drinking habits, or may even encourage it, yet become vocal when the implications of drinking are mirrored in negative outcomes involving family disputes, vehicular accidents and direct infraction of the law.

It is argued that heavy drinking by itself is not caused by a disease since many alcoholics deemed "diseased" have returned to normal drinking, if we mean by disease, "once an alcoholic, always an alcoholic." This suggests that to become an alcoholic one certainly has to drink, but other factors, including a sufficiently high degree of irresponsibility, ensure that an abuser continues in his or her ways.

It is further argued that the disease model and the impression it conveys to the man in the street is that the alcoholic needs professional help. Here is an individual who cannot help himself but is wreaking havoc on society and destroying it in the process.

Yet, there is no attempt on the part of the alcoholic, that is, through his/her own volition to seek treatment, nor do the authorities call for mandatory detoxification of these alcoholics in most cases. In either case, alcoholics remain at large in the society and they use this "freedom" because of the level of social irresponsibility which pervades modern society, as far as drinking is concerned.

When "social irresponsibility" is shifted to individuals instead of society, we do not recognize that some individuals can bring themselves to become "responsible." When the authorities adopt a wait-and-see attitude, they abandon not only the irresponsible drinker (who needs their assistance) but also those whom he is influencing, namely adolescents and younger adults.

"Responsible" and "irresponsible" behaviors may be subjective concepts. However, "responsibility" and "irresponsibility" are two sides of the same coin and we recognize that what might be considered "responsible" in one setting may be viewed as "irresponsible" in another. Nonetheless, we must recognize that "responsibility" can be measured objectively, that is, by societal and individual standards of behavior.

We are also cognizant of the possibility that once we divide alcohol abuse into "responsible" and "irresponsible" groups, we may be supporting a certain level of drinking, once it is done responsibly. This is exactly what we want to do since there could be no total ban on alcohol consumption.

Once we translate the association between "irresponsibility" and "disease" to one of individual, societal and governmental "irresponsibility," alcohol abusers may think twice before engaging in alcohol consumption. Special attention should be paid to non-drinkers and problem drinkers. These are the individuals we would need to target to prevent them slipping into the "alcoholic" category. A number of categories of alcohol consumption have been identified. They are: frequent heavy drinkers; frequent high maximum; frequent low maximum; infrequent; occasional; and abstainer, or social drinker; problem drinker; and alcoholic.

Genetically, those who argue that alcohol is a disease have not shown how it is transmitted. What is it that is transmitted? No one has come up with a credible answer. One compromise is what is called the "environmental trigger" leading to genetic predisposition.

These, and other questions, must be answered by scientists before there could be any resolve to seriously tackle the alcohol problem. And it is our ambivalence in dealing with alcoholism, which compromises at times the behavior of alcoholics to take cover under the disease model. It is a behavior, which invokes sympathy and "understanding" from an otherwise unsuspecting and tolerant public.

---

[1] The term alcoholism here is used interchangeably with alcohol consumption and alcohol dependency. According to the World Health Organization (WHO 1982): "a scientific definition cannot be fixed for all time but will be influenced by the state of our knowledge and particularly advances in research technology". British Journal of Addiction 77, p. 5.

[2] A drink means 1 oz of spirits, a 4oz glass of wine or a 12 oz can of beer, each of which contains approximately 9 g of absolute alcohol.

CHAPTER 2

Alcohol Studies: The Genetic Argument

Introduction

What is an Alcoholic?

> An alcoholic is a very sick person, victim of an insidious, progressive disease, which all too often ends fatally. An alcoholic can be recognized, diagnosed, and treated successfully. An alcoholic cannot be cured of his disease so that he can drink normally again. But his illness can be arrested so successfully that he can lead a perfectly normal and happy life without drinking. All of this can take place provided he is recognized as an alcoholic, and brought to recognize this fact himself. And, as in any other illness, the sooner alcoholism is recognized and treated, the better for everyone concerned (Mannis 1958, p. 17).

The above quote, like so many others, sets the stage for the contestation of alcoholism as a disease. No other social disorder has commanded so much attention over so long a period of time as alcoholism. Since the 1940s it has remained one of those problems, if not the only problem, which have continued to defy scientists in understanding the full etiology of its existence. At any one time, it is considered a disease, a social disorder, a psychological problem, a cultural entity, even an economic good (Walsh 1990).

Alcoholics Anonymous Membership Objectives

The repeal of Prohibition in 1933 had set the stage for the modern "disease theory" of alcoholism aided and abetted by Alcoholics Anonymous (AA), but as will be shown later, AA was not too concerned about getting rid of alcoholism. It was preoccupied with keeping its members on a tight rein of membership and commitment to its rules and regulations surrounding abstinence, notwithstanding ethnic differences in the reported reasons for the services of Alcoholics Anonymous (Kaskutas et al. 1999).

Genetic Studies

A number of scientific studies have been etched in the minds of the general population concerning the issue of a genetic connection to alcoholism. The results of these studies while revealing and very important in furthering our understanding of alcoholism, must be detailed if we are to fully understand the meanings and the implications of this "disease." We note that once something has made an impact, people tend to run with it, reconceptualize it, distort it, and sometimes even over-generalize its specificity.

Goodwin (1990) summarizes the phases or developments which have taken place in the genetic camp. He recalls that the first of these studies took place with "55 Danish males who had a biological parent with a hospital diagnosis of alcoholism and who had been adopted during the first few weeks of life by non-relatives." These offspring were compared with controls who were subsequently interviewed by a psychiatrist for any related symptoms that would have predisposed them to alcoholism.

Goodwin noted that 10 out of the 55 sons of alcoholics turned out to be alcoholics, while only 4 out of the 78 controls were alcoholics. However, there were no differences found for heavy drinking between the experimental group (sons of alcoholics), and the control group (sons of non-alcoholics). Goodwin concluded that sons reared apart from their biological parents would still become alcoholics, although having an alcoholic parent did not increase their risk of having psychiatric disorders.

Two observations must be made from the above; firstly, that both males of alcoholic parents and males of non-alcoholic parents were equally likely to be heavy drinkers, and secondly, both were likely to have depressions, drug abuse and sociopathy as reported by the study.

Epidemiological Importance

Epidemiologically speaking, the question remains, what is the likelihood of the control group (which shares equal predisposition with the experimental group in heavy drinking and sociopathic behaviors) to develop alcoholism, particularly when it is intertwined with environmental factors or left to develop by itself (presumably without genetic factors)?

The second phase of the genetic claim was put to the test when the brothers of the sons of alcoholics were scientifically tested to see how they stood up to "the disease," alcoholism. According to Goodwin, "The 30 sons raised by their alcoholic biological parents also had a high rate of alcoholism" when compared with non-adopted men who were raised by non-alcoholic parents. Clearly, this experiment was to determine whether alcoholism is an inherited trait. According to the report, there "was no greater...[difference]...than was the rate observed in their brothers..." The study questioned the belief that alcoholism really emanated from children with alcoholic fathers since alcoholism appeared in both children raised by alcoholic parents and non-alcoholic parents. It also challenged the view that alcoholism was inherited. In short, "exposure to the alcoholic parent did not appear to augment this increased susceptibility" (p. 39).

Finally, a comparison was made between alcoholics and non-alcoholics who came from broken homes. It was found that "62 per cent of the alcoholics had an alcoholic biological parent compared with 20 per cent of the non-alcoholics..." (p. 42) but this development took place irrespective of social contact with the alcoholic parent.

The Genetically Protected, the Genetically Unprotected

However, before we claim any sort of victory over the genetic argument we must listen to Goodwin (1990). He argues that genetic factors can operate in two ways, namely by those who are "protected" and those who are "unprotected." In the first instance, we must know which persons have "aversive physiological and subjective reactions...even in small quantities." In the second instance, the unprotected individuals experience "varying degrees of positive reinforcement from the substance followed quickly by aversive effects...." When this happens, the individual has to take the drug/substance once more in order to relieve the aversive effects which were produced by the same substance in the first instance (Goodwin 1990).

Environmental Factors

While conceding that environmental factors play a part, Goodwin (1990) however plays down the strength of it:

> The agent obviously must be available, and this does not necessarily mean that it is the agent being legal and commercially available. Prices, legal ages of buyers, prevailing attitudes toward the substance, and a multitude of other social and cultural factors influence the use of the agent. There is no question but that availability, in the broadest sense, influences use (Goodwin 1990, p. 48).

Biological Association/Genetic Transmission

It would appear, therefore, that the real problem with understanding the alcohol problem or alcoholism for that matter is not biological association but its transmission. For example, that which is transmitted from father to son. Presumably, how do hereditary genes cross over from one generation to the next?

> The interesting familial aggregation of alcoholism does not, of course, necessarily imply that any genetic mechanism is operating. Theories implicating the adverse effects of certain family practices and attitudes to alcohol could equally well explain such findings. Furthermore, because the genetic predisposition of alcoholism is likely to arise from the effects of many genes (polygenetic inheritance) it would be expected that the incidence of alcoholism in second degree relatives of alcoholics would be lower than in first degree relatives. In fact, the incidence of alcoholism in second degree relatives is higher than would be expected on the basis of strong polygenic predisposition.... This fact implies that familial and environmental pressures are probably operating to increase the amount of alcoholism in second degree relatives.... In addition, the high incidence in second degree relatives can also be partly explained by assertive mating for alcoholism and there is evidence that this occurs, for example Bleuler (1955) found that 29 per cent of alcoholic men had spouses who were also alcoholics (Gurling and Murray 1984, pp. 128-129).

Again, Roe (1944) has observed "that children of alcoholics can be taken out of harm's way if they are brought up away from their parents" and this takes place, even when alcoholism appears to develop more frequently in children of alcoholics. "This has added to the belief that alcoholism is related more to environment than to genetic factors" (National Institute of Mental Health 1969, p. 24).

But this will not put the genetic argument to rest, an argument which will be used by both academics and alcoholics to further their own ends. The geneticists will argue that familial alcoholism is caused by fathers or parents being alcoholic, but "theories implicating the adverse effects of certain family practices and attitudes to alcohol could equally explain such findings" (Myers 1984, p. 128).

The Challenge to the Disease Theory

According to Peele (1985), the disease theory can be challenged by social science on the following grounds: (1) laboratory studies have shown that "alcoholics'" patterns of drinking do not conform to the loss-of-control model" (Marlatt et al. 1973), (2) clinical research has demonstrated that efficacy of techniques were capable of moderating problem-drinking, (3) longitudinal studies have demonstrated that outcomes can be treated successfully, and (4) the demonstration that a principal component in alcoholism was the social and belief systems, as demonstrated by various ethnic and cultural studies.

Genetic and Social

The interest in a genetic link to alcohol consumption is not new. As far back as 1860 there was some notion and interest that it was a degenerative disease (Brynum 1984). Whatever the causes of the problem, the phenomenon can be narrowed down to two competing models, namely, the genetic and the social, or, put another way, nature versus nurture. The debate has raged on, driven in great measure by the plethora of empirical research undertaken in the past five decades. The findings from these studies have set up wittingly or unwittingly, a race to determine final outcomes.

In the early to mid-twentieth century, the disease concept held sway, but this approach was never able to convincingly prove that alcoholism, or dependent alcohol consumption, was genetic in its origin. Further, it begged the question that, if alcohol dependence has some of its variance explained by genetic predisposition, controlling for genetics would explain a significant portion of "alcoholism." This it has failed to do. This leaves us with the social/socio-cultural aspects to determine that a greater portion of alcohol consumption has its origin in behavioral relatedness.

Landmark Studies on Alcohol

Numerous genetic studies and hypotheses have been undertaken and discussed. Some of the more important ones include: Hilgard and Newman (1963); Goodwin (1971); Goodwin et al. (1974); Keller (1976); Kaij and Dock (1975); Bohman (1978); Schuckit et al. (1972, 1980, 1982, 1983, 1984, 1985, 1994); Schuckit et al. (1995, 1996, 1997); Cadoret et al. (1980); Crowe (1985); Hesselbrock et al. (1985); Peele (1986); Clair and Genest (1987).

It is to some aspects of the above studies that we will now turn and the arguments that researchers put forward in support of their findings. However, it should be pointed out that family studies of alcoholism "consistently emphasize its high prevalence among the relatives of alcoholics" (Cotton 1979). This position is supported by Wolfgang (1997) who notes that researchers have identified "the basic environmental and genetic components" which are responsible for the risk of alcohol use and abuse. According to Wolfgang, research has shown that genetic factors contribute substantially to vulnerability for the disease. Schuckit also leans towards this position.

> There is no one single cause of alcoholism. However, if this disorder is carefully defined and if those individuals with other major pre-existing psychiatric disorders (i.e., secondary alcoholics) are excluded, the remaining primary alcoholics appear to have a genetically influenced disease...(Schuckit 1982, p. 791).

The investigator went on to point out that there is a lack of concordance for alcoholism between identical twins which questions the suitability/relevance of the genetic model to fully explain alcoholism. For the purpose of comprehensiveness, we point to a description of alcoholism by Hanlon and Pickett (1984):

> [A]lcoholism may be defined as an acquired chronic progressive [disorder] involving the compulsive intake of excessive amounts of alcohol and leading, in its more advanced stages, to certain psychological, social, and physical determination sequelae. It affects predominantly men to the ratio of 3 or more to 1, ...[It] is particularly common in certain occupations...it is significantly greater in urban areas and is more frequently found in certain nationalities, especially Scandinavian, Nordic, Celtic, and Polish, in contrast to its infrequency among Italians, Czechoslovakians, and Jews (p. 461).

Heredity Studies Classification

According to Goodwin (1971) hereditary studies in alcoholism can be grouped into five (5) areas, namely, family studies, twin studies, adoptive studies, genetic marker studies, and "self selection" animal studies, that is, where animals are placed under experimental conditions and are likely to make free choices between water and alcohol solutions (p. 545).

He states:

> Without known exception every family study of alcoholism, irrespective of country of origin has shown much higher rates of alcoholism among relatives of alcoholics that apparently occurs in the general population (p. 345).

In the above article, Goodwin (1971) argues that "after a century of studies and speculation" the mode of familial transmission is unknown. However, he does believe that genetic predisposition cannot be ruled out simply because a genetic factor cannot be located and concedes that there might exist an environmental "trigger."

In 1972, Schuckit, Goodwin and Winokur examined the incidence of alcoholism in children raised by non-alcoholic parent figures, but who actually belonged to alcoholic parents. Those were compared to children with and without biological parents. The findings "supported" the genetic model, that is, alcoholism appeared to develop more readily with the genetic factor than environmental ones.

The researchers reported that "alcoholism was seen fairly frequently in most relatives but most often in the male relatives" (p. 124).

> [T]he alcoholism rates for half siblings[1] were consistently higher when their childhood environments were not shared with probands. The difference was not significant, however, and further suggests that different genotypes, i.e., full siblings versus half siblings who shared the same childhood environment, developed

alcoholism along the lines of their genetic load rather than of their shared environment (Schuckit, Goodwin, and Winokur 1972, p. 124).

The researchers noted that the only consistent predictor of alcoholism in half siblings was the presence of an alcoholic parent. They entertained the possibility that in some subtle way a non-alcoholic biological parent influences the alcoholic outcome in children raised by neither of the biological parent.

Opposing Viewpoints

While these studies have convincing statistical significance, there are opposing viewpoints (Fingarette 1988; Keller 1976).

According to Keller:

> Some people feel that they cannot be sure alcoholism is a disease so long as what causes it remains uncertain (1976, p. 1708).

The author went on to reveal that social scientists want to find out how people who drink heavily for one reason or another and then stop suddenly, the same way they started, should be classified. Do all of them have the "disease" called alcoholism? Keller (1976, p. 1709) suggests that we speak in terms of "types and degrees of drinking behaviors and consequences." It is for the same reason that

Goodwin posed the question: "...why should a binge drinker start drinking again after experiencing horrendous effects from previous binges?" (1990, p. 45), and Schuckit talks about the possibility of "an enhanced risk for future alcoholism in young men with alcoholic relatives" (Schuckit 1982).

However, one should take note that environmental studies have been of great concern to the proponents of the genetic theory. Schuckit (1985, p. 31) noted that when biological factors were controlled, alcohol consumption did not increase, thus justifying the need for the continued search for the alcohol gene. It should be remembered also that although alcoholism may be "a family disorder," family does not mean that genetic factors are at work. If this were the case why would there be the high likelihood of polygenetic inheritance in second degree relatives of alcoholics? Some theorists believe this development can take place by personality factors or a psychiatric illness, holding the possibility of hereditary and environmental interaction.

Family Studies of Alcoholism

Therefore, for the benefit of the reading public, it is noteworthy that family studies fall under a number of headings: (1) family studies, that is, family values on alcohol transmitted to children and other members of the family, (2) twin studies, (3) adoption studies, and (4) genetic marker studies. To date, adoption studies are "the most productive method for distinguishing nature from nurture in man..." (Goodwin 1971 p. 545).

Questions Raised on Genetic Studies

In order to put the genetic argument into perspective I will examine the opinions of some of the experts in the field. Fillmore (1988) raises some issues with three adoption studies, conducted by Goodwin (1979), Bohman (1978) and Cadoret and Gath (1978). He recalls that in the study by Goodwin (1979) there were a number of problems. Firstly, "the sex of the biological parent with alcoholism was not always stated" and secondly, there was the problem of control. Two control groups were combined (when they should not have been); it was discovered that one of the men had biological parents who had been hospitalized for psychiatric problems. Again, "the most serious criticism had to do with the measurement criteria for alcoholism." This criteria included infrequent drinking, parental disapproval of drinking and a single traffic arrest for drinking (Fillmore 1988, p. 73).

> These criteria do not appear very strict but nevertheless produce a curious anomaly. If the cut-off point for abnormality is widened to include not just alcoholism but also problem drinking, then evidence for any genetic predisposition vanishes... (Murray et al. 1983, p. 42. Cited in Fillmore 1988, p. 74).

The study by Bohman et al. (1978) was criticized on the grounds that males selected from Temperance Boards "were more likely to be psychopathic than alcohol abusers known in the general population who had come to the Board's attention." Again, the methodological concerns cast doubt on the validity of this study. The third investigation, that of Cadoret and Gath was conducted on children who were placed for adoption in the state of Iowa between 1938 and 1962. Alcohol problems were assessed "by interviews with adoptive parents" and partly through a telephone interview "with the adoptees themselves." Fillmore (1988) argues that although there were obvious relationships existing between alcoholism and biological parents, he had some concerns with a number of noted irregularities, namely, diagnosis of alcoholism, sample loss, use of parents' interviews to diagnose alcoholism, among others.

The above were landmark studies in the genetic thrust, but there have been others like Butts and Chotlos (1973), El-Guebaly and Offord (1977) and Maes et al. (1999).

Research has also shown that children of alcoholic fathers were more likely to become alcoholics themselves, although it was felt that they had little will power or weak personalities.

But as the alcohol debate moves into another phase, it is interesting to note the findings of one study (Schuckit 1983) that when additional data from resource persons testing for alcoholism were analyzed the number of non-alcoholics dropped from 56 percent to 41 percent. When information from resource persons was omitted the number of those identified as alcoholics increased.

> It is possible that for some subjects the serious alcohol-related pathology coincided with pre-existing affective disorders (e.g., some of the subjects might have had primary affective disorder with secondary alcoholism). It is also possible that these subjects were studied years after the onset of severe and pervasive antisocial problems... (Schuckit 1983, p. 439).

Sample Selection, Methodological Concerns

According to Schuckit (1983) the problem might lie in the sample selection. He questions why approximately "one-half to two-thirds of alcoholics relate no family history" of alcoholism (p. 439).

Notwithstanding the above concerns on alcoholism, there is still the notion that if we "medicalize" a potentially devastating social problem, which seemingly has no cure, then at least we can treat it with "magic bullets." Thus, there are obvious limitations to the disease model. Another problem appears to be that there has been no 'genetic mechanism' to take into consideration the accumulation of alcohol data (Peele 1986, p. 63).

Fillmore (1988, pp. 71-72) observes:

> There are similarities between the science postulating hereditary links in alcoholism at the turn of the century and today. In neither time did a "critical experiment" emerge to demonstrate beyond a shadow of a doubt that a biological basis for alcoholism exists; in both periods, the existing data on the matter was assumed to prove the thesis. In contemporary times, three "adoptee" studies (and, to a lesser degree, twin studies and half- sibling studies) have laid the groundwork for an explosion of U.S. studies seeking to locate the "biological marker or markers" which will hypothetically point to this genetic factor.

Thus, it would not be without foundation to lay claim that the variance on alcohol consumption may not increase within the coming years or decades of scientific research, even if a biological marker were to be found.

Alcoholism and the Medical Profession

Genetically speaking, it has been argued that the medical profession has a stake in treating people for alcohol consumption as if it were a disease arising from some physical causal agent(s). However, the medical profession has achieved its results from severe cases of alcohol abuse (detoxification) and relapse. Their best efforts have produced minimal results. Alcohol consumption remains a troublesome issue for the medical profession. Admittedly, there are a lot of variables like family, order of children in the home, peer pressure, and the socio-economic cultural position which impact on alcohol abuse.

If one were to control for hereditary factors globally, one would find that the variance for alcohol abuse still remains extremely high, as opposed to if one had to control for all the socio-economic and cultural factors. One may find that the variance would drop significantly, indicating that more weight is attached to social factors, than the genetic or medical one, as indicated earlier. Clearly then, the more possible and practical option must be to scrutinize the social factors.

The disease model, whose underlying concept is that alcoholism is a disease over which the individual has no control, allows the alcohol industry worldwide to rake in billions of dollars in profits without assuming social responsibility for its effects. As long as the concept of alcohol as a disease remains both in the minds of caregivers and the general public, then it provides a breeding ground for the individual to continue to drink and for the alcohol industry to sell. They both need each other, but they are both engaged in irresponsible behavior.

Genetically-Driven Model Overplayed?

There is no doubt in my mind that the biological/medical approach to alcohol has some salience brought about by respectable research which identifies a causal relationship between hereditary factors and alcohol consumption. There are also those who support the model based on the need to treat alcohol consumption as a disease and to subject the patient to treatment mode akin to other treatable diseases. Cooper (1983, p. 66) argues:

> The biological model focuses on internal determinants as a causal factor for alcoholism, the socio-cultural models focus on environment and social effects.... Drinking behavior has been correlated with age, socio-economic status, urbanization, ethnic origin, and religion.

Schuckit (1985), argues that the biological and genetically influenced factors may have been overplayed. He agrees that environmental factors like experience with alcohol, environmental stress, culture, and modeling were important factors to be considered in alcohol consumption. Schuckit went on to explain that it was the complex interactions between genotype and environment which makes it difficult to determine cause and effect. When we look at broken homes and other factors associated with alcoholism, particularly where "more recent studies have asked whether both childhood environment problems and adult alcoholism might be related to a third factor" (p. 33), we realize that we are dealing with a complex problem. Schuckit (1985) supported the view that once the presence or absence of an alcoholic biological parent was controlled, there would be little or no association between negative childhood experiences and adult development of alcoholism.

Summary

Alcoholism is brought about by a number of factors, chief among them being social factors. But because social factors are responsible in large measure for alcoholism it runs into contention that it is a genetically driven disease running in families. Goodwin argues for the genetic camp by identifying a number of significant studies. They include adoption studies; sons raised apart from their alcoholic biological parents; and comparison studies between alcoholics and non-alcoholics coming from broken homes.

Because of shortcomings in some of those studies, Goodwin agrees that environmental factors do play a part in furthering our understanding of alcoholism. The central problem for the geneticist is how to explain "the transmission" of the alcohol gene. In addition to this difficulty, the disease theory can be challenged on a number of grounds: laboratory studies, which are at variance to the "loss-of-control" thesis, in addition to clinical research, longitudinal studies and the findings of ethnic and cultural studies. All of these, according to Peele (1985), have challenged the disease concept since they moderate alcohol consumption.

In the main, therefore we have a situation where some percentage of the variance on alcohol abuse can be attributed to genetic factors but the vast majority of the variance remains spread among the socio-cultural and social camps.

The reason alcohol abuse remains a "confusing" issue is because science is combined with traditional beliefs, feelings and expectations.

Suggested Readings

Hulpieu, H.R.; and Versa V. Cole. 1946-47. "Potentiation of the Depressant Action of Alcohol by Adrenaline." Quarterly Journal of Studies on Alcohol 1:89-97.

Stabenau, James R. 1985. "Basic Research on Heredity and Alcohol: Implications for Clinical Application." Social Biology 32, nos. 3-4: 297-320.

Turner, Thomas B.; Esteban Mezey; and A.W. Kimball. 1977. "Measurement of Alcohol-Related Effects in Man: Chronic Effects in Relation to Levels of Alcohol Consumption. Part A." The Johns Hopkins Medical Journal 141:235-48.

---

[1] *half sibling is defined as one related to the proband through only one biologic parent*

CHAPTER 3

The History of Alcohol Consumption

Introduction

> No one can say with certainty how or when alcohol beverages were discovered, but they have known to exist in most civilizations throughout recorded history.... In our society today, alcoholic beverages are readily available in many homes as well as in stores, bars, and restaurants. Drinking is permissible in many public facilities such as parks, theaters, and stadiums. Distillers, wineries, and breweries spend vast sums of money to advertise in newspapers and magazines and on television with messages implying that life without alcoholic beverages is incomplete. Good times, glamorous friends, and personal success are depicted as part of what people experience with alcoholic beverages (Jung 1994, p. 2).

Colonialism and Alcoholism

Jung notes, with specific reference to the United States, that in colonial times, alcohol was considered a beverage and a home remedy, not the cause of social problems. But as alcohol abuse increased, there were growing indications that from the 1700s to the mid 1800s shifts were taking place as the country moved from an agrarian economy to an industrial one. During the Temperance and Prohibition era, one had the distinction of labeling alcoholics as "skid-row bums," casting a blind eye, according to Jung (1994), to other citizens who were engaging in the habit and who were at the same time, gainfully employed. Demonstrably, therefore, alcohol abuse, not only has a long history but also a checkered one. Morally, "excessive drinking was sinful behavior and reflected a lack of will power" (p. 7).

But the moral model was superseded by Alcoholics Anonymous (AA) which was formed by two alcoholics themselves, Bill Wilson and Bob Smith, the first a stock broker, the second a physician. This movement, according to Jung, gave alcoholics a "spiritual reawakening." But the AA had its limitations. It continued to operate clandestinely and so encouraged the stigmatization that alcoholics should be known but not seen. In fact, the AA, the disease model and some institutions, both private and governmental, are now embarking on a mission, if not to eradicate alcoholism/alcohol abuse, to sensitize all those who wish to know more about the "disease." Yet institutionally, there is a lack of coordination and this is because alcoholism is served and championed by separate interests which have different views on how alcohol should be consumed and how people should behave towards it.

The Influence of the Disease Concept

As the history of alcohol consumption will show, there have been serious and ongoing attempts to grapple with the alcohol problem from the time alcohol was considered a "disease." This is because more people bought into the disease concept and respectable folks came to accept that some of them had a disease, not a personality or social problem ascribed to lower class people who were found at the end of life's opportunities.

Yalisove (1998) points out that the disease concept of treatment evolved through the Alcoholics Anonymous (AA) informal facilities such as mental hospitals, alcoholism units, and detoxification programs.

The Implications of Jellinek's Model

Since 1952, however, with the introduction of Jellinek's disease model, scientists and theorists alike began to move increasingly towards the disease or biological model of alcohol abuse. This spurred the momentum to locate the genetic link to alcohol abuse. Mannis (1958) looked at alcohol as a progressive disease which could not be cured, but which could be treated successfully, enabling the person to live a life of normalcy. Also, Bohman (1978) looked at a sample of children (those who were up for adoption as against those with alcoholic fathers).

The results showed that those sons who were from alcoholic biological parents fared worse than their counterparts (that is, those who grew up in foster homes) in becoming alcoholics. Again, Goodwin (1979) argued that "familial alcoholism" might be valuable as a method in preventing alcohol abuse. He examined the various biological studies, like the genetic twin and adoption studies, and found inconsistencies in them. The route to genetic cause, therefore, would seem to be located in family studies.

On the other hand, do alcohol and ethnicity indicate evidence of genetic culpability? Not really, the verdict is still inconclusive. For one, the predisposition of certain groups, say Blacks for instance, to abuse alcohol is tied up with the claim of social and discriminatory practices that are meted out to them in society. In looking at the social derivatives of alcohol consumption therefore, one has to think of roles and role-playing, that is, how people interact with others based on their perception of each other's position/role within the social milieu, and how they interact with one another based on people's expectations of them.

The Transmission of Cultural Norms

Research by Steinglass (1976) underscores the need to look for alcohol abuse within the broad parameter of "social irresponsibility." Budd et al. (1985, p. 145) suggest that the norms of drinking are passed on within the family setting. Also, that heavy drinkers will seek peer group support rather than their parents. Although their study examined the life style of the young drinker, it did bring out some important aspects in the dynamics of social drinking. For example, there were notable sex differences in social setting drinking as opposed to uniformity among the sexes (Budd et al. 1985). The researchers observed that 80 percent of adolescents between 11 to 16 drink at social settings. Girls aged 14 were less likely to drink at social settings than boys.

In their discussion they found that "the majority of adolescents who drink, have tasted their first drink before the age of 10 (p. 155). In addition to learning to drink at home, other social implications for drinking were religion, socio-economic status, and rural-urban residence. Catholics and Jews appeared to drink slightly more than Protestants, the probability of drinking increased with socio-economic status, and urban adults appeared to drink more than their counterparts in the rural areas.

The Effects of the Social Structure

Commenting on teenage drinking, Maddox (1962), had this to say:

> One cannot understand the drinking or abstinence of teenagers in the United States without recognizing the teenager's position in the social structure and how this position is conceived both by the teenagers themselves and by the adults to whom, somehow, they must relate themselves....In addition to prescribing certain occupational and other behavioral expectations, placement in a particular age category provides an individual with patterns of behavior which are proper for his relationship both with peers of his age and with those in other age categories (p. 42).

According to the National Institute of Mental Health (1969):

> Many people do feel that the alcoholic may be no more responsible for his drinking than, for instance, a tuberculosis patient is responsible for his coughing. They believe, however, that such patients must be brought to understand that they have a moral responsibility to seek treatment and to make all possible efforts to help themselves (p. 7).

Time, Manner and Reason as Factors in Drinking

Experts have now agreed that what is very important in the study of alcoholism is when, how and why a man drinks. These are more powerful factors in explaining alcoholism than the amount he drinks (Public Health Service 1969, p. 8).

When temperance thinking gave way to the forces of modernization, some scholars argued that the disease concept resurfaced to function as a device, an "alibi," deflecting attention from liquor itself and toward the especially sensitive alcoholics infected by the "disease." Defining the central problem chiefly in terms of treatment and placing major responsibility for the alcohol problem with the medical profession, allowed the alcohol trade to flourish in the wakening consumer era. By definition, the alcoholic's behavior, controlled as it was thought to be, by dependence on alcohol, would be utterly impervious to attempts by the state to regulate the overall sale or use of alcohol beverages (Walsh et al. 1989, p. 55).

So, although quite a number of scientific studies have been conducted suggesting a genetic linkage, particularly among twins, these findings cannot be generalized to the wider population of alcoholics. Further, the view that alcoholics lose total control cannot readily be accepted (Fingarette 1988).

The Sick Role of the Genetic Model

Without a doubt, then, the effect of the disease model is to place alcoholics in the sick role, which, in effect, legitimizes their behavior (Roman and Trice 1968), and thus takes them out of mainstream socialization to receive specialized health care. However, it is a sick role with a difference. These alcoholics are not removed from society and placed under the care of a physician until validated "well."

"The essentials...of the post-Prohibition understanding of alcoholism first emerged in American popular thought at the end of the 18th and beginning of the 19th century" (Levine 1978, p. 143; Peele 1985, p. 30). It was around that time, Levine points out, that a new paradigm, the disease paradigm model was defined. Basically, the model argued that alcohol was a progressive disease where loss of control was eventually identified as one of the main symptoms, and where abstinence was seen as the only cure (Levine 1978, p. 144). However, the "disease" etiology shifted from family orientation to one which was saloon-based, where mainly women congregated (Peele 1985, p. 30). It was during this time also that drinking took on the image of a "male prerogative" (Peele 1985). What is Alcoholics Anonymous's (AA's) role in all of this? Not very well defined. According to Bufe (1991), AA's members have shown little interest in professional help and non-religious self-help programs. This, the author contended, was because of the organizational principle which insists on the submission of the individual to the will of God. It views itself as "the exclusive holder of the truth" (p. 10).

The Various Forms of the Disease Model

The disease model, it must be remembered, takes various forms, both in terms of its perception and application. In the first instance, it is seen as a disease of the body; that is, there are indicators of "loss of control" and physiological addiction. These conditions are either inherited or may be the result of changed physiological response emanating from drinking over long or extended periods of time (Ward 1980, p. 5). It is also seen as a disease of the will.

Smith contends that the amount of drinking which takes place today is not as much as in earlier times. This contention sums up our attitude towards doing something about alcohol as wishy-washy, as compared to the attitudes earlier in our history. Smith addresses the issue of why problem drinking has emerged as a serious issue for public debate:

> [P]roblem drinking is associated with something in modern industrial life, rather than with the drinking behavior itself and the amount of alcohol consumed. Indeed, significant increases in the prevalence of problem drinking have been found in countries where industrialization has been rapid in this century, such as Japan and some socialist and Third World countries. China-watchers expect to see a similar trend as a result of recent modernization efforts in that country (Smith 1986, p. 16).

Consistency and Responsibility

It has been said that alcohol has been with us as far back as 1500 B.C. and in order to understand alcohol's role in our society we have to examine the history of attitudes and practices involving alcohol (Jung 1994). Jung was referring specifically to American society but he may as well be speaking on behalf of most societies of the world. This brings us back to our central theme, namely, that our responsibility is really conditioned by our attitudes and practices or behavior.

We may ask, have our attitudes in the past been consistent with our responsibility towards ourselves, our family and society? Will our attitudes and behaviors be in keeping with what we consider responsible behavior? Consistent with this thrust the family, the individual and society are seen as the determining influence in drinking patterns. These are the three populations that I feel can alter significantly the prevailing alcoholic landscape around the world.

Summary

No one can, with certainty determine when alcohol was discovered. However, during colonial times it was considered a beverage. Later through the 1700s to the 1800s alcohol as a problem began to emerge. The history of alcohol will show that initially most people bought into the disease concept which gained impetus following the Jellinek disease model of 1962. Other notable researchers in the early period contributed to and supported the disease concept.

Scientific studies on children given up for adoption and twin studies further bolstered the claim of a genetically driven alcoholism. Steinglass (1976) on the other hand called for a broader conceptualization of alcoholism. He suggested looking at norms, values and socialization, even the social structure. In this regard when one recognizes one's place within the social structure and how one relates to another by virtue of expectations based on occupation, age and other criteria the cause of alcoholism becomes a bit clearer.

The disease model takes various forms. First, it is regarded as a disease of the body evidenced by "loss of control" and physiological addiction. Yet we witness that as drinking is increased or remains at stable levels it may be due to something in modern industrial life (Smith 1986).

The author of this book believes that we need to examine three areas of alcohol consumption to arrive at a definitive conclusion, namely the family, the individual and the society.

Suggested Reading

Porter, Roy. 1985. The Drinking Man's Disease: The 'Pre-History' of Alcoholism in Georgian Britain." British Journal of Addiction 80: 385-96.

CHAPTER 4

The Issue Before Us

Introduction

The issue before us is clear. How do we move ahead with research and policy guidelines to deal with the alcohol consumption threat, or alcohol for that matter? Should we remain as we are in a "multidisciplinary theoretical" and seemingly static quagmire, or should we decide that we should use the "irresponsibility approach," that is, that alcoholics are responsible for bringing on their own condition, and that steps should be taken to stop it; if so, who will stop it?

The Path of Least Resistance

The irresponsibility approach would be the path of least resistance, since the general public, according to the literature, has little positive attitude or tolerance, for that matter, toward alcoholics. It would be more difficult to deal with the medically diagnosed alcoholics, where it is believed that the condition is not caused by behavior per se, but by genetic factors. As such, it could be argued that the individual has little or no responsibility for his/her condition, since it is inherited.

In this respect, we must be clear on what we want, a clean society in which our children are free of alcohol abuse especially those that are behaviorally driven. Therefore, we must identify the alcoholic and develop our programs accordingly. One of the things we know is that people have "widely differing notions as to whom they should consider to be an alcoholic" (Glatt 1969, p. 16).

> For some he is a man who is always drunk or who cannot leave drink alone, the person who is rolling drunk in the gutter, or the man who habitually beats up his wife. These misconceptions usually result in even heavy drinkers not thinking of themselves as alcoholics because their behavior does not "come up" to these expectations (Glatt 1969, p. 16).

Alcoholism: A Complex Phenomenon

According to Glatt (1969), some people can drink a bottle of whisky a day without becoming an "alcoholic," others will drink less and qualify for the term. Further, many drink because of what they feel alcohol does for them, while others see only what it does to them. Therefore, depending on one's perspective, both parties—the alcoholic and the observer—might be interpreting alcohol consumption differently. Glatt (1969) alludes to the multidisciplinary approach to alcoholism by suggesting that it is a complex phenomenon with more than one cause operating in almost all cases.

When a phenomenon is regarded as multidisciplinary in its approach and treatment mode, it does not mean that it cannot be treated successfully. It simply means that there are competing independent or predictor variables. The problem appears when one discipline feels that it has the variance "fully" explained, either through methodological procedures specific to its discipline, while choosing to "ignore" other empirical factors, or when, through logical argument and theoretical significance, theorists feel driven to follow an argument constructed by their own line of thinking, in the first instance.

This approach, while valid from an intellectual point of view, does not do us any good when we are looking for practical solutions to a problem which has been with us for well over sixty (60) years.

Political Implications

When we have crossed the intellectual outcome hurdle, we must face the influence of political factors. In large measure, one suspects that there has not been a genuine worldwide effort to tackle alcohol as a dangerous drug which puts families and societies at risk. One wonders why there hasn't been a "consistent yearly worldwide effort," with particular reference to alcohol abuse; or why there hasn't been inter-government collaboration for the control of alcohol, limiting its use by teenagers, the aged, the mentally incapacitated, or the economically and physically challenged? What there has been however, are attempts to raise consciousness of the "bad effects" of drinking, leaving it up to the individual to choose. This, to me, is constructing "irresponsibility," not responsibility. First of all, proponents of free choice and "the right to enjoyment of property" will argue that individuals have a "right" to decide if they want to drink or not. However, no attempt is made to identify those "free choicers" who are at risk, or who will put others at risk.

Whatever the reasons, alcohol consumption changes the physical texture, and the internal mechanism of the body; it may not be noticeable, but it could certainly be felt, even by those who find comfort under the headings "abstainers" or "social drinkers." Therefore physiological changes intersect with behavioral ones.

The Age of Responsibility

It must be clearly pointed out that unless individuals take it upon themselves to stop drinking, alcoholism will always remain a problem. We have reached the age of "responsibility," responsibility for our health, our well-being, our duties to our families, and our actions. We must now take responsibility for our drinking. The drink is now in our hands! We can stop alcoholism.

We have reached the age where we must be held responsible for ourselves and our families as far as drinking behavior is concerned. Any other type of behavior within the drinking scenario must be seen as counter productive to the individual, the family and society.

We therefore have to contend with issues that have far-reaching effects both for ourselves and the wider society. In adopting this position we cannot assume an individualistic position: we must be cognizant of the fact that there are a number of individuals who are not concerned whether alcohol remains a problem. Once the problem does not appear on their doorstep they tend to leave it for others to deal with.

Accompanying this position is the feeling that societal problems remain the "responsibility" of governments and organizations with special interests. This view cultivated in the past, flourishes today because of the prevalence of individualism.

However, those who harbor such philosophies must be reminded that it is a collection of individuals which comprise a society. Further it goes against the prevailing public health paradigm of community responsibility and empowerment.

We all must concern ourselves with public health issues or abandon our commitment to community membership. We can participate in a number of ways: (1) sourcing materials on alcohol abuse, (2) attending or arranging group discussions on the effects of alcohol consumption in the home, (3) lobbying for legislation surrounding the sale of liquor to minors and introduction of the breathalyzer, (4) requesting that adequate statistics be provided on alcohol-related deaths, ranging from domestic abuse to suicides, and (5) linking alcohol abuse to chronic diseases and non-inherited personality disorders.

It is to be noted that there is evidence of an increase in risk-taking behaviors on the part of many individuals. It is as if life holds no more natural challenges to motivate man and that he must start constructing his own.

We do not have the space to delineate some of the underlying reasons for such behaviors in this book. However, it is sufficient to note that alcohol and other related drugs are suspected to be the agents used in creating the environment for this type of misleading behavior.

Summary

The multidisciplinary approach to understanding alcohol consumption must be seriously considered against the background of not only finding a "cure," but for determining the efficacy of policy measures and guidelines. This becomes necessary to introduce and sustain any movement from irresponsible to responsible behavior on an individual basis.

It is true that not everyone is concerned about having a clean society; they leave these "larger issues" for governments whose responsibilities are clearly defined.

Another aspect of alcohol abuse has to do with the political influence of interest groups. Governments around the globe are influenced, sometimes heavily by interest groups and class perspectives. Negative impact on sales affect not only workers but the lifeblood of some industries. In this respect governments and regions across the world hold a global rein on alcohol abuse by arranging conferences and workshops in the hope that sensitization in this way will gain peoples' attention. This approach, I believe does not have the far-reaching effects that it might have had if it were not for the influence of interest groups. Thus governments must come up with innovative approaches to get the message across more effectively.

Another point to consider is risk-taking behavior. These new trends and emerging attitudes place a strain on accepting what we term "responsible behavior" and it creates a vacuum in our consciousness as far as empowerment is concerned. In its place is the tendency to believe that "if anything goes wrong" there are people around who can "fix it." Clearly, these individuals are referring to the vast array of specialists churned out by modern society. But as it is well known, physicians are not necessarily researchers and the nature and distribution of chronic diseases mean that increasingly we will have to know the nature of the health disorder before we treat with it.

More and more in the face of a growing inadequacy to find a "cure" for alcoholism, we will have to take responsibility through education and promoting health awareness. And we will have to view alcoholism as behaviorally based rather than genetically driven.

Suggested Readings

Navratil, L. 1959. "On the Etiology of Alcoholism." Quarterly Journal of Studies on Alcohol 20, no. 2:236-44.

Smart, Reginald G.; and Robert E. Mann. 1995. "Treatment, Health Promotion and Alcohol Controls and the Decrease of Alcohol Consumption and Problems in Ontario: 1975-1993." Alcohol and Alcoholism 30, no. 3:337-43.

CHAPTER 5

The Relevance of the Alcoholic Models

Introduction

A model is a simplified version of a phenomenon. It takes into consideration a particular theory seeking to explain in a logical and rational manner, a puzzle. The phenomenon in question here is alcoholism. A model demonstrates relationships among variables and hypothesizes outcomes. Each discipline may construct its own model of alcoholism, attempting in the process to show some salient features as to why its model best elucidates the issues surrounding the phenomenon called alcoholism.

Competing Models

In examining the various models then, one would come away with an understanding of the model and the impact it has made, both on the individual and on a number of research endeavors. No doubt individuals will be swayed by the contribution that model makes in explaining the problem. In this regard, researchers keep alive their claim to "the best approach" for understanding and explaining alcoholism.

The test of every model is the reality it brings to bear on the research experience. Specifically, the question is always asked: to what extent does the model account for the majority of alcoholics both within the home and outside of it. That is the real test of the model. The medical model explains alcoholism from a genetic perspective and the sociological model explains alcoholism from a group perspective. The question is: which is the more relevant of the two models?

As mentioned before, at one time the medical model held sway. Today other models, namely the sociological and psychological, seem more relevant (empirically speaking) in explaining alcoholism in varying degrees. In the past, and to some extent the present, the medical model laid claim to a certain amount of scientific information regarding alcoholism, namely, that alcoholism could be treated at hospitals and medical facilities. As such, many alcoholics responded. However, it is believed in many circles that the whole issue of a medically-treated alcoholic has outlived its usefulness, although it doggedly remains in the minds of many.

Once an Alcoholic, Always an Alcoholic?

Most researchers and lay people pay very little attention to the various divisions or categories of alcohol consumption in terms of its various levels of intoxication. The general feeling is that once you are an alcoholic, you are "always an alcoholic." However, we need to make observations and place them within a better-understood system of factual events (Tarter and Schneider 1976, p. 77).

The Different Models Discussed

Tarter and Schneider (1976), looked at the various models of alcohol consumption and identified certain complexities associated with them. Under the medical model it was found that there is the search for genetic, endocrinological, dysfunctional brain patterns or biochemical explanations.

On the other hand, the psychological model seeks to determine alcohol's existence and prevalence, and personal and subjective factors, namely, psychodynamism (discharging images consistent with his/her self-image).

The learning theory explains alcoholism through reinforcement, (among other things), such as a history of drinking, and the cultural and social acceptability of same.

The model of personality theory seeks to explain the reason for drinking by identifying what might be termed "disturbed personalities" dealing with, among other things, low self-esteem, perfectionism, and poor interpersonal relationships.

Sociological models examine the impact of the environment and the influence of social groups in determining or explaining alcohol dependence.

Cultural theories seek to explain the existence of alcoholism as one in which culpability is found to reside in the culture itself, where, for example, according to Bales (1946), drinking can be explained by the manner in which the culture sanctions it, (for example, how it is interpreted, and under what conditions it is accepted). A culture, which is very stressful with no outlet for the release of tensions, would by necessity encourage alcoholism (Tarter and Schneider 1976).

Thus, alcohol consumption in its extreme forms represents a problem. That problem has to do with measurement of the social/environmental factors, the family and the society. The individual is central to all of this. I will now turn my attention to the evidence obtained from empirical research conducted on the social factors of alcoholism.

Psychodynamic theory (Gomberg 1985; Levy 1958; Talashek 1987) postulates that the individual has certain inhibitions and must drink to pacify or overcome them; it is a response to certain needs within the individual. Talashek (1987) examined the Eriksonian theory of ego development and found that adolescents with alcoholic parents scored lower than their controls on ego identity; those without an alcoholic parent were more likely to be considered problem drinkers than those with alcoholic parents, although the findings were not statistically significant. The younger the children the lower were their ego identity.

Another theory, the learning theory, explains how some persons have a disturbed equilibrium brought on through anger, fear and depression—mainly by individual, interpersonal or societal pressures. The overall aim is to reduce such pressures. Studies by Kingham (1958); Masserman and Yum (1946); Conger (1956); Bandura (1969); Russell and Mehrabian (1975) and Bergler (1946/1947) support the learning theory in one way or another. Basically, the individual learns about alcohol through modeling, frequency, devotion, and intensity because of the psychological benefits it affords him. This process has to do with reinforcement, stimulus, response and rewards.

Other researchers point to the social-psychological factors of all persons in general, and explain that one should be cognizant of the fact that there are intervening

variables which can mediate the outcome of the effects of the psychological factors and the response/behavior of the individual. These effects may also determine whether long standing personality traits are brought to the fore by certain drugs.

In examining the socio-cultural approach to alcoholism one must take into consideration the effects that the wider culture has on, and to a certain extent facilitates the individual to drink excessively. The socio-cultural approach argues that man is both a social and a cultural entity. Socio-cultural theories arose out of an examination of subcultural and cross-cultural differences in the rate of problem drinking (White 1985).

This approach emphasizes a responsibility for safe drinking practices. It argues that some of the problems of alcohol consumption are based on the lack of norms or appreciation of safe drinking in a particular society (O'Connor 1984).

Further Bales (1946) contends that individuals within society are faced with two options, that is, the need to drink and the opportunities offered them to drink. Individuals differ in their behavior based on the environment in which drinking takes place. Bales (1946) argues that there is a great amount of tension occurring in society; tensions that are culturally induced, producing guilt, anxiety, conflict and suppressed sexual tensions. If society did not throw up these tensions, individuals would not drink excessively. In short, there is a direct correlation between societal tensions and alcohol abuse.

This is one of the reasons according to Bales why the Irish culture found outlets for their tensions in drinking. It was brought on by the anxiety of growing old on the farm, a bleak occupational outlook, and suppressed aggression and anxiety.

Different Types of Cultural Drinking

Bales (1946) identifies four different types of drinking attitudes found in different cultures. They are: complete abstinence, as for example, that practised by Moslems; ritual attitude, as that practised by the Jews; convivial attitudes, as those practised by politicians, businessmen, pilgrims, and the like; and the utilitarian attitude, whereby drinks are used to seal a bargain, (whether in the market place or in marriage arrangements).

Again, in examining social factors, one needs to look at the drinking habits across the entire country to determine variability. In 1985, Linsky et al. undertook a study of 50 states in America. The results indicated that stress alone accounted for some of the variations in alcoholism. The researchers pointed to differences in culture as one of the factors responsible for their findings. Some cultures are considered more stressful than others.

A second study conducted by Linsky et al. (1987) confirmed Bales' theory that cultural norms in a society encourage alcohol consumption. Stress was most strongly related to the amount of alcohol consumed. Likewise, death by cirrhosis was linked to states which were more "permissive" in alcohol consumption.

In 1986, Linsky et al. used an index of 50 states and computed the percentage population residing in legally dry areas, degree of legal restrictions on the sale of alcohol consumed and the percent of Mormons or Fundamentalists residing in those states, rate of calculation of liquor outlets per million population, and the degree to which sale of alcohol was restricted by way of special hours on Sundays.

Religion was correlated in the direction predicted and was also highly correlated with dry areas, sales restriction and liquor outlets.

Zucker (1979) on the other hand, argues that one's socio-cultural background (that is, one's community, socio-economic status, ethnicity, religion, neighborhood values, availability of alcohol, and the values attached to drinking) can be instrumental in determining the propensity of the individual to drink.

Zucker (1979) criticizes socio-cultural studies as they suggested that the culture of the family remains constant over a long-term period and that the family maintains its social and ecological disposition without any upward or downward movement. He argues that post-industrial societies alter the community in which the family resides. In addition, alcoholics claim that they were beset by divorce, parental loss, and disagreements. Zucker also points to the influence of the school in the individual's pre-adolescent years.

It would appear, nonetheless, that the most enduring pieces of research on socio-cultural influences on alcohol consumption are those conducted by Bales (1946) and validated by Linsky et al. in three separate studies 1985, 1986 and 1987.

What makes the study of alcohol consumption so multi-factorial? Why are there so many variables responsible for alcohol consumption? We may never know the full reason, but it does not prevent us from etching ever so closer to the real reason. It is the author's view that alcohol consumption has many predictor variables most of which are interrelated. The task is to note which variables appear first in order of priority, and which through time, interact with other variables, camouflaging and confounding the original or underlying causal agent(s), and sending conflicting messages leading to multiple and/or ambivalent interpretations.

This entire moving scenario or shifting dynamics of alcohol consumption has led to a series of landmark studies, both genetically and sociologically driven, in an attempt to unravel the complicated causes of alcohol consumption.

Genetic Culpability, Social Irresponsibility

The author wishes to make the point and to deal conclusively with the issue that: it is either genetic culpability or social irresponsibility. In so doing, he attempts to put the matter to rest and at the same time give the academic community and the layman an indication of what are the main factors at work, and where future research is headed.

For example, some people find comfort in drinking, when they lack confidence in themselves or have misgivings about their ability to deal with ordinary life situations or problems. Johnson and Mâtre (1974) tested the relationship between anomie and use of alcohol among both urban working class Mexican Americans and Anglos. By so doing, they brought to the fore empirical evidence of the relationship between, not only class and nationality, but urban- rural relationship. Booth et al. (2000) comparing a community of rural-urban, at-risk drinkers report that rural drinkers are associated with regular alcohol disorders and medical problems. However, they note that there is a greater use of supportive and intervention mechanism (help for their drinking, outpatient services, and treatment) for their problem than their urban counterparts.

Summary

A model is a simplified version of a phenomenon and alcohol consumption is one such phenomenon. Because alcoholism by its nature is very complex, many models attempt to explain its etiology. These models are representative of the various disciplines using various approaches to understand the problem. At the same time they set up a form of competition for belief and behavior, since they are supported by empirical evidence.

The medical model explains the genetic or familial variance of alcoholism and the sociological model explains alcohol from a group perspective. Basically, it explains alcohol abuse from a number of social factors.

There is a saying: "once an alcoholic, always an alcoholic" but this cliché cannot be substantiated in the face of towering evidence to the contrary.

The psychological model focuses on things like self-image and repressive forces while the learning theory explains patterns of reinforcement; the history of drinking, and learning to drink from other drinkers. Personality theory, on the other hand, seeks to explain drinking behavior from among other things, poor interpersonal relationships or the "disturbed personality" thesis.

Cultural theories of alcoholism locate their reason for abuse within the culture itself. Bales (1946) was one of the first persons to measure the cultural effects of alcoholism by comparing drinking among various states. Psychodynamic theory seeks to predict alcohol abuse from the inner needs of the individual which has to do with ego identity.

Still, some of these theories like the social-cultural, the psychodynamic and psychological share boundaries on alcohol abuse or alcohol consumption. When all the various models are taken into account we (arguably) are left with the two main contenders—the genetic model and the sociological one.

Suggested Readings

Christian, Joe C.; Terry Reed; Dorit Carmelli; and William F. Page. 1995. "Self-Reported Alcohol Intake and Cognition in Aging Twins." Journal of Studies on Alcohol 56, no. 4:414-16.

Johnson, Richard; and Roger William. 1985. "Genetic and Environmental Factors in the Individual Susceptibility to the Development of Alcoholic Liver Diseases." Alcohol and Alcoholism 20, no. 2:137-60.

Kozaric-Kovacic, Dragica; Vera Folnegovic-Smalc; Zdenco Folnegovic and Ana Marusic. 1995. "Influence of Alcoholism on the Prognosis of Schizophrenic Patients." Journal of Studies on Alcohol 56, no. 6:622-27.

Ojehagen, A.; M. Berglund; C. P. Appel; K. Andersson; B. Skjoerris; and A. M. Wedlin-Toftenow. 1992. "A Randomized Study of Long-Term Out-Patient Treatment in Alcoholics." Alcohol and Alcoholism 27, no. 6:649-58.

CHAPTER 6

The Family and Alcohol-Related Problems

Introduction

Alcoholism or alcohol dependence runs strongly in families, without a remarkable familial rate of most other psychiatric disorders such as schizophrenia and manic-depressive disease (Cotton 1979). Works by Bohman (1978); Cadoret et al. (1980); Goodwin et al. (1974) and to a certain extent Schuckit et al. (1972) have significant bearings on genetic influences on alcohol dependency. It has been observed that "ninety percent of the people in the United States have had experiences with alcoholic beverages" (Schuckit 1994), but a greater percentage in developing countries might not only have alcoholic beverage contact, but may be alcoholics themselves after having failed to overcome the initial temptation of alcohol consumption.

No Perfect Tests for Alcohol Dependence

Schuckit (1994) raises some concerns on the alcohol problem when he indicated that "there are no perfect tests for alcohol dependence" (p. 6). In any event, it "requires carefully defining the stage of the alcohol history in which biological factors might contribute to the vulnerability to alcohol dependence" (p. 6).

In fact Schuckit (1994), argues that there are two considerations for the detection of inheritance patterns, namely the polygenic and multifactorial. The first deals with a number of genes having a particular propensity to significantly increase one's risk. The second "indicates a high likelihood that both genetic and environmental factors influence the development of alcohol dependence" (Schuckit, p. 7).

> The magnitude of the genetic impact on alcoholism is not easily established for several reasons. Study results are affected by the definition of alcohol dependence, the decision to combine all severe alcohol-dependent pictures together or to focus on those occurring in the absence of severe psychiatric syndromes, the potential impact of environmental events and the probable existence of genetic heterogeneity within different pedigrees of primary alcoholics (Schuckit 1994, p. 14).

Some of the environmental factors that influence levels of alcohol use include family upbringing, peer groups, job status, and marital stability. From a larger perspective, your culture and social class also have an effect on your drinking habit (p. 112).

The Reality of Alcoholism

Anyone can become an alcoholic; you do not have to be born an alcoholic. Sociological and environmental factors may do the job! Social irresponsibility will complete it.

No scientific study has confirmed that alcoholism is a disease. To this end, the competing argument of the sociological factors impacting on alcohol consumption within the family becomes particularly inviting. Even as we do so, we still have to ask the question: what are the peculiar circumstances within the family which set up this constellation of factors leading to drinking patterns? The literature points to a large body of research which can help us examine relations between family members and alcohol consumption.

The alcoholic in the family certainly creates some problems; the social drinker, or non-alcoholic must be taken seriously. It has to do with the responsibility of status and roles and perception between and among family members.

Keller (1976) describes alcoholism as the condition where an individual is unable to give up drinking in spite of the hurt it is causing himself healthwise, socially and economically. In other words, the individual has reached a path of irresponsibility. In short, he is addicted to the substance.

Others believe that the shift in alcoholism treated as a disease was due to the movement away from free will toward one of determinism. In this respect it is believed that there is some sort of ideological influence at work.

Even as we make this observation we note that the rise in abuse of alcohol has assumed alarming proportions, and the societies afflicted by this problem seem to be at a loss to determine how to even start dealing with it, far less to adopt measures to bring the problem under control.

Compelling "Evidence"

Jellinek's (1960) study was perhaps the most compelling "evidence" that alcoholism was a disease. His study showed that loss of control was an indiscretion that the victim was not exhibiting normal patterns of behavior, and that he/she needed medical intervention.

Since that time, Jellinek's work significantly influenced many alcohol researchers who were trying to prove their hypothesis, that alcohol consumption (mainly in its extreme frequency) will produce alcohol-related problems, the solutions to which will be found in a medical treatment facility.

In 1960, Jellinek identified various types of alcohol addiction. They are Alpha alcoholism-characterized by heavy drinking with no loss of control. This was followed by Beta alcoholism, Gamma alcoholism, Delta alcoholism and Epsilon alcoholism (Blum 1984). The last stage-Epsilon alcoholism is characterized by explosive drinking, resulting in tissue damage and illness.

It is important to note that while Jellinek had set the stage for the loss of control thesis via the genetic route, the thesis may be interpreted from a social irresponsibility approach. We note that all alcoholics are actually out of control or are likely to be "out of control." We must be able to dichotomize through empirical evidence whether such out-of-controlness is genetically or socially or personally driven.

Polich et al. (1981) compared subjective and objective responses of biological sons of alcoholic men and controls; sons showed lower somatic symptoms than the controls.

Schuckit et al. (1972), compared children who had alcoholic biological parents raised by non-alcoholic parents with those who had non-alcoholic biologic parents raised by alcoholic parents. They observed that alcoholism was found more often among half siblings with an alcoholic biological parent. However, when genetic loading was held constant there was no significant increase in the incidence of alcoholism in the offspring of alcoholic parents.

Goodwin et al. (1974) attempted to further endorse the linkage between genetics and alcohol consumption: the sons of the alcoholics were compared with their brothers. One set of brothers was raised by non-alcoholic parents; the other set was raised by alcoholic parents. The findings indicated that both groups had high rates of alcoholism, suggesting that parentage had nothing to do with alcoholism or alcohol development for that matter.

Also, Cadoret et al. (1980) reported that male adoptees raised separately from their alcoholic parents developed symptoms similar to those of their male counterparts who were raised by alcoholic parents.

Alcoholism and Close Alcoholic Relatives

Parents who had close alcoholic relatives (first degree relatives) were found to develop alcoholism, and to have drug and psychiatric problems more readily than their controls, even when similar alcohol intake and demographics were held constant (Schuckit 1982).

But Goodwin et al. (1981) lamented the problem with family studies dealing with the genetic approach. His concerns were with patients' records, questionnaires and interviews. He suggested that one had to screen different individuals with different backgrounds for honesty and validity of information. Could one trust second hand information from patients? Under these circumstances, how adequate will the sample be? Further, alcoholism and its problems were unevenly distributed within the population (Goodwin et al. 1981).

Looking at twin studies, Goodwin et al. (1981) observed that too hasty an assumption is made in believing that identical and fraternal twins have equally similar environments:

> Generalizing from twins to non-twins is hazardous. Twins represent a genetic selected population. They have higher infant mortality, lower birth rate, slightly lower intelligence, and their mother's ages are on the average higher (p. 161).

Inadequate Measurement Techniques

Kaij and Dock (1975) observed that there were no substantial differences between groups of grandsons and the transmission of alcoholism. Difficulties also lay ahead when controlling for environmental factors. Part of the problem had to do with inadequate measurement techniques and delays between the event and the consequent behavior (Schuckit et al. 1985, p. 32).

In examining adoption studies, Goodwin et al. (1981) observed that there must be reliable information on the biologic adoptive parents, the non-biologic adoptive parents, and information on the adoptees. He pointed to five conditions that should be present when undertaking studies of this nature:

(1) Comparability of psychopathology

(2) Socio-economic and demographic variables

(3) Separation of adoptees soon after birth (possibly a few months); in addition to being matched for age and sex

(4) Non-contact with parents following separation of child from parent

(5) Adoptees should not be at the age of risk when they are under scrutiny for alcoholism

Standardization of Research Process

Thus, consistency across studies represents one reasonable way of dealing with an area of study which is fraught with problems (Goodwin et al. 1981).

Alcohol triggers expectancies in people even before one drink is taken. Placing a mug of water on a table in front of a group of persons, elicits a different reaction as opposed to placing a mug of alcoholic beverage on it. And if the persons seated around the table were of different cultures, we would witness different behaviors based mainly on different perceptions of alcohol.

> It is intellectually exciting, just as it is scientifically relevant and practically useful to consider this single substance that is used by people throughout the world in very different ways for very different purposes, and with very different consequences.... It is an ideal realm for trying to sort out the distinction between what is cultural and what is biological, what comes from nature and what comes from nurture (Heath 1995, p. 2).

The Family and Alcohol

From time immemorial, the family has existed as the pillar of society. It is a form of social support, emotional support, societal obligation, a means of understanding the psychology of individuals: how they express their emotions, their commitment to themselves, to each other, and to society.

The family therefore occupies an important position within the society; it keeps family members together, and it influences behavior within the family unit. Most importantly, however, is that it is the primary agent of socialization where norms are passed on from one individual to another. Both disciplinary actions and nurturing tendencies are central features within the family. The unit is akin to a small society. Goals, rewards, punishment, and the planning for the future stability of the family and its members also take place. The family may also grow smaller or become larger; some members of the family leave home with the intention of setting up families of their own, others go their individual ways.

The Family and External Threats

Each family may have its own peculiar way of dealing with external or internal threats to its existence. Some cope more efficiently than others. Some problems destroy families or render them incapable of functioning normally. Alcohol consumption is one such threat. It can threaten the existence of the family both from within and without.

When alcohol threatens from outside, it usually takes the form of penetration into the homes via the electronic and print media. However, the most powerful influence is the electronic media. Television has an impact upon the minds of persons, which other instruments do not have. For example, in order to influence teenagers to drink, the media may portray drinking as a form of camaraderie, a social outing, hanging together, or simply a significant milestone like attaining the age of eighteen.

This perception can quickly reach the teenager in the home and tempt the "restless youth" who being adventurous, may flirt with the notion of drinking, even if it means drinking by himself/herself. For the child in the home to be detected, it would require some vigilance on the part of other siblings, or on the part of the mother or father themselves.

Negative Perception of Alcohol in the Family

When alcohol consumption takes place within the home in large measures, and frequently so, and it is "supported" by the father or mother, then it produces some negative perceptions within the community. There is role confusion and abandonment. The father is no longer seen as a role model and the mother, having to take on both roles, that of mother and father, is no longer seen as the nurturer.

Research has shown that sometimes the problem is controlled, (sometimes exacerbated) when the mother takes on both roles and realizes the extent of the power she has within her hands. It has been argued that when a father drinks and becomes an alcoholic he brings shame and disrepute into the family.

Women Drinking Surreptitiously

Women drinking, on the other hand, may be a bit secretive, drinking when the husband and the children are away at work or at school. A large body of empirical evidence reveals the behavior of women alcoholics in and out of the home, their ability to maintain families, their work relationship patterns, and their social relationships.

Women drinking excessively (alcoholics) and men drinking excessively (alcoholics) have differing impacts on the family although both their actions can put the family at risk of disintegration. This is because men and women are seen differently. As a result, expectations and behaviors are constructed differently.

The image of a female alcoholic evokes more "understanding" and sympathy from the community and members of the general public than a male alcoholic. Males are seen as more "irresponsible."

Who influences whom? We are yet to understand empirically who is more influenced in an alcoholic family setting—who is able to withstand social and peer pressure, and who is more likely to succumb. Is it the boys or the girls? The whole question of expectation and coping skills come into play, not to mention the composition of the family. Fathers may influence boys more than mothers, while mothers may have more influence on their daughters than sons. However, where coping is concerned, research has shown that daughters and mothers cope more when the father becomes an alcoholic. The father himself may not be able to cope and may sell the family valuables to ensure the continuation of his drinking habit, while the wife and daughter attempt to keep the family together by assuming roles formerly occupied by the father.

Implication for Family Composition

Depending on the composition of the family, the ability to deal effectively with excessive drinking comes to the fore. Clearly, in a single family with one father and two daughters, the ability to cope effectively will be challenged, more so, if the daughters are not yet teenagers. Alternatively, a family with both mother and father in the home and children above teenage years is slightly more effective in controlling alcohol consumption, though not significantly so (Marshall 1992).

We need to obtain more information about the socio-economic position of families and their ability to contain high levels of drinking within their homes: what are the differences, if any, between upper class Blacks and upper class Whites; between upper class Blacks and lower class Blacks; between upper class Whites and lower class Whites, when family composition is controlled? How are roles shared between various age groups? Who is more likely to seek professional help privately as opposed to those likely to seek help in the public domain? Can findings in a Black/White society be inferred to multiethnic societies?

These are some of the questions which need to be answered before making a comprehensive analysis of the alcoholic within the family. Only through this method also, can we determine if the vast majority of individuals defined as alcoholics were nurtured and "socialized" in an environment which placed them at risk very early in their lives.

For example, "in a home where one or both parents are actively alcoholic, family life has a distinct character" (Gravitz and Bowden 1985, p. 9). The authors point out that such a family is characterized by inconsistency, unpredictability, arbitrariness and chaos.

The Family as the Unit of Analysis

The family as the unit of analysis gives us the golden opportunity to observe how norms and values are passed on from one generation to the next. It demonstrates how its members are endowed with a sense of value. Such values, it is hoped, is in the best interest of the survivability of the species. However, parents sometimes pass on values that may be detrimental to the healthy growth and development of their offspring.

Alcohol use is one such practice which can alter the behavior of a young child. Zucker (1979, p. 217) argues that family characteristics are tied in with the socialization process and will determine whether, or how, a child will drink. Part of the problem relates to how parents perceive alcohol use. Jackson et al. (1999) believe that many parents view alcohol use as a problem of adolescence and as such, are not as vigilant as they ought to be with their children.

However, a lot of work still needs to be done. Although much has been accomplished on family studies in terms of understanding the etiology of alcohol use, most researchers have neglected to look at the effects of joint families in the assessment of drinking.

Stress and the Family

In examining the relationship between joint families and alcohol use, research has also been conducted in assessing the moderating effects of stress on alcohol use. In view of the fact that prior research on the nuclear family (to a great extent) and on the extended family (to a lesser extent) has reported a relationship between family interaction and alcohol use, it becomes necessary to assess the moderating effects of stress on alcohol consumption within the family structure, and consequently on family relations.

As alluded to before, we believe that the family can help the alcoholic, by preventing him from becoming worse, or they can bring him to the point where he remains totally helpless and unable to discharge his familial duties, no matter how marginal these duties may be. Further, "family therapy" is only one of the many methods the social psychiatrist has at his disposal (Esser 1971, p. 251), that is, having the support of a brother, a sister, a grandparent, or persons who will maintain the "balance" within the family.

Taking Cover

In addition, the family while providing a fertile breeding ground for alcoholics, can effectively deal with the offspring who is genetically at risk to alcohol consumption. If we are to accept the claim by the proponents of the disease model, then we can identify those "genetically" predisposed families and take care of them in the same way an offspring of an alcoholic is raised by a male non-alcoholic parent, instead of a biological father. Although children raised by both alcoholic and non-alcoholic parents may be at risk, those raised by alcoholic parents are additionally at risk since they are more exposed to alcohol-induced behavior. In other words, there is a peculiar type of socialization they experience. The argument is that it can be consciously and deliberately stopped, once we determine the risks a priori.

Taking Control

In one study, Jackson (1959) relates how the wives of alcoholics were interviewed with a view to determining the problem stages of their alcoholic husbands. The pattern that emerged was one in which the alcoholic progressed from social drinking, to excessive drinking, followed by emotional stress and disturbance of both the wife and the children. Finally, the wife would take control of the home as attempts to positively influence the husband's drinking prove futile.

As a realistic probability, the alcoholic may recover, but not fully into his former role of husband/father provider. According to Jackson (1959), he may eventually become so full of Alcoholics Anonymous (AA) activities that he may literally forget his home, paying little attention to his wife. This in turn can become a new source of concern to the household, unless the wife can attend AA meetings herself to articulate her own grievances and get them addressed.

In this respect, the family "finds itself in an unstructured situation which is undefined by the culture" (Jackson 1959, p. 585).

The Married Alcoholic

Further, the alcoholic in marriage poses serious problems to the social order of the society. "Middle and upper class male alcoholics have been found to marry at about the same rate as the general population, but they have higher rates of broken marriages than their male counterparts in the general population" (Bailey 1961, p. 83). Indeed, wives drinking appear to be related positively to husbands drinking, particularly those in a higher economic level and those happy with marital life (Demers et al. 1999).

There are a number of social interactive activities taking place among the married alcoholic; e.g. a bossy or dominant wife, who encourages her husband to drink or is bent on removing any support he is attempting to build in order to improve his situation. There is also the position that wives suffer just as husbands, particularly from stress and loss of identity. A breakdown in the family through alcohol can be reflected in social strains and problems at the societal levels, requiring professional assistance, with all the necessary loss in time and human potential it brings. For example, loss of earnings, loss of self-esteem and confidence, adolescent and motivation problems, accidents, spousal abuse and general violence.

> Family breakdown and disorganization caused by alcoholism create a void in the family structure. As a result, children may attempt to meet the needs of their parents or siblings, thus encountering demands and stresses that are inappropriate for anyone of their age (Jacob et al. 1978, p. 1236).

But, there is also the issue of "the ratio of prodeviance to anti-deviance..." Bahr et al. (1995) point out that it may not be simply whether one was socialized positively or negatively, but the extent to which one was exposed to these types of socialization which, depending on the ratios, might cancel out the effects of one over the other. In this case the good over the bad.

In testing family bonds, family drug use and age on the one hand, and educational commitment, peer drug use, alcohol frequency and alcohol amount on the other, the researchers found that "when compared to adolescents, lower family bonds tend to have stronger educational commitment and fewer close friends who use drugs" (p. 464).

The Comprehensiveness of Family Studies

All these outcomes carry "staggering social and psychological consequences" (Steinglass (1976, p. 98). But family studies are wide as they are varied and they are approached from many different angles, namely the alcoholic himself, the family of the alcoholic, the family per se, alcoholism and the wider culture, not to mention the "alcoholic woman." Some of the more prominent studies on the families of alcoholics are Stanton et al. (1978); Jackson (1959); Keil (1978); Levenson et al. (1987); Jacob et al. (1978).

An interesting line of argument is constructed by Cotton (1979, p. 104), who argues that "other than alcoholism, depression appears to be the mental illness most frequently reported in relatives of alcoholics." Reviewing the literature on the incidence of family alcoholism, the investigator notes that research is concentrating on "recognizing alcoholism as a primary disease" in the first instance, and as a "secondary complication" of other conditions such as depression, schizophrenia, psychopathy and other psychiatric illnesses. One of the problems in examining the relationship between mental illness and alcoholism is to establish that mental illness is a factor to be considered before alcoholism develops, that is, independent of excessive drinking (Cotton 1979, p. 104). This position is also borne out by Schuckit (1983) when he commented on the relationship between alcoholic men with no alcoholic relatives.

However, amidst all the studies which have been undertaken so far, one has to ask the question "is there a peculiarity with men as alcoholics in the home as opposed to women as alcoholics in the home?" One view is that in a capitalist society, men have certain egotistical and identity problems as far as "being in control of the household" is concerned. It would be interesting to note whether the higher predisposition for males to become alcoholics is really a function of their given social status within society, and consequently, whether alcoholism is really a combination of social factors emanating from the home through the workplace leading to excessive drinking, not necessarily hereditary factors acting alone.

Women, Social Pressures and Alcohol Consumption

Women, on the other hand, may have some social pressures of their own at home, whether they are employed or not.

> Today, more women drink than ever before, and alcohol dependence among women has grown steadily. ...Women of all ages and socio-economic background, fall victim to alcoholism, which, among women, as among men, knows no boundaries. Adolescents and those advanced in years, housewives and executives, the rich and the poor, the single and the married are all susceptible to alcoholism. The alarming statistic is that the number of alcoholic women has been growing much faster than the number of alcoholic men (Fellios 1989, p. 12).

The author cautions that the female alcoholic is the homemaker "who hides her bottle in the house and who is protected by other members of her family" (Fellios 1989, p. 12). Pointing to a study by Broham (1981), Fellios argues that the study identifies adopted daughters who had alcoholic biological parents to be three times more likely to abuse alcohol than adopted daughters who had non-alcoholic parents. But it was only one of many factors which may combine to cause alcoholism (Fellios 1989, p. 13). Some other problems which affect women and increase their risk of alcohol abuse included infertility, premenstrual and menstrual problems, miscarriages, lack of sexual interest and related problems (Fellios1989, p. 17).

Fellios also observed that the largest population of female drinkers were those in professional, technical and business jobs, while the lowest were found in the semi-skilled and laborers category.

In addition, women who were seeking work and those who were married, as opposed to those who were single, had more alcohol problems than those who were home (that is, not seeking work and not married).

All this points to the view that women may worry more, domestically and socially, than men, and this provides a greater risk to alcohol abuse, and to becoming alcoholics.

Social Psychological Factors

In other words, the social psychological pressures might be heavily skewed against women unlike men, and although many women derive great satisfaction from a full-time career as mother and home-maker, others may find it difficult to adjust to the pressures and use drinking as one form of escape.

However, there are some factors that seem to be inherent to women and that is, because they have less muscle tissue they do not have sufficient water in their bodies to break down the alcohol (Fellios 1989, p. 114). The researcher also found that one's weight, metabolic rate, emotional state and experience were risk factors for alcoholism, in the first instance.

In addition, research needs to be undertaken on the impact of these factors to which women are predisposed when they have alcoholic husbands. In short, the question must be asked: to what extent are some of these factors indirectly impacting on their alcoholic husbands? All this could be undertaken in a longitudinal setting. Miller-Tutzauer et al. (1991) found that prior to marriage, alcoholics begin to moderate their drinking habit (which may be stabilized after marriage). What does "stabilization" mean? Under what conditions does "stabilization" prevent alcoholism? The researcher did not elaborate.

Abusive Relationships

Abuse and abusive relationships have figured prominently in relationships between parents and offsprings, but little comes to light scientifically. Only when children grow up do we hear of their experiences and the consequences, which have followed them into adulthood. Widom et al. (1995) matched abused and neglected children with non-abused and neglected children "and followed them prospectively into young adulthood." The researchers found that neglect, not sexual abuse was significant for women, but not for men. This finding suggests that women are at risk to alcohol problems later on due to neglect at an earlier stage of their lives, and although men drinking greater amounts of alcohol than women have learned the contradictions of control (Connor et al. 1999), it is not quite certain if women have been sensitized to this scenario.

Similarly, longitudinal studies undertaken by Johnson et al. (1995) examining the development of behavioral problems from 10-12 years found that "boys and girls had different initial levels of conduct problem behaviors" (p. 661). In support of this finding, O'Farrel et al. (1999) report that there is a greater frequency of husband-to-wife violence. In a study to determine the effects of marital therapy, the researchers reported that relapse to violence occurred more frequently among couples who discontinued their therapy, than with those who continued it.

Gender and Pleasure

Thus, the literature is quite clear about the risk of alcohol consumption to women very early in their lives. It also suggests that researchers of late onset drinking patterns of men and women should take these factors into consideration and weight women more "favorably," so as to standardize the risks for both sexes before making comparisons of drinking behavior. It also holds implications for unsanctioned drinking problems: the more unsanctioned or unsupervised the drinking, the greater the risk of related problems later in life. However, under certain conditions this risk may alter. For example, males have been found to be more implicated in pleasure-seeking and risk-taking after using alcohol than females (Stoduto et al, 1998). Some of these studies on alcohol and adolescent behaviors suggest that some children may have some deficits, as far as interpersonal skills are concerned (Senchak et al. 1996), or that they need to be exposed, early in their lives to some form of coping skills development. However, for this to take place, children must be initially supervised. Baumrind (1985) observed that the most significant finding in the adolescent literature on substance abuse is that the conservative, traditional way of rearing children protects them from early exposure to illicit drugs.

While parents have been implicated in children's alcohol problems (Baer et al. 1998), the question of social status further seals the issue (Alterman et al. 1998).

Families Over-emphasized?

Callan and Jackson (1985), however, suggest that parental alcoholism may not be a strong predictor of the quality of parent-type relationship in alcohol dependency. In their study they report that there were hardly any differences in the "levels of functioning and adjustment between families of recovered alcoholics and that of non-alcoholic families in the community" (p. 182).

Jackson (1959), in studying the adjustment of the family to alcoholism, hypothesizes that all family members believe in some measure of relief. In this respect, the cultural definition of alcoholism and the role of solidarity come to play an important part. In her study, Jackson identifies a number of stages that the alcoholic family passes through. These are the denial stage, the isolation stage, the disorganization stage, the reorganization stage, and the escape stage; each stage becomes progressively worse as members attempt to turn the situation around (Jackson 1959, pp. 569-579; Moos and Moos 1984).

Regardless of what is the etiology of alcoholism, it is suggested that women have more to lose than men. They have a high degree of denial and some even hide their alcoholic behavior from friends. In addition, the woman has to consider her job and her family, and these may negatively impact on her continuing her alcohol treatment (Fellios 1989).

In one study, Moos and Moos (1984) determined that spouses of relapsed alcoholics had more work to do than those who had alcoholic husbands. In addition, the spouses of relapsed alcoholics found that their partners performed fewer household tasks. This prompts a reshuffling of roles for the betterment of the family. When we examine the figures, we find that Black women have higher alcohol rates than their white counterparts. Some women may also drink because they feel helpless (Levin 1990). Also, it is reported that drinking problems are negatively associated with female problems than male problems (Johnson and Glassman 1999).

Women at Greater Risks?

The consistency of women drinking having the prospects of being more disadvantageously placed than male drinking however, means that some situations might be more high risk than originally thought, sometimes leading to fatal consequences. Some studies indicate that women are more at risk in the adolescent years, particularly if they were sexually abused as children. It was reported that women who were being treated for alcohol abuse had "higher rates of child sexual abuse" than women afflicted with other problems (Miller et al. 1993). This finding was later supported by Wilsnack et al. (1997) when in a national survey on drinking, they found that women's history of bad sexual experiences may in fact be a risk factor for substance abuse later on in life. In fact, Curran et al. (1999) reported differences in socioeconomic status of women as they relate to family history of alcoholism and alcohol dependence symptoms in later life.

When we examine the family and alcohol consumption, we feel that there are family members who can contain the extent of their drinking, while others cannot; some are not supposed to drink and do; others who can, don't. Byles (1978) found that violence among alcoholics in the home constituted an assault on the wife, children and property. This not only traumatizes young children, but it can breed new alcoholics. In an environment where drinking is "acceptable," the message taught is that alcohol is "good" (Esser 1968). However, where it is "not acceptable," the power that the drug has over individuals to force them to do things they would not normally do is itself an influence that might be considered negative.

This behavior may act as a relay to peers. Having had the initial "baptism of fire" from their households, children may now seek the advice, suggestion and sanctuary of their equals. It is here that peer pressure is demonstrated as the adolescent leaves home and strives to become independent, and where close associates become important sources of support (Brown 1990). It may also provide the opportunity to engage in deviant behaviors. Clearly then, a (new) family must therefore deal with two major issues: (1) there must be a delineation of internal and external boundaries where drinking is concerned, (2) the family must rally around a shared set of beliefs, values and rules of behavior (Steinglass et al. 1987).

Adult Children of Alcoholics

It is further observed that whether the children in the family are young individuals or older ones, they suffer from the consequences of the presence of alcohol just the same. In large measure, research has shown that adult children of alcoholics (ACOAs) are significantly more anxious and depressed than their counterparts from non-alcoholic families (Tweed and Ryff 1991). This indicates the telling effect that alcoholism has on the family. In one study Gerra et al. (1999) found that adult children of alcoholics score significantly higher on guilt and resentment subscales; hysteria, hypochondria and paranoia.

Not all children of alcoholics (COAs) however, suffer from the risk of alcoholism or psychological disorders. Hussong and Chassin (1977) determine that there is some measure of support for the "buffering" hypothesis. In this respect their study points out that a well-organized family with appropriate behavioral patterns should prevent adolescents falling prey to their parents' drinking. Still, the question must be asked: how many alcoholic families in that study had appropriate measures in place but witnessed family disintegration anyway? Put another way: what strength of cohesion is necessary for one to overcome alcoholism within the family, or is it the issue of different combinations of family units versus levels of alcohol consumption? (Marshall 1992). Is the family's equilibrium maintained or are members stigmatized as helpless and incompetent? (Peele 1985).

Motive versus Irresponsibility

After all is said and done, it may come down to motive for drinking (Carey and Correira 1997). Positive reinforcement or negative reinforcement rewarded by one's peers or societal culture, appears to be the culprit in predisposing people to drink alcohol. Here, it becomes a problem—personally and socially, thus precipitating "irresponsibility" first within the family and among close associates and second within the wider society.

These social factors, empirically tested, normally come up against the strongest arguments for a genetic link to alcoholism within the family. As a result, it sets the stage for social factors versus the genetic ones, and a test of genetic culpability against social irresponsibility.

Summary

There is no doubt, based on the evidence before us, that alcoholism runs in families. It underscores the genetic aspect of alcoholism. As pointed out by Schuckit (1982) "the data supporting a genetic role in alcoholism come from a variety of studies carried out in different countries and using diverse methodologies."

One of the difficulties however, has to do with the polygenic and multi-factorial patterns in respect to the development of alcohol dependency. Central to this concern is the likelihood of both genetic and environmental factors influencing the inheritance patterns.

It is instructive to note that no study has confirmed that alcoholism is a disease. Jellinek's study on the various stages of development of alcoholism must be seen as the most important aspect in furthering the disease concept of alcoholism. His model of alcoholism ranging from Beta to Epsilon alcoholism had significantly influenced professionals, treatment practices, research and models. Jellinek's main thrust was that an alcoholic was someone who had "lost control."

This "loss of control" thesis however, has not been accepted unconditionally. One of the research problems involved in alcohol investigation at the hereditary level is the validity of patient records and secondary data, not to mention the health condition of those providing the information. Questions of recall has to do with adopting too hastily a belief that identical and fraternal twins experience the same environmental conditions.

Family studies are important, for the family provides us with an important role within the society, among them the socialization of values which keeps the family unit together. Families may therefore be seen as microcosms of the wider society.

Media can penetrate families with suggestions of alcohol consumption and persuade the teenager or the adventurous youth to go on a path of drinking. They influence the teenager in various ways namely, creating a false sense of camaraderie at social settings, constructing scenes of "significant events" and suggesting that the "time was right" to drink.

Research has shown that when father becomes an alcoholic it is different to when mother becomes an alcoholic. Father brings shame and disrepute in the family; women evoke sympathy and understanding. It has to do with how perceptions are constructed and played out in the wider society. Not to be discounted is the composition of the family, the socio-economic position of the family and the sharing of roles within the family unit.

Alcoholics may recover but there is the general feeling that once recovered they may not be fully incorporated into their conventional role of husband/father provider. Involvement in other activities such as Alcoholics Anonymous (AA) may influence them unduly.

Family studies are very comprehensive in identifying the underlying causes of alcohol abuse. One point of view is that men seem to be more predisposed to initiate abuse than women. The question is asked: are men's vulnerability to alcohol consumption a function of status, ego and social factors? On the other hand, women may face more psychological pressures on a daily basis than men and this may create a susceptibility to alcohol abuse. Also to be taken into consideration is the whole question of abusive relationship, including abuse on children. Widom et al.

(1995) reported that neglect was a main factor in determining alcoholic outcome among abused children, particularly women as opposed to men.

In this respect there may be a gender risk to alcohol abuse and this may have implications in later life. However, Callan and Jackson (1985) warn that we may be overplaying family alcoholism since research has shown that there is hardly any difference in the levels of functioning and adjustment between families of recovered alcoholics and non-alcoholics. Further, not all children of alcoholics run the risk of becoming alcoholic or psychologically prone to becoming so.

The more immediate concern is to determine the use of drugs within the home and the motive for drinking as it relates to positive or negative reinforcement.

Suggested Readings

Baer, Paul E.; Lisa Garmezy; Berg; Robert J. McLaughlin; Alex D. Pokorny; and Mark J. Wernick. 1987. "Stress, Coping, Family Conflict, and Adolescent Alcohol Use." Journal of Behavioral Medicine 10, no. 5:449-66.

Baumrind, D. 1985. "Familial Antecedents of Adolescent Drug Use: A Development Perspective." In Etiology of Drug Abuse. Implications for Prevention, edited by C.I. Jones and R.J. Bartjes, 13-44. NIDA Research Monograph 56. Washington D.C.: US Department of Health and Human Services.

Bennett, Linda. 1989. "Family, Alcohol and Culture." Recent Development in Alcoholism 7:111-27.

Dumka, Larry E.; and Mark W. Roosa. 1995. "The Role of Stress and Family Relationships in Mediating Problem Drinking and Fathers' Personal Adjustment." Journal of Studies on Alcohol 56, no. 5: 528-37.

Fecaces, M.; Thomas C. Harford; Gerald D. Williams; and Eleanor Z. Hanna. 1999. "Alcohol Consumption and Divorce Rates in the United States." Journal of Studies on Alcohol 60, no. 5:647-52.

Hernández, Anthony C.R.; Michael D. Newcomb; and Jerome Rabow,. 1995. "Types of Drunk Driving Intervention: Prevalence, Success and Gender." Journal of Studies on Alcohol 56, no. 4:408-13.

Johnson, Fred W.; Paul J. Gruenewald; J. Andrew Treno; and Gail Taff Armstrong. 1998. "Drinking over the Life Course within Gender and Ethnic Groups: A Hyperparametric Analysis." Journal of Studies on Alcohol 59:568-80.

Kaplan, Howard B. 1987. "Substance Abuse Patterns and Their Relationship to Family Attitudes and Values." Health Values 11, no. 2:40-46.

Koller, K.M.; and J.N Castanos. 1969. "Family Background and Life Situation in Alcoholics." Archives of General Psychiatry 21, no. 5: 602-10.

Orford, Jim. 1984. "The Prevention and Management of Alcohol Problems in the Family Setting: A Review of Work Carried Out in English-Speaking Countries." Alcohol and Alcoholism 19, no. 2: 109-22.

Öström, Mats; Harmeet SjöGren; and Anders Eriksson. 1995. "Role of Alcohol in Traffic Crashes Involving Women: Passenger Car Fatalities in Northern Sweden." Journal of Studies on Alcohol 56, no. 5:506-12.

Paolino, Thomas Jr.; Barbara S. McCrady; and Sharon Diamond. 1978. "Statistics on Alcoholic Marriages: An Overview." The International Journal of the Addictions 13, no. 8: 1285-93.

Waterson, E. J.; and I. M. Murray-Lyon. 1989. "Drinking and Smoking Patterns amongst Women Attending an Antenatal Clinic - I. Before Pregnancy." Alcohol and Alcoholism 24, no. 2:153-62.

CHAPTER 7

The Psychology of Alcoholism

Introduction

It is said that some people drink to reduce stress; others have argued that alcoholism itself may produce stress.

The concept of alcoholism as a learned response, a habit, may be as old as alcohol itself. Certainly alcoholism as "a habit" forms the core of the general public's present thinking about "the disease."

> Most people who have no personal or professional interest in alcoholics and alcoholism have no clear idea of the strength of the habit and... those who do not have an interest are often hard put to understand and explain the extreme resistance to change which this response exhibits (Kingham 1958, p. 320).

Learning Theory

Learning theory, as far as alcoholism is concerned, was developed by Masserman and Yum (Kingham 1958). In an experiment, the scientists trained cats to obtain food then shocked them by placing electrodes in the path of the food to determine their responses. This was followed by giving the cats small doses of alcohol, which eventually overrode their fear of the shocks, to obtain the food (Ervin et al. 1988).

In extending the understanding of psychological effects, researchers compare children of alcoholic fathers and normal mothers with children having two normal parents. Some researchers have discovered that children with one normal parent and one alcoholic parent have deficits in the areas of intelligence tests, cognitive development and academic achievement (Tarter and Edwards 1988; Ervin et al. 1988).

Conflicting Images

Bergler (1946/1947) examines the alcoholic personality in terms of the "undigested unconscious conflicts with his (the alcoholic's) image of the pre-oedipal mother" (p. 356). In this, the researcher explains how the drinker passes through various phases from the pre-to-post stages of drinking. According to the writer, the alcoholic is at first in a depressive mood, then he is in a jocose mood, then a morose mood, and finally an aggressive mood, followed by sleep and hangover. All this, according to the author, is the result of inner conflict within the alcoholic.

> He is fighting, intraphysically, his attachment of a masochistic variety, to the fantasy of a "bad" "depriving" and "refusing" mother..... The main characteristics of that (alcoholic) personality can be summarized in the word "refusing". For their wives and children they refuse, either directly or indirectly, stability and security on a financial or social level; along with this goes damage to their reputations (Bergler 1946/1947, pp. 356-57).

In comparing psychopathy and personality disorder, Windle (1999) reports that those alcoholics with a personality disorder were diagnosed as having a higher

prevalence of familial alcoholism and engage in higher levels of criminal activities, among other things.

Mood Swings

An underlying theme appears to be the emotional predisposition to alcohol consumption by the alcoholic. "Writers as divergent as poets and learning theorists have assumed that alcohol can improve a drunkard's mood" (Russell and Mehrabian 1975, p. 108). Such mood can range from morbidness to pleasure, triggering or inducing happiness.

As a matter of fact, alcohol consumption has been implicated by anxiety (displeasure, high arousal, submissiveness), and depression or boredom (displeasure, low arousal, submissiveness) (Russell and Mehrabian, p.1514).

Yet, one has to realize that one of the most enduring notions of alcoholism is the stress/anxiety reduction thesis and that "the possible associations of stress, drinking, and drugs have become major issues in the public mind and the scientific literature" (p. xix).

Forms of Stress

The stress literature, though, has some very important dimensions. Stress can take many forms, ranging from situational stress to personal stress. According to researchers, "the fact that alcohol can act as a tranquilizer for individuals should be reflected in broader relations between the intensity of strains existing in a society and the level of alcohol consumption in that society" (Pearlin and Radabaugh 1976, p. 652).

Quite a lot of work has been done on stress and tension reduction, using alcohol as the predictor variable. They are Conger (1956); Heien and Pompelli (1987); Steffen et al. (1974); Allman et al. (1972); Linksy (1987); Linsky et al. (1985); Stockwell et al. (1982); Neff (1985); Cappell and Herman (1972); Williams (1950); Livingston (1985); Arbuckle et al. (1994); Sher et al. (1997); Powers and Kutash (1985).

Stress, Tension and Alcohol Consumption

Among the many works on stress and alcohol consumption, two studies stand out. The first is an article titled "Stress and Alcohol" (Powers and Kutash 1985) in which the researchers investigate the whole issue of alcohol as a reliever of stress. The researchers point out that the concept behind stress and tension is not the same, and that previous works by Masserman and Yum (1946) and Conger (1956) had to do with a tension reduction hypothesis (TRH). In other words, alcohol was posited to be a reducer of tension but in reducing tension it, however, reinforced the drinking response (Powers and Kutash 1985, p. 462).

> Recently the assumptions of the TRH have been challenged. In a number of laboratory studies with human subjects, alcohol use has produced an increase in anxiety or no change...subjects with free access to alcohol over several days showed an increase in anxiety, as well as an increase in hostility and aggressiveness. On the basis of such findings, several prominent researchers...have concluded that the TRH cannot be supported. At present however it appears premature to abandon the TRH... Recent evidence indicates the TRH may be supported under certain circumstances...(Powers and Kutash 1985, p. 462).

However, "stress" is often times used in a broader sense than "tension," although both "tension" and "anxiety" have often been used interchangeably (p. 463). "Tension or anxiety is but one prominent type of stress response." In this respect, a stress reduction hypothesis (SRH) must be distinguished from a tension reduction hypothesis (TRH). Therefore, when studying tension, one is focussing on one aspect of stress response, but when using the stress response hypothesis (SRH) one is examining a wider range of stress responses, namely, depression, lowered self-esteem and anger (p. 463).

The Buffering Effects of Alcohol

The second landmark study on stress was conducted by Neff (1985) in which he sought to identify the link between the "Stress buffering properties of alcohol consumption and depressive symptoms of abstainers and heavy drinkers." His hypothesis was to determine the relationship between the stress-buffering role of alcohol consumption and variation by type of event and symptom. The results of his investigation supported his hypothesis and showed, among other things, that both heavy drinkers and abstainers reported increases in drinking when life events increased. However, drinking decreased (with occasional drinkers) when non-catastrophic events rose.

> While neither life event nor drinking pattern had significant main effects, the interaction effect between non-catastrophic events and drinking patterns was significant. The event - distress profiles for the different drinking pattern groups indicate monotonic increases in CES-D (Center for Epidemiologic Studies Depression Scale) scores with increasing events among both abstainers and frequent - heavy drinkers. Among occasional drinkers, CES-D scores decrease monotonically with more non-catastrophic events (Neff 1985, p. 39).

Ego, Self and Alcoholism.

We now turn to another contentious area in the psychology of alcoholics, that is, the ego, self and alcoholism. Quite a number of observations have been made by researchers in this regard. Among them are Frankel and Murphy (1974); Drake and Vaillant (1988); Levenson et al. (1987); Jacob and Leonard (1986); Johnson and Mâtre (1974); Newell (1950); Butts and Chotlos (1973); Talashek (1987); Kastl (1969). There are others, but these are the more prominent ones.

Newell hypothesized that people, who are at greater risk from alcohol, whether by nature or nurture, would have more pleasure than others when they drank. As a result, these people will perceive drinking as more rewarding than others. Also, a reinforcement pattern will be set up and this will eventually lead to "a more rapid progression along the path toward alcohol dependence," and alcoholism. The results of the investigation concluded that high-risk subjects (those receiving greater result from alcohol by virtue of nature, that is, having an alcoholic parent) experience significant reinforcing effects from alcohol than those with low risk and personality deficits.

But the psychological aspect of alcohol studies does not stop here. A father can cause serious disturbance to the young child, particularly the son who is likely to adopt the father's image, by transmitting conflicting and inconsistent messages when he is sober as opposed to when he is drunk. It is quite likely therefore, that a child under such conditions would display "ambivalence, inconsistencies, antagonisms and touching overtures of affection" (Newell 1950, p. 92).

The Alcoholic Personality

There is no alcoholic personality, or put another way: there is no set of "personality factors" which predisposes one to become an alcoholic, or to drink excessively, for that matter.

> The extensive search for the "alcoholic personality" has been fruitless. It can be stated with confidence that there is no special set of personality characteristics that is to be found in all alcoholics... This is not to deny that some alcoholics display abnormal personality characteristics, but this may well be a consequence of alcohol abuse. Given that no single "core of alcoholic personality" exists, the question becomes one of whether certain characteristics of personality predispose individuals to become alcoholics. It is reasonable to expect personality to play some part in the making of an alcoholic but personality is one factor amongst many" (Eastman 1984, p. 116-117).

We have arrived at one of the most popular perceptions of alcoholism, that is, the psychological predisposition for drinking. Within this concept, we find that those who have a "natural" predisposition to do so, by virtue of their personality, must drink; their personality presents a risk in itself. In addition, the interpretation of psychological factors that are external to the individual must also be taken into consideration. The combination of those factors may make the individual react and drink excessively.

The Theory of Reinforcement

Many theories have been developed under the psychological label. One such theory is reinforcement theory. Reinforcement theory has do to with learning, and the proffering of rewards for the response(s) elicited. However, there have been problems in testing these hypotheses. For example, in looking at the relationship between stimulus and response, cats trained to open a box in order to receive food, then given negative punishment (air blasts) to deter them from receiving the reward (Masserman and Yum 1946), had their responses analyzed in the following manner: (i) Alcohol suppressed other drives, including fear, (ii) competing responses were brought about by the depressive nature of alcohol with the possibility of different effects of alcohol consumption occurring (Conger 1956, p. 303).

In this way, therefore, and in direct reference to humans, there have been responses which alcohol might fail to repress, such as sexual and apprehensive behavior.

It is nevertheless evident from a large body of empirical findings and knowledge of behavior maintenance mechanism, that the search for personality dynamics that supposedly control excessive drinking is a futile pursuit.

> Just as persons who differ markedly in personality attributes can learn to use tobacco excessively, so, given appropriate social-learning conditions, persons who possess diverse personality characteristics, can be taught heavy drinking of alcoholic beverages (Bandura 1969, p. 528-29).

Alcohol—the Situational Tension Reducer

Even as we pursue our elusive search for an alcoholic personality, it is clear that it is no longer useful to ask whether alcohol reduces tension, but rather, to investigate under what condition, at what quality, and by which measures it reduces tension (Wilson et al. 1980, p. 263). In fact, the search for an alcoholic personality does not reflect the outcome of a vast number of research findings, and may represent ongoing attempts to come to grips with overwhelming evidence that alcoholics are not genetically driven, but are socially inclined to consume large doses of alcohol, either intermittently or consistently.

"Extensive research failed to identify a single personality type to which alcoholics conform" (Cotton 1979, p. 104) but, like the genetic argument it is hard to accept this, no doubt driven by years of exposure to the concept that reality is what the vast majority of people think it is and that not every thing can be measured consistently within the confines of the laboratory.

Coming out of the literature on alcoholism, one notes that stress, hypertension, tension-reduction and coping are major variables, which impact on an individual's concentration. For while there is the general view that alcohol reduces stress, others say it controls anxiety. Still others (Arbuckle et al. 1994) contend that cognitive deficits and psychological distress are not so much responsible for social drinking, but due in part to neuropsychological drinking measures. Tweed and Ryff (1991), support this line of reasoning. Using a self-report standardized instrument of psychological well-being, emotional distress and personality characteristics, they concluded that adult children of alcoholics (ACOAs) score significantly higher on anxiety and depression measures than do those from non-alcoholic families.

Psychological Impact of Alcohol Consumption

There is, however, a growing body of literature which suggests that there is some significant psychological impact in explaining alcohol consumption. Some of these factors are personality disorders (Windle 1994; Drake and Vaillant 1988). In addition, the role of exposure to stressors could explain alcoholic disorders, for example, between father and offspring (Sher et al. 1997). This behavior is demonstrated and inflicted on them through sibling and parents interaction gone awry with excessive drinking. What we do know also is that individuals displaying antisocial behaviors, tend to have higher rates of substance abuse than persons in the general population (Kwapil 1996), just as those who have had a history of psychiatric problems.

Expectancy Outcomes

Consistent with this view is the whole issue of expectancy outcomes. (Wall et al. 1998); Marshall (1999) reports that alcohol produces expectancies of sexual functioning for males, and assertiveness for females. However, men remain the subject of stress inquiry following consistent excessive drinking. A person's sensitivity to alcohol is "a good predictor of who does and who does not develop alcoholism" (Wolfgang 1997, p. 278).

Stress and personality factors have also implicated stressful situations in persons' lives to determine where heavy drinking can be located. So great is the association between stress and drinking that researchers tend to focus on interactions played out between stressful situations, ego identity and personality in understanding not only the question of the "alcoholic personality", but reactions to situations which are inclined towards drinking.

For example, stress found in family relationships and college campuses may be one of the many factors of significance in furthering our understanding of distress, stress and excessive drinking. Yet, the question must be raised: why do stressful situations (perceived or real) make the vast majority of such individuals want to abuse substances? It might be a fundamental factor in all human beings to want social support "in times of crises," and so, instead of hypothesizing relationships between stress and alcohol abuse we should be looking at how stress is perceived, manipulated and controlled.

The Ever Presence of Alcohol

The reason why there is an "association" between stress and alcoholism is simply because the alcoholic beverage is ever present and within easy reach of the vast majority of sub-populations which are at risk, by virtue of their social situation, in the first instance. Skog (2000) in measuring the change in over-the-counter to monopoly outlets in Sweden found that increased availability of alcohol led to increases in consumption. It may also have to do with the intoxicant nature of alcohol to temporarily relieve the stress.

In addition, the external environment may be responsible for changing the mood of drinkers, for example, anxiety and alienation in the workplace (Phillips 1976), interpersonal intimate relationships, job security, high unemployment and the general lack of planning and predictability in the social and political environment. These may be temporary conditions, not habit forming, but carry implications for alcohol use as a temporary respite, especially at the end of the workweek.

High Expectations

Some individuals are placed or find themselves in social positions where expectations are high, but for which they are not yet prepared, or for which they are ill-prepared. Others may react to alcohol intake depending on life-styles or the nature of their organizational affiliation, suggesting that the image of an institution may determine one's behavior outside of it. Forney et al. (1988) found that "white males and those who attend church infrequently are more likely to be frequent or heavy drinkers" (p. 777). In addition, their fathers were reported to be heavy drinkers themselves. The study was conducted among first-year medical students in order "to identify students" who were likely to engage in heavy drinking.

The Effects of Memory on Drinking

Vannicelli (1972) on the other hand, investigated whether alcoholics who experienced increased anxiety while drinking recalled such experience when sober.

It was hypothesized that those alcoholics who had increased levels of anxiety when drinking would develop a "disgusting and distasteful" attitude or feeling, resulting in making poor predictions when sober as it related to their intoxicated behavior. Alternatively, it was predicted that those alcoholics who found themselves having decreased anxiety when drinking "are more capable of making predictions when sober" because they do not reject themselves when they are drunk, based on their reduced anxiety.

Vannicelli (1972) reported that when drinks were held constant, there were no significant differences between three groups tested, particularly following the first drink. However, anxiety-prone alcoholics showed a greater level of anxiety following the second, third, and fourth drinks. Therefore, alcoholics can display different responses to alcohol.

The researcher also found that it was more accurate to make predictions about the sober self when drunk than about the drunk self when sober, prompting discussion that the alcoholic, when sober, may not make a valid representation of his actions or behaviors when he was in his drunken state. It is more likely that the reverse is true, that is, that the alcoholic may make a better presentation of his sober behaviors when he is drunk. If this is the case, then, there are certainly some psychological imperatives that we cannot easily dismiss. The question to be asked is: can these findings be generalized to the wider community of alcoholics?

Rewards and Punishment

The above revelation has implications for understanding results of self-report data collection from alcoholics in their sober state about their drinking. Particularly, it may help in understanding why alcoholics (in their sober state) may be predisposed to "not remember" their behaviors, because it carries uncomfortable impressions. This behavior allows him to prevent the transmission of his bad experience from one condition to the other (that is, from sober to drunken state and back to sober state), and in the process, prevent the effects of an occurring negative reinforcement which might reduce his drinking:

> It would appear that the drunk self is relatively inaccessible to the sober alcoholic-perhaps because the ability to judge evaluate, verbalize, etc. is impaired in the drunken state (Vannicelli 1972, p. 356).

It is instructive to note that in the continuing search for clarification of the relationship between stress and alcohol consumption, Perkins (1999) finds that college students' stress-motivated drinking is more prevalent in the undergraduate years, but drinking for stress-reduction becomes increasingly significant in the years following college life. A similar finding is described by Wood et al. (1997) who examine the relationship between problematic alcohol use with that of academic problems. The researchers determine that alcohol use is correlated with academic problems particularly at the freshman level.

Summary

The literature supports conflicting hypotheses on stress and alcoholism. Some researchers argue that stress leads to alcohol abuse; others contend that alcohol abuse leads to stress.

Learned behavior from a scientific point of view began with Masserman and Yum who proved that alcohol militates inhibition. In addition, Bergler (1946/1947) suggests that drinking is associated with unconscious conflicts represented by the changing moods of the alcoholic personality.

Two studies on alcohol and stress stand out. They are "Stress and Alcohol" by Powers and Kutash (1985) and "Stress Buffering Properties of Alcohol Consumption..." by Neff (1985). The first examines the contention that alcohol is a reliever of stress. The researchers argued that previous stress research had to do with, not stress per se, but tension reduction. Therefore one had to distinguish between stress reduction and tension reduction.

The second by Neff (1985), on the other hand, argued for the stress-buffering properties of alcohol consumption as it related to the depressive symptoms of drinkers on either end of the continuum—abstainers and heavy drinkers. The researcher reported that heavy drinkers had significantly more life events than abstainers. This suggests that life events which were stressful predisposed one to engage in heavy drinking.

Persons who are psychologically predisposed to alcoholism have been seen to have an extra increment of pleasure when drinking. Likewise an "alcoholic personality" can be developed by the transmission of conflicting messages from father to son; on occasions when he is sober to occasions when he is drunk.

However, there is no set of personality factors within which to locate the "alcoholic personality." These factors must be seen within the external environment and on an individual basis.

The most practical aspect of alcohol consumption as a tension reducer must therefore take into consideration certain things, namely, the conditions surrounding drinking, quantity drunk and the measures by which it reduces tension. Yet, a growing body of literature contends that personality disorders, exposure to stressors and type of parental socialization and psychotic persons tend to show greater rates of substance abuse.

Not to be discounted in this scenario is expectancy and sensitivity to alcohol. Therefore a personality disorder compounded with expectancy can have above-normal consequences. Also, prevailing circumstances in society such as job insecurity, unstable political environment, alienation and intimate relationships produce alcohol behavior that may be considered serious.

The question of remembering things from an alcoholic state when in a sober one, or put another way, remembering things done in a drunken state, has interestingly come to the fore.

Vannicelli (1972) reports that the alcoholic may be in a better position to understand his sober behavior when drunk rather than about his drunken state when sober.

Suggested Readings

Abrams, David B.; and Terence G. Wilson. 1979. "Effects of Alcohol on Social Anxiety in Women: Cognitive Versus Physiological Processes." Journal of Abnormal Psychology 88, no. 2:161-73.

Breslin, Curtis F.; Michele Hayward; and Andrew S. Baum. 1995. "Stress and Alcohol: The Moderating Effect of Chronic Stress on the Acute Stress-Intoxication Relationship." Journal of Studies on Alcohol 56, no. 5:546-52.

Brown, Sandra A.; Peter W. Vik; Thomas L. Patterson; Igor Grant; and Marc A. Schuckit. 1995. "Stress, Vulnerability and Adult Alcohol Relapse." Journal of Studies on Alcohol 56, no. 5:538-45.

Cooney, Ned L.; Mark D. Litt; Priscilla A. Morse; Lance O. Bauer; and Larry Gaupp. 1997. "Alcohol Cue Reactivity, Negative-Mood Reactivity, and Relapse in Treated Alcohol Men." Journal of Abnormal Psychology. 106, no. 2:243-50.

Gottheil, Edward; Keith Druby; Steven Pashko; and Stephen Weinstein.1987. Stress and Addiction. New York: Brunner/Mazel Publishers.

Ham, Hazen P.; and Oscar A. Parsons. 1997. "Organization of Psychological Functions in Alcoholics and Non-alcoholics: A Test of the Compensatory Hypothesis." Journal of Studies on Alcohol 58, no. 1:67-74.

Liguori, Anthony; Ralph B. D'Agostino; Steven I. Dworkin; Don Edwards; and John H. Robinson. 1999. "Alcohol Effects on Mood, Equilibrium, and Simulated Driving." Alcoholism Clinical and Experimental Research 23, no. 5:815-21.

Mundt, James C.; M.W. Perrine; and John S. Searles. 1997. "Individual Differences in Alcohol Responsivity: Physiological, Psychomotor and Subjective Response Domains." Journal of Studies on Alcohol 58, no. 2:130-40.

Rada, Richard T. 1984. "Alcoholism and the Child Molester." In Psychological Approaches to Crime and its Correction, edited by Irving Jacks and Steven G. Cox. Chicago: Nelson-Hall.

CHAPTER 8

CHILDREN OF ALCOHOLICS (COAs)

Introduction

Children continue to hold the spotlight as far as the deleterious effects of alcohol abuse are concerned. Children of alcoholics need special consideration, especially when we consider that a child is literally defenseless against unhealthy socialization, particularly when that kind of socialization leads to greater problems in the future. "Adolescence is a very special time" (Olson and Gerstein 1985, p. 70). It is a time when children are bombarded by the media and popular culture; it is also a time when they tend to be more loyal to their friends than themselves. Teenagers have many problems to work out. What is even more critical is when "most students reach the minimum drinking age in an environment marked by ready access to alcohol and great personal freedom," (Olson and Gerstein 1985, p. 72) things can happen.

Children and Symbols of Alcohol Consumption

It should be noted, however, that those who are socialized into families exposed to heavy drinking would be so influenced whether through symbolic interaction, or, observational learning, or modeling (Lawson and Lawson 1989). Symbolic interaction means that people assign different meaning to objects or things, depending on the importance or significance of these things. Someone may view an object as a weapon, another may view it as an ornament, still, another may interpret the same object as a reminder of some pleasant or unpleasant incident.

Observational learning also called modeling is developed by observing another's behavior, and can lead to the acquisition of interpersonal skills (Michener et al. 1986 p. 17).

> According to the National Association for Children of Alcoholics...about 25 million Americans have at least one alcoholic parent, and 52% of those alcoholic parents come from alcoholic families themselves (Fox 1968, Cited in Lawson and Lawson 1989, p. 139).

Thus, there is a high risk for these children to develop alcohol drinking and related problems. However, the greater presence of alcohol in homes does not necessarily constitute an at-risk situation for all children. Certain conditions militate against children becoming alcoholics themselves. They are:

- The exposure early in life to alcohol as a religious aspect or component of religious rituals
- Parents drinking moderately
- Non-alcoholic beverages in the household
- Beverages considered food and consequently consumed with meals
- Drinking with no moral meaning attached to it
- No image of masculinity or adult behavior attached to drinking alcohol
- Abstinence is accepted, socially, speaking while being drunk is not accepted
- All members of the family having the same standards for drinking (O'Connor 1975)

It seems, therefore, from all indications, that containing the image and symbol of alcohol within the home plays no small part in the conditioning of behavior, as far as alcohol abuse is concerned.

Once alcoholism seeps into the household, it can create lasting feelings into adulthood of loss of control, fear or abandonment, and feelings of anger (Lawson and Lawson 1989).

Pandina and Johnson (1989) find no relationship between offspring of families having a history of alcoholism, that is, frequent intoxication and escape-drinking, and those without a positive history of alcoholism. However, those children from families having a positive history of alcoholism were more likely than the children of those without a positive history, to succumb to problems related to drinking and the taking of drugs.

The Importance of Early Experiences

"Early experiences, particularly those originating from parental example are likely to be relevant for the future of children's development" (Casswell et al. 1985, p. 191).

Casswell et al. (1985), looking at children's (8-9 years) attitude towards alcohol, observed that they all had negative feelings towards alcohol consumption. However, where these children were aware of alcohol-related problems in their environment the negative attitude was increased, as opposed to those children who were unaware of problems in their immediate environment, even though their parents drank. In other words, having a positive or negative attitude towards alcohol consumption was dependent upon one's awareness/unawareness of alcohol problems. This finding suggests that it is not what you do but how you do it. Not what, or how much you drink, but what accompanies the drinking. Is drinking associated with quarrel, strife and lack of responsibility, or is it accompanied by praise, special consideration, or general contentment, following some achievement?

It has been further posited that children in the family might exacerbate the effects of alcoholism. According to Jacob et al. (1978), the presence of children may make the father recognize "his failure" and become guilty. No doubt, the suggestion here is tied up with the father's sense of responsibility in the home; the child stands as a silent reminder of the alcoholic father's "failures." But Curran and Chassin (1996) in examining the relationship between maternal, parental behaviors and the negative effects coming from paternal's alcoholic behavior, found data supporting the hypothesis that both parents could influence child development alcohol outcomes.

Age and Alcoholism

The young are particularly vulnerable to alcohol abuse/alcoholism. Of particular concern is disillusionment which young people harbour for "the establishment" (Glatt and Hills 1968). Following Jellinek's (1960) line of argument that a widespread acceptance of heavy drinking increases the risk of individuals becoming alcoholics, Glatt and Hills (1968) contend that, similarly, the case of young teenagers' drinking increases the likelihood of a large number of adult drinkers later on in life (p. 186). In fact, early drinking represents the breeding ground of future alcoholics.

Teenage Drinking, Normal Drinking

The writers observe that one should not confuse "normal drinking" among teenagers with that of "dependent young drinkers." For example, "normal" drinkers do not drink for "fun," they drink for social acceptance, on certain occasions. On the other hand, those who are "dependent" may have a distorted view of their own situation, or they may be angry with their parents, or they may wish to emulate the (drinking) behavior of adults in society.

> The teenager's perception of adult behavior coupled with descriptions of first drinking experiences in the home both emphasize drinking as legitimate behavior for adults and at least some teenagers under some circumstances (Maddox 1962. Cited in Pittman and Snyder p. 231).

Glatt and Hills (1968) point to certain factors which fall under the socio-pathological heading. These are recounted here for the benefit of clarity and perspective:

(1) Early emotional deprivation, representative of physical and emotional trauma

(2) Evidence of heavy drinking by one parent, followed by dominance and submission of the other

(3) Sexual problems, including confused sexual identities

(4) Identification of behavior with parent who drinks

(5) Overcompensation, when there is a deficit or perceived deficit, leading to withdrawal from society followed by anti-social behavior

(6) Difficulty in accepting role of adults

Most of these observations are consistent with the work of other researchers, namely: Budd et al. (1985); Potvin and Lee (1980); Maddox (1962). However there is hope. As mentioned before, there is evidence to support the thesis that not all children of alcoholics are relegated to a life of problems and social malfunctioning. Callan and Jackson (1985), report that children of recovered alcoholics rate their parents positively, and that those children disagree with the view that alcoholics lack will power and have weak personalities. This signals that the children themselves recognize the negative aspect of drinking and its consequences and are prepared to deal with them.

Further, Segrin and Menees (1996) contend that there is little or no relationship between "parental problem drinking and various aspects of young adult children's social skills."(p. 31) However, the question of dysfunctional communication patterns still played a part. Families with an alcoholic parent exhibit greater dysfunctional patterns than those without, they reported. It should also be remembered however, that there may be some blurring of the boundaries between family studies (that is, children of alcoholics) and alcoholism among the young who are not under parental control or guidance, or among teenagers who live with their parents. What is striking about the literature on young drinkers is that it is divided up into "family studies of alcohol", "children of alcoholics," and "young drinkers."

Young Drinkers

As regards the first, that is, family studies, the literature is quite clear, the unit of analysis is either the parent, the family or both; in studies on children of alcoholics (COA) the unit of analysis is the children who reside within homes where alcohol is abused. On the other hand, studies on "the young and alcohol abuse" must be clearer, both in terms of their content and specifically their title. For example, Glatt and Hills (1968) speak about alcohol abuse among the young and they point out that it involves the young in various settings, that is family settings, "alcoholic unit settings," and "addition unit" settings.

Others are not so explicit: Budd et al. (1985) theorize about the "young drinker," by incorporating and implicating family drinking as part of life style behavior leading to "young drinking." "Heavy drinkers will be experiencing more stress than light, moderate or non-drinkers..." and "will perceive themselves as doing worse in school," (Budd et al. 1985, p. 145) in addition to having conflict with their parents. Williams and Lillis (1986) examine "changes in alcohol consumption

by 18 year olds," without controlling for parental influence. Notwithstanding, the researchers report that alcohol consumption by 18-year-olds, (as well as 17-year-olds) decreased significantly when the minimum age for purchase went from 18 to 19 years. Using a three-stage, stratified, proportionate random sample, eighteen hundred 16-20-year-old New Yorkers were selected using anonymous telephone interviews. This was done before the age to purchase was raised to age 19. One year following the introduction of this legislation the researchers took a second sample before arriving at their conclusion.

Controlling for Different Classes of Young Drinkers

When looking at the young and alcoholism, one should identify whether these youngsters are living alone or living with parents. Merely pointing out that the method of selection was done on households says very little in as much as teenagers live with their parents or apart from them.

Other studies that look at drinking during the teenage years, while focusing on the teenager as the unit of analysis and not attempting to separate adult home pressure from teenage peer pressure, must determine what factor is interacting with other factors and which factor is more predominant?

El-Guebaly and Offord (1977) advanced the suggestion that we look also at children of alcoholic parents who do not seem to be at increased risk for psychosocial illnesses. This suggests identifying factors, which these "successful" children have in common in order to determine whether these factors could be developed in those children of alcoholics who are negatively affected.

Citing a study by Jones et al. (1995) the authors showed how that particular study identified risk factors among offspring of alcoholic mothers, among them being perinatal mortality, fetal alcohol syndrome, adverse pregnancy outcome, and lower IQ. They determined their findings by examining the records of 55,000 pregnant women and their offspring from which 23 alcoholic mothers were chosen. Each alcoholic mother was matched with 2 control non-alcoholic mothers. Those maternal variables which were controlled were age, race, socio-economic class, education, marital status and parity.

Epidemiological Studies

What is seriously needed is an epidemiological study of two groups of young children from childhood to adulthood (early forties); with one group having alcoholic parents, and another group having non-alcoholic parents. This helps determine whether genetic predisposition, peer pressure, psychological pressure, environmental factors, social and cultural factors, are responsible for non-alcoholic as opposed to alcoholic outcomes. This study should be controlled for genetic factors, (environment and other factors may mitigate the "genetic risk," particularly

particularly in the long term), psychological factors, peer pressures, cultural factors, toward adulthood. One such study having this potential is the one currently in operation (Schuckit et al. 1998). In reviewing results from an ongoing prospective study, it was found that 20-year-old sons of alcoholics exhibited a low level of response to alcohol abuse. This finding might be viewed as critical to understanding the full etiology of alcoholism.

Also, Seppa et al. (1999), examining heavy or problem drinking among 40-year-olds, found that most of them either reduced their drinking in previous years or had maintained the same amount of drinking five years later. This confirms that middle-aged men could make conscious decisions to reduce their consumption level of alcohol or to prevent its increase. Epidemiologically speaking, studies on alcohol abuse will allow us to determine the point at which "remission" commences, thus identifying powerful factors, which can counter the alcohol addiction. These studies can also highlight the point at which dependency sets in, thus identifying when overload is followed by a combination of factors in the individuals' lives. This suggestion is borne out by Budd et al. (1985, p. 155) when they observe that:

> [Over] 90% [of adolescents] report that they drink with their parents, most adolescents are introduced to drinking in the family setting...while the number of adolescents who drink at home remains constant with age, the number who drink in social settings outside the home increase sharply from about fourteen years of age onwards.

It would appear from the above that children maintain their level of alcohol consumption within the home, which may be a function of the stabilizing effect of socialization. On the other hand, children who drink outside the home in social settings tend to have their alcohol consumption fuelled by peer pressures and certain situations.

Predicting Future Drinking

It is clear that children of alcoholics are an at-risk population (Roosa et al. 1987), and that something should be done at the family and the public policy levels. Indications are that a life events scale (Roosa et al. 1987) could measure these at-risk children of alcoholics. In examining factors responsible for alcohol abuse among the young, Koch-Hattem and Denman (1987) found that among University students, mean age "at the time of the respondent's first drink was 14.3 years" and that a "number of family stresses during the previous year led to increase in alcohol abuse."

But Casswell et al. (1985) argue that parental influence have much to do with children's future drinking. Still, the data show that problem drinking among children is very common and in no way signifies an entry into adult drinking (Levin 1990, p. 94). One study (Keefe 1994) reports that friends who pressured others not to drink decrease with age. In other words, as age increases peer influence on drinking decreases. Another study (Curran et al. 1998) examines the changes of marital status on alcohol use trajectories in young adults. Results show that becoming married for the first time had a negative impact on alcohol use. This was particularly significant for Whites as opposed to Blacks.

College Student, Adolescent and the Alcoholic Child

> Heavy drinking among college students continues to concern college administrators and counselors...Surveys indicate that 45% of college seniors consume alcohol once a week or more..., and at least half of college students are moderate to heavy drinkers...Furthermore, as the quantity and frequency of drinking increase, the risk of alcohol-related problems also increase (O'Hare 1990. Cited in Carey 1995, p. 287).

Yet, not all drinking on campus carries implications. Carey (1995), suggests that heavy drinkers are at risk in situations where there is social pressure to drink, for example, during "pleasant times," but these same drinkers were not at risk of "loss of control," or in situations involving "unpleasant emotions."

The college student may be no different from the adolescent in his/her drinking pattern when we take into consideration that most adolescents are in school continuing their maturational development. The perceived differences in these two groups may stem from the fact that one may be in a school setting where peer pressure and other factors may predispose one to greater influence of alcohol abuse, or some other problem arising from other students' drinking (Wechsler et al. 1995).

The whole question of expectancy, therefore, becomes quite relevant when we take into consideration that the actual socialization process can confirm or reinforce such tendencies or expectations. In short, children are socialized into expectations and societies continue to reinforce these expectations, (Aas et al. 1995), irrespective of the effects of the agent of socialization which they may encounter at every stage of their development.

Understanding the Theory of Planned Action

The theory of reasoned action (TRA) explains the relationship between attitudes and actions, and actions towards behavior. O'Callaghan et al. (1997) report that university students quizzed on attitudes, subjective norms, perceived behaviors, past behaviors and intentions to drink, provide good predictors of their intentions to drink, and this normally translates into actual behavior.

One study (Carey and Correia 1997), tests the motive for drinking among college undergraduates. Results indicate that both negative and positive reinforcement motives are mediated by maximum daily quantity, although both positive and negative reinforcement motives "retained unique predictive powers" (p. 100). Simply put, the analysis indicates that depending upon one's motives for drinking, that motive becomes significant only to the extent of the amount of drinks drunk. Further, motive itself can be a predictor variable even when mediated by "maximum daily quantity."

Friedman and Humphrey (1985) argue that collegiate life governed by norms, permit drinking to a certain extent. The researchers constructed a model comprising (1) race, sex, and population of students' hometown; (2) father's occupation, parents' marital status, and closeness to a problem-drinker, and (3) the onset of student drinking, that is, age at first drinking and extent of drinking. Drawing a 10 percent random sample of undergraduate students from two state supported universities, the researchers reported that there were similarities in drinking patterns among White males and White females, especially in the lower academic classes. But White college students drank more than their Black counterparts. In addition, "the level of alcohol consumption by undergraduates on a given drinking occasion was associated with race (Whites drinking had the following correlation ($r = 0.29$), fathers' skills, managerial, or professional positions ($r = 0.21$)," or when undergraduates' drinking began before the age of 16 ($r = -0.16$).

Much has been written on children of alcoholics; this interest is relevant because children of alcoholics can be traced from the home right through college years. It also indicates that these children may have had the drinking habit passed on to them without having time to develop sufficient coping skills. Equally intriguing is the suggestion that the family remains the cradle for identifying the development of alcoholism from a "genetic predisposition" and from "adverse effects of certain family practices and attitudes to alcohol" (Krasner et al. 1984, p. 128), although "familial...is not synonymous with genetic" (Goodwin 1990).

Nature and Nurture

It is quite possible to separate nature from nurture by empirical testing. Those individuals who are at risk could be removed soon after birth and followed through adult life. Yet, the debate remains significant for there is a strong feeling that children can unwittingly "inherit" alcoholism from their familial setting. In short, we are focusing on children becoming victims of adult alcoholic behavior.

Summary

Children are extremely important in understanding alcohol abuse. In this respect children of alcoholics must come in for special consideration. One factor in alcohol abuse is socialization; it makes for the passing on of the alcoholic habit. Adolescence is a particularly trying time for individuals for they are buffeted both by internal and external forces.

Symbolically, those who have been socialized into alcohol consumption would ascribe certain meanings to the drinking of alcohol. It is therefore important to fashion the kinds of positive images that are being constructed in the home.

There remains conflicting findings surrounding alcohol consumption in the home although children coming from dysfunctional alcoholic homes may succumb to problems related to drinking and the taking of drugs. In this respect early experiences may foretell the future.

Symbolically, all these negatives could be invalidated. Good symbols will mitigate the negative effects of alcohol abuse. Early drinking is the breaking ground for future alcoholics. Teenagers' perception also play a part in teenage drinking. Early emotional deprivation, dominance and submission, sexual problems, over compensation and role acceptance can lead to teenage drinking.

Not all is negative, where alcohol consumption within the home is concerned. Research has shown that children of recovered alcoholics rate their parents positively, indicating a certain amount of sympathy for their parents, while inhibiting cognitive objective thinking in the process.

In examining literature on young drinkers one has to consider "family studies," "children of alcoholics," and "young drinkers," since there is some blurring of the boundaries. Some studies identify their unit of analysis, others do not; still others do not control for "other variables" to determine if, following control, the variance among the "young drinkers" will decrease.

A suggestion is made by this writer to undertake an epidemiological study that will allow us to control for genetic factors, psychological factors, cultural factors and peer pressure. This will allow us to locate the point of "dependency."

Expected outcome is a significant factor in alcohol abuse. Children literally learn what to expect from a particular behavior. The theory of reason action (TRA) explains the relationship between attitudes, actions, and behavior.

The family remains the cradle of alcoholism either from a "genetic predisposition" or to adverse effects perspective within the family.

In sum, children can become victims of adult alcoholic behavior for more reasons than one.

Suggested Readings

Black, Claudia. 1983. "Children of Alcoholics: Young-Adolescent-Adult." In: Alcoholism, edited by P. Golding. Boston: MTP Press.

Cameron, James R. 1977. "Parental Treatment, Children's Temperament, and the Risk of Childhood Behavioral Problems." American Journal of Orthopsychiatry 47, no.4:568-76.

Donohew, Lewis R.; Rich H. Hoyle; Richard R. Clayton; William F.Skinner; Susan E. Colon; and Ronald Rice. 1999. "Sensation Seeking and Drug Use by

Adolescents and Their Friends: Models for Marijuana and Alcohol." Journal of Studies on Alcohol 60, no. 5:622-31.

Donovan, John E. 1993. "Young Adult Drinking-Driving: Behavioral and Psychosocial Correlates." Journal of Studies on Alcohol 54, no. 5:600-63.

Harvey, J. M.; D. L. Boswell; and J. S. Romans. 1995. "The Relationship of Self-Perception and Stress in Adult Children of Alcoholics and Their Peers." Journal of Drug Education 25, no. 1:23-29.

Kress, Yvonne. 1989. "Special Issues of Adult Children of Alcoholics." In Alcoholism and Substance Abuse in Special Populations, edited by Gary W. Lawson and Ann W. Lawson. Maryland: Aspen Publisher Inc.

Maxwell, Delmas M. 1989. "Impact Analysis of the Raised Legal Drinking Age in Illinois." In Evaluation in Practice: A Methodological Approach, edited by Richard D. Bingham and Claire L. Felbinger. New York & London: Longman.

Nezlek, John B.; Constance J. Pilkington; and Kathryn G. Bilbro. 1994. "Moderation in Excess: Binge Drinking and Social Interaction among College Students." Journal of Studies on Alcohol 55, no. 3: 342-51.

Palmer, N. 1997. "Resilience in Adult Children of Alcoholics: A Non-Pathological Approach to Social Work Practice." Health and Social Work 22, no. 3 : 201-209.

Smith, Gregory T.; Denis M. McCarthy; and Mark S. Goldman. 1995. "Self-Reported Drinking and Alcohol-Related Problems among Early Adolescents: Dimensionality and Validity over 24 Months." Journal of Studies on Alcohol 56, no. 4:383-94.

Thomas, Richard W.; and David R. Seibold. 1995. "College Students' Decisions to Intervene in Alcohol-Related Situations." Journal of Studies on Alcohol 56, no. 5: 580-88.

Wagenaar, Alexander; Traci L. Toomey; David M. Murray; Brian J. Short; Mark Wolfson; and Rhonda Jones-Webb. 1996. "Sources of Alcohol for Underage Drinkers." Journal of Studies on Alcohol 57, no. 3:325-33.

Warder, J.; and Ross, C. J. 1971. "Age and Alcoholism." British Journal of Addiction 66:45-51.

CHAPTER 9

The Socio-Cultural Aspects of Alcoholism

Introduction

The study of alcohol abuse represents an intriguing challenge to every student of sociology (Bourne and Fox 1973). Every student of human behavior must recognize the challenge faced by alcohol abuse. It is a challenge mixed with social and cultural factors, one where individuals and groups alike lay claim to it being a recreational past-time, or a necessary habit, sanctioned by society and encouraged by the culture.

The Strength of Sociological Base

That alcohol abuse has a strong sociological basis cannot be denied; that the behavioral approach remains the main (strongest) claim from which alcohol abuse has and continues to have significant outcomes, both from a statistical (quantum) point of view and from a recovery point of view. This is the main contention of this book. In short, it is the pathway to understanding irresponsible behavior.

The conventional wisdom or experience points to the fact that alcohol abuse has many variants reflected in supportive arguments, including the genetic, the ethnic, in addition to even the structural and cultural. However, it is instructive to note that of all the competing theories, the sociological one is the one which most often will be employed in order to explain alcohol recovery, even when the abuser has an at-risk (genetic/biological) predisposition.

The sociological approach basically deals with group behavior towards alcohol abuse. It encompasses the impact the environment has upon individuals. In examining the sociological approach, one cannot ignore the core sociological variables. They are age, race, sex, religion and socio-economic status. One may argue, and rightly so, that living in any environment may necessitate some sort of social activities, (including drinking) since man is basically social, and other variables such as age, race and sex explain individual nuances as well.

Alcohol and Its Ability to Straddle Different Populations

The difference with alcohol abuse is that unlike other forms of abuse, it straddles different populations from young to old. These populations all have 'valid' reasons to engage in a practice that is deleterious to their health, notwithstanding varying degrees of alcohol awareness programs throughout the world. One of the reasons for this is that alcohol cuts across the various sociological explanations, namely socialization, familial, group, situational, symbolic and conflictual. Researchers who try to understand alcohol abuse come up normally with patterns of behaviors that give meanings and insights into various aspects of sociological theories.

How then do we understand alcohol abuse in different situations? For example, in a situation where a man gets a "high," feeling good, with friends or all by himself and he moves to a "low, " where he feels badly about himself as he enters his home, and proceeds to abuse his spouse. Alternatively, he drinks, becomes depressed because of a problem he cannot cope with, but ends up "high" anyway.

In the first instance: can it be argued that the individual had the motivation to be abusive earlier on? Secondly, can it be argued that the drinker would have experienced euphoria or gratification later regardless of his interactional experience which followed his drinking?

Elsewhere (Marshall 1992), it has been stressed that the genesis of alcohol abuse can be located within the family structure, where parents' interaction with siblings set up a demonstration effect impacting the youngest members of the family unit. In this scenario, customs and norms are passed on from mother to daughter, and from father to son. However, these factors may be contextual (Keefe and Newcomb 1996).

The Context of Sex

We may ask the question how "contextual" is sex, ethnicity and socio-economic status? These are variables which may display various levels of variance inside and outside the context in which they are analyzed, but in the main they are relatively consistent where drinking is concerned. Across the board, and generally speaking, male drinking and female drinking show more or less consistent patterns of behavior.

Further, family influences take place long before peer influence (Zucker 1979). As pointed out before, one researcher reports that the age of alcohol influence takes place between fourteen and fifteen years (Maddox 1962) and this appears to be a consistent finding throughout the literature. This means that even if the teenager escapes home drinking he/she may not escape the influence of peer drinking or some aspects of it.

What then of social irresponsibility? Does it mean that anyone who is not "genetically" at risk and is an abuser of alcohol, is engaging in social irresponsibility? The answer is both yes and no, depending from which angle you approach the question.

For those persons who are not aware of the social factors responsible for their behavior we can excuse them, like adolescents trapped in a social environment, where they model their drinking from their parents, or where they are under peer pressure to identify with members of the "in-group." For those who are aware and continue to refuse counseling and other methods of treatment, we have to be wary of their behavior, whether they find solace, escape or bravado in continuing their high level of alcohol consumption. They should not only be warned, but be "punished" for their "social irresponsibility."

Social Irresponsibility Not New

Remarkably, the issue of responsibility was around since the Temperance Movement in the 19th century. Supporters of Temperance were hard on moderate drinkers, not on abusers. They felt the abuser, not the moderate drinker was a

victim. Later they changed their stance to one of "irresponsibility", that is, they saw an "abuser" as a pest or nuisance to society. This change of heart took place during prohibition.

Heavy Drinking

Heavy drinking takes place at greater levels within the lower socio-economic groups. Middle-and upper-class people tend to report drinking more frequently, but they are less prone to heavy consumption.

Middle-and upper-socio-economic Blacks drank similarly to their White counterparts, suggesting class differences in alcohol consumption. However, Levine (1978) makes an important point in this regard:

> Contrary to much writing on the Temperance movement...I want to suggest that, in the 19th century, temperance was not only an attempt by one class or status group to change the behavior of another. It was also a quite self interested activity... Members of temperance organizations were deeply concerned with the pernicious effects of alcohol on their own group-primarily the Protestant middle class; they worried about themselves, their relatives, friends and neighbors (p. 259).

Throughout the history of alcoholism, the "irresponsibility" theme comes through: what would my friend say? How will I look? What effect will it have on my family, relatives and friends? This struggle of "responsibility" over "irresponsibility" tends to find a niche in adopting the disease model (a victim who is not responsible for his condition), or a "pest," that is, one who cannot control his drinking and therefore escapes responsibility.

As pointed out earlier, the complexity of alcoholic behavior or drinking patterns for that matter becomes easy once it is dichotomized into the genetic and social camp. These two share boundaries by using the same unit of analysis, the family, for the etiology of alcoholism, but the similarity ends there. The weight of social factors is the true focus in which to locate the "victim" and the "irresponsible." For one, it is determined that males differ in their drinking patterns to their female counterparts (Olenick and Chalmers 1991), or among their own sexes (Herd 1997).

For another, Cahalan and Cisin (1968) point to Italian-Americans who, although consuming a great deal of alcohol, have little alcoholism or problem drinkers in their society. Similarly, the Jews have a history of sobriety and this is attributed to the traditional manner in which they use alcohol within the home, at celebrations, and at religious ceremonies. This, according to the author, was viewed as an attitude towards alcohol consumption.

Group behavior towards alcoholism deals with a number of issues. For one, there is the personality factor and the meaning attached to group membership.

The interactive model explains the combination of psychological and sociological variables in precipitating alcohol consumption.

Deviance Theme in Alcoholism

Other sociological theories used for explaining alcoholism is the labeling theory; the individual is seen as a deviant and is compelled to continue to drink because of this label, notwithstanding the cross-cultural differences in the rates of alcoholism. Under this approach, cultural norms, and the individual's relation to the particular culture determine how he will drink. Furthermore, public policy towards alcoholism is impacted by the prevailing cultural values than actual consumption levels (Smith 1986, p. 16).

Bales Theory of Alcoholism

Bales' (1946) theory is probably the most comprehensive when it comes to explaining the socio-cultural approach to alcohol consumption. He defines the ways in which culture and social organization can influence the rate of alcoholism. The first is the degree to which the culture creates inner tension or acute needs; the second is the attitude towards drinking which the culture imparts to its members in terms of norms, ideas and sentiments. The third factor is the degree to which the particular culture provides alternatives to cope with acute distress.

The socio-cultural theories of alcohol consumption provide the main framework under which the etiology, prevalence and incidence of alcohol consumption is predicted and interpreted. It is particularly relevant for explaining high levels of drinking among Blacks, the incessant and abnormally high rates of homicides and suicides among native Americans, and the inordinate abuse of alcohol among Hispanics, not to mention the high incidence of prenatal and neonatal care that Blacks experience, relative to their White counterparts. As mentioned before, Blacks' drinking in America might have sprung from a social situational position where, since slavery, the legacy of stigmatization has been responsible in part for their exclusion from jobs, housing, access to health care and for institutional racism. Blacks tend to be over-represented where diseases are concerned, although they remain a minority in the general population.

Bales (1946) noted that it was the inability of the society to provide alternative mechanisms for the relief of these tensions and stresses which is responsible, in no small measure, for the extent of alcohol consumption in the United States, and other countries.

The findings of Johnson and Mâtre (1974, p. 897-901) is instructive in this regard. Mexican-Americans regard a "real man" as one who could "hold his liquor." More Mexican-American men than women believe that having "a few beers" was a good way to unwind. On the other hand, ethnic differences remained high among the two groups even when the researchers controlled for drinking habits, religious beliefs, and occupational status. Also, Heien and Pompelli (1987) found that divorce, unemployment, income, prices of alcoholic beverages for the period 1968-1977 (excluding 1972), cultural factors (such as ethnic background), and stressful conditions have a strong influence on cirrhosis deaths.

Differences in Alcohol Rates among Social Groups

Still, the most important issue which causes quite an embarrassment to the proponents of the genetic model is their inability to explain the enormous differences in the rates of alcoholism between groups like the Jews and the Irish.

These two groups are from different cultures and are superimposed by the American drinking culture. The Jews drink heavily, but are not alcoholics, while the Irish drink heavily and have alcohol problems.

The Real Reason for the Genetic Model

When we add to this, the lack of concordance between twins from alcoholic fathers and other methodological problems consistent with the genetic model, together with the haste in some quarters to promote greater sensitization of alcoholism as a disease, then one is left to wonder what are the real reasons behind this move. Is it one of economic and political influence, or the frustration of the geneticists in obtaining a "cure?" Alternatively, is it the old issue of attempting to medicalize social problems, or is it more convenient to deal with the genetic model than to confront the cost of implementing a strategy that will have to address a host of social factors within the broader parameters of the economic, political, and cultural relatedness?

It would appear then, that the disease model of alcoholism has been over-emphasized. Further, while this writer views as significant the entire thrust of alcohol consumption by some researchers to locate a cure, and the tenacious hold of medicine over alcohol, it could be seen as another attempt to defend a theory that can no longer explain behavior towards this substance. It may very well be that the large body of genetic interests which has been built up around this theory will not go away without a fight, making it difficult to release these long held views of alcoholism and alcohol dependency. When a new theory explains more than the old only when it is tested by the intellectual and the general community then it begins to grow to replace the old (see Kuhn, *The structure of Scientific Revolutions*, 1962).

The Myth of Alcoholism

The myth of alcoholism as a medical problem must be exposed once and for all. The overall real cure lies in the social factors and social programs, not medical treatment! Clinical tests on the other hand may be a reinforcer to aid to any behavioral assessment.

The amount of research conducted on the social/cultural aspects of alcoholism needs to be highlighted. It would be impossible, on account of space, to list all of them. However, some of the prominent ones stand out:

Clinard (1974); Mulford and Miller (1960); Knibbe et al. (1987); Johnson and Mâtre (1974); Caetano (1984); Bowman et al. (1975); Linksy et al. (1986); Bales (1946); Weiner (1981); Room (1985); Negrete (1973); Casswell (1985); Feeney (1981/1982); Beauvis and La Boueff (1985); Miller and Agnew (1974); Schuckit (1985); Pearlin and Radabaugh (1976); Bruun (1959); Phillips (1976); Blumberg et al. (1971); Edwards et al. (1973); Benjamin and Benjamin (1981); Nofz (1988); Walsh (1990).

Most, if not all of these studies sought to argue through observation, theory and research, that the socio-cultural factors are the main determinants in heavy drinking. The problem is that the ever-present socio-cultural predictors make it almost impossible to identify the strength of one over the other, especially in social settings which change ever so often. Still, one thing stands out: there are some core variables which, most times, seem to engage the attention of researchers. They are age, income, education, sex, employment status, marital status and religious application (Caetano 1984, p. 36).

Implications of Under-Reporting

In terms of the robustness of the socio-cultural models, under-reporting poses a serious problem in the data collection stage of any investigation. It may be that the stigma attached to drinking deters heavy drinkers from reporting their problems. As such, we are left with broad assumptions that younger people drink more; men drink more than women, and manual workers drink more than non-manual workers.

In this regard, one researcher is calling for the separate study of Blacks in order to uncover variation within these groups. In short, a recognition of Black values and life-styles becomes necessary. Also to be taken into consideration is, not only individual drinking, but group drinking, that is, the powerful influence which groups exert on their members. Bruun (1959) found that group norms exert tremendous influence over the behavior of drinkers, in terms of the quantity or pattern of their drinking.

On the other hand, cross-cultural research has quite a number of hurdles to cross because of the amount of biases needed to be addressed. Some of these areas are standardization of questionnaires and psychological tests, non-standardization of ages between cultures, not to mention the need for historical questionnaires seeking reasons for the breaking of norms (Westermeyer 1974). Further, it is argued that clinical studies may provide "the best" answers to objectivity via withdrawal, toxicity, alcohol metabolic rate, breathalyzer and serological tests. These could be used to narrow the loss of socio-cultural variables when assessing their significance.

Summary

The study of alcohol abuse, alcoholism, or alcohol consumption for that matter, represents an intriguing challenge to every student of human behavior.

Alcohol abuse has a strong sociological basis, within which is found the behaviorist approach representing the most significant factor or set of factors yet in understanding this phenomenon.

We may call this *the pathways to understanding irresponsible behavior.*

The sociological approach has to do with behavior. It is the only theory which could be employed to explain all others (even as we use variants of it, such as family background, relationships, personality behavior and the like) in addition to alcohol recovery. Some basic sociological concepts have remained robust in alcohol research. They are age, race, sex, religion and socio-economic status.

Alcohol consumption straddles different populations the old and the young at different points on the continuum. If we study the family structure we have to deal with parental effect. Customs and norms are passed on from parent to child, although the family situation can be seen as taking place within a particular context. Again, we can argue that some variables, such as sex, ethnicity and socio-economic status may be subject to contextual interpretation while in other conditions they may remain consistent, broadly speaking. One has to be careful, therefore, about placing all family units into contextual situations. In short, some variables may over-ride the claim to contextuality, or any attempt for that matter, to indicate that the family can behave in predictable ways in different contexts.

Social irresponsibility means anyone who is not "genetically" at risk and who "loses control". However, it depends on the angle from which you examine it. Some individuals, particularly the young, we give the benefit of the doubt.

"Social irresponsibility" is not a new concept; it has been in the literature for quite some time, since the Temperance Movement. What has changed is its meaning, having been held hostage by the "geneticists" for quite some time.

Heavy drinking is heavier in the lower socio-economic groups and middle-to-upper class people tend to report drinking more frequently. Blacks drink more than Whites. Proponents of the genetic camp and those belonging to the behaviorist camp share boundaries in terms of the unit of analysis—the family and the individual. But the similarity ends there; the weight of social outcome variables towers over the genetic ones.

The sociological argument can extend itself to deviance theories including a reaction to public policies which take their cues from the prevailing socio-cultural state of affairs.

Bales' theory is probably the most comprehensive when it comes to understanding the socio-cultural approach to alcohol consumption. He identifies a number of variables, namely, the degree to which the culture creates inner tension, the culturally-driven attitude towards drinking, and the degree to which the culture provides coping mechanisms to deal with cultural stress.

One of the most significant examples of the importance of social/sociological variables is the fact that the Jews and the Irish drink heavily, yet one, the Jews do not have problems with alcoholics, but the other has. When we add to this, the lack of concordance between twins from alcoholic fathers and other methodological shortcomings consistent with the genetic argument one can have genuine concerns about the genetic thrust.

One wonders whether the reasons behind the genetic argument is one of political or economic opportunism, or frustration with finding a "cure?"

It is advanced that the disease concept is over-emphasized and that there is a desperate struggle, as Kuhn (1962) would argue, between an old theory and a new one with the reluctance of the old to embrace the new. It clearly is a myth to view alcohol as a disease for its overall cure lies in the manipulation of social factors, not biological ones.

The sheer tower of social and sociological research into alcoholism, or alcohol abuse dwarfs the genetic researches. Even when undertaking the genetic researches there are social and sociological variables that cannot be kept out because they are ever-present factors in alcoholic behavior.

One of the greatest hurdles to alcohol research is the problem of under-reporting, leaving us with broad and sometimes faulty assumptions. In addition to these, there is the problem of cross-cultural biases or non-standardization of measurement, and the reasons behind the breaking of norms and values. So far, clinical studies have provided "the best" answers to objective indicators, that is, withdrawal, toxicity, metabolic rate, and breathalyzer tests. These could be used in a supportive way to deal with problems of biases arising out of the examination of socio-cultural variables.

Suggested Readings

Holubowycz, Oksana T.; and Jack A. McLean. 1995. "Demographic Characteristics, Drinking Patterns and Drink-Driving Behavior of Injured Male Drivers and Motorcycle Riders." Journal of Studies on Alcohol 56, no. 5:513-21.

Lowe, George D.; and Alan L. Ziglin. 1973. "Social Class and the Treatment of Alcoholic Patients." Quarterly Journal of Studies on Alcohol 34:173-84.

Murray, David; and Brian Short. 1995. "Intra-Class Correlation among Measures Related to Alcohol Use by Young Adults: Estimates, Correlates and Applications in Intervention Studies." Journal of Studies on Alcohol 56, no. 6:681-94.

Smart, Reginald G. 1996. "Behavioral and Social Consequences Related to the Consumption of Different Beverage Types." Journal of Studies on Alcohol 57, no. 1:77-84.

CHAPTER 10

The Hidden Alcoholic

Introduction

Hidden alcoholics are those who surreptitiously and frequently consume alcohol in large amounts, but who do not face the public glare. They seldom appear in public places, although they may take part in some celebration or personal event—a wedding, an achievement or some other significant occasion.

Alcoholics and Their Relatives

These alcoholics are more or less "controlled" by their relatives and friends. Their behavior is "understood" and they do not readily seek treatment, either in the form of group therapy or in the form of social/psychological counseling. As such, they remain hidden. If they have to access expert treatment, they do so privately.

White Collar Alcoholism

These "hidden alcoholics" commit what might be called "White collar alcoholism." Because of their socio-economic position and the status they hold in society, they get away with a lot. As a result, their behavior is glossed over as "not serious." When their actions get "out of hand," as it sometimes does, it is viewed as the "exception," not the norm. This happens basically because these alcoholics never accept that alcohol is harming them socially. In short, the drinker undergoes a period of denial which may be aided and abetted by friends, relatives, close family members, and even the society, or culture. The most difficult problem with an alcoholic is for him to admit that he is drunk (McCormick 1982, p. 9).

The alcoholic is often "hidden" because he suffers from a disease of denial—by himself, his family, society, and sometimes, the medical profession. Self-recognition of the illness in its early stages is rare; admitting it to others is still rarer. Admittedly, many early alcoholics do not appreciate that alcohol is harming them. However, even when they realize the true situation they are unlikely to hurry to their family doctor for help (Wilkins 1974, p. 202).

No doubt, hidden alcoholics prefer to go unnoticed; the social cost of shame and loss of status may be too much for them to bear. In addition, for all of the efforts by these professionals, addressing their alcoholic behavior is not seen as a priority. Some drink away from the public glare but shy away from outwardly damning behavior.

The Hidden Alcoholic Defies Assessment

The hidden alcoholic defies assessment. Little work has been done on the "hidden" alcoholic. As the name implies, "hidden alcoholics" are out of public view and escape the scrutiny of observation by researchers. Not all "hidden" alcoholics remain hidden, however; some by virtue of their excesses, start to outwardly manifest symptoms of chronic alcohol use, but others may continue shifting between moderate drinking to heavy drinking for years without receiving behavior modification treatment, or admitting that they need to have their behavior adjusted.

It is these alcoholics who are the most worrisome to public officials. They refuse to stand up and be counted. Government programs designed to deal with the spiraling population of alcoholics—the youths, teenagers, and the elderly—may have only a superficial effect, relatively speaking, and may represent a chip of the alcohol iceberg.

Research on Hidden Alcoholics

Researchers (Cornel et al. 1996) undertook a study of "hidden alcoholics" using practices instead of direct alcohol-related questionnaires. They found that 6 percent of a group of drinkers regarded as non-problem drinkers were in fact problem-drinkers or potential alcoholics. The researchers, using general practitioners' files, distinguished four areas which predispose persons to higher risk of alcoholism. They were gender, life events, smoking and reported alcohol consumption. Moreover, these patients were originally (officially) defined as non-problem drinkers. Males had the highest ratio of drinking, followed by "smoking," "life events" and the use of "sleeping pills." Added to this was the presence of chronic social problems in which problem drinkers could be identified from the population of drinkers, some of whom were "hidden alcoholics." These and other studies underscore the type of problems encountered by researchers when undertaking work on special populations. As mentioned previously, there are good reasons for some alcoholics to remain hidden. Many qualify as community leaders, fine family figures, successful job holders (McCormick 1982, p. 11).

> Whereas previously alcoholics were conceptualized as homeless, jobless, physically ravaged individuals with meager psychological resources, it is now clear that this "end stage" alcoholic is most unrepresentative of the patient population that abuses alcohol. A significant, if not major proportion of the alcoholic population continues to function, within...intact and stable family systems, a natural clientele for the family therapist (Steinglass 1976, p. 98).

Women as Hidden Alcoholics

Hidden alcoholism appears to be a feature among women as among men. Women face greater cultural pressure to imbibement (Cotton 1979). But the hidden alcoholic also seems to be a function of drinking itself. The psyche of the human mind appears to know when it is doing something wrong, or when society's disapproval is strong. According to Beauchamp (1980), one of the basic functions of alcoholism is to hide the role of the alcoholic in society's alcohol problems. The idea, he explains, is to try to locate "a small minority who unaccountably cannot control their drinking" (Beauchamp 1980, p. 49).

> [T]he irony is that this idea of alcoholism not only hides the role of alcohol but also helps drive the alcoholic further from view (p. 49).

The Secrecy of the Hidden Alcoholics

But the whole structure put in place to deal with the alcoholic has much to do with secrecy. For example, when we examine the organization of Alcoholics Anonymous (AA), we find one "class of organizations that utilize mechanisms of secrecy and concealment" (Beauchamp, p. 52).

> The anonymity (of the AA) is not only a protective measure against stigma of alcohol problems, but also the ideological function that alcoholics themselves are largely responsible for society's alcohol problems (Beauchamp 1980, p. 68).

Thus, the idea, nay, the prevalence of the hidden alcoholic finds fertile ground. It is the way in which alcoholism is regarded and secondly, the manner in which it is treated. In more ways than one the true picture of alcoholism, who is hiding behind it, and who is hiding it, is hidden. We are yet to learn from official statistics the true figure of fatalities on the road by persons regarded as non-drinkers. So too is the national figure of total man-hours lost on account of workplace drinking by alcoholics on the job.

Stealing a Drink

The presence of hidden alcoholics in society adds to the pleasure of "stealing a drink" in the comfort and privacy of one's own home; adds to the relish of being able to conceal a habit that carries social sanctions outside of an event; adds to being "responsible" while engaging in irresponsibility.

The hidden alcoholic runs the continuum from social drinker to problem drinker, to alcoholic. The sad fact is that the hidden alcoholic may not know on which point of the continuum he lies. He is hardly afforded the type of scrutiny that comes with "going public." In this regard, he runs the risk of drinking himself into a stupor without becoming aware of how close he comes to harming himself and others.

The Family and Hidden Alcoholism

The vast array of literature on alcoholics within families indicates that some of these may be hidden alcoholics, and the message they send to their families may

be one that not only encourages them to hold the secret, but threatens the stability of the family if the secret is let out. Thus, for years family members may agonize between seeking help for the victim on the one hand, or risking the disintegration of the family, on the other. Under these circumstances, it is usually the wife who carries the weight of these decisions. She carries the "emotional maintenance" of the husband, regarded as "strategic importance to the urban individual, as other avenues of emotional redress have become extinct" (Seldin 1972, p. 98). The image of the spouse may be changing from one of aggression "to that of a woman who may or may not react to the stress of her marriage with personality dysfunction" (Edwards et al. 1973, p. 112).

Hidden alcoholism seems to be a feature of various populations in which monitoring does not come easily or is seen as an invasion of privacy.

> According to a report...between 22,000 and 36,000 U.S. doctors in practice today are alcoholics, recovering alcoholics or soon-to-be alcoholics. Some doctors are reluctant or unwilling to report impaired colleagues thus increasing the possible risks of harm to patients (Mackey 1988).

Modern Society and Hidden Alcoholism

It is important, however, to understand not only doctors, but also the vast number of alcoholics who remain hidden for one reason or another. Some professions are so highly stressed with expectations of workers running so high, that it becomes almost impossible to keep away from drugs or alcohol. Modern society has developed into a complex monolithic structure with increasing demands on individuals, and very few legitimate or convenient outlets to discharge these pent up stresses arising out of these demands. Conveniently, a drink is always there to be taken in the comfort of one's home or can be purchased at any convenience store, in any quantity, and as frequently as one feels to have it.

Changing Scenarios of Skid Row

Skid row was a place where one could easily locate alcoholics: it was the home, the urban part of the city where unskilled men and low standard of consumption resided side by side, a place where "drunken bums" congregated, and where "alcoholic derelicts" had produced a form of social control (Rubington 1971, p. 125). However, Rubington argues, the skid row scenario had produced a form of social control which backfired. It had two purposes: it actually encouraged drinkers to the site, but it also "provided camouflage for millions of problem drinkers in the United States..." (Rubington 1971, p. 125). But skid row is still with us, for while in the past it provided different things to different categories of drinkers, today the symbol of denial, the major defense of the alcoholic is found among millions of the nation's alcoholics.

> This false syllogism provided cover for "hidden" alcoholics, confusion for moderate drinkers, moral superiority for abstainers, and a rationale for at least some skid row alcoholics... Most alcoholics are hidden rather than overt, and all but a small fraction of the nation's alcoholics do not live on Skid Row... But the symbol probably encouraged more people to continue their own appropriate drinking conduct than it helped others either to abstain from or curtail such drinking... The alcoholic can say to himself and to others..."since you have never seen me drunk on the streets, what makes you think I'm an alcoholic?" (Rubington 1971, p. 123, 125).

Denial, the Root Cause

In large measure, therefore, denial mechanisms constructed by society, the family, and the alcoholic himself are the root cause of "hidden" alcoholism. In short, the alcoholic has the disease called denial. Alcoholism is still a disease of stigma and shame (Wilkins 1974, p. 202). Modern day alcoholic organizations still possess the ability to keep the alcoholic out of public view, prompting concerns that they are a specialized group, with different kinds of problems, needing professional attention. So the enigma continues, inadvertently preventing the alcoholic from returning to a state of normalcy.

> Until that time part of the mystique stems from the "other worldly" experience that surrounds many of these social problems. It is no accident that we often refer to recovery from alcohol or drug problems as the "journey back" or the way out.... Deviance in all societies is not only an object of stigma and isolation but also a source of endless fascination (Beauchamp 1980, p. 51).

Summary

Hidden alcoholics are those persons secretly drinking alcohol in large amounts. However, as the name implies they do not face the public glare. As a result, they are not known. One of the problems of the hidden alcoholic is that they are "managed" by relatives and friends who protect or help them protect their drinking habits; they do not seek treatment readily. They commit "white collar alcoholism."; their actions do not receive sanctions as their counterpart in the pub.

Hidden alcoholics, for the most part have high status positions and their image remains "untouched" by stigma or negative perception so long as they remain hidden. Because of this and because they do not believe that alcohol is causing, or can cause them harm, the hidden alcoholic undergoes a period of denial, supported by himself, his family and sometimes, even the medical profession.

But there is a social cost to shame and loss of status if the "hidden" alcoholic goes public. He therefore defies assessment and little scientifically is known about the behavior and attitude of this individual. However, it has been advanced that there may be good reasons for some alcoholics to remain hidden. They may be community leaders, fine family figures, important role models. Going public carries a heavy cost. At the same time somebody, most likely the public, is being duped.

Hidden alcoholism is a feature of men as it is of women and this is so because generally we tend to hide the role of the alcoholic in society (Beauchamp 1980). If we can locate a small minority of persons who are alcoholics who cannot "control" their drinking, then the pressure is removed from the hidden alcoholic.

The hidden alcoholic finds fertile ground because of the way in which alcohol is regarded, the manner in which it is treated and the protection it receives from Alcoholics Anonymous.

The hidden alcoholic is a phenomenon, a contradiction. He may be in a "responsible position," but practices irresponsible behavior by his actions of denial and secrecy. By his actions he can hurt himself and his family and friends.

Hidden alcoholics may come from populations or professions that are highly stressed.

These individuals have little or no outlets to discharge pent up pressures. They can be akin to skid row bums and like skid row their behavior provides a camouflage for millions of problem drinkers.

Because of their status and their mystique, even their deviance, the hidden alcoholic may be seen as a "source of endless fascination."

Suggested Reading

York, James L. 1995. "Progression of Alcohol Consumption across the Drinking Career in Alcoholics and Social Drinkers." Journal of Studies on Alcohol 56, no. 3:328-36.

CHAPTER 11

The Elderly Alcoholic

Introduction

Alcohol abuse has been identified as one major response to the stresses associated with aging (Dupree et al. 1984). According to research undertaken among persons fifty-five years and over, approximately 10-15 percent of them use alcohol. The Gerontology Alcohol Project (GAP), assessed the subjects on the basis of physical health, mental health, family and social adjustment, financial stability and legal status.

Goodwin et al. (1987) found that there was a positive relation between male gender, income, level of education and alcohol intake, but that there was a negative association between age and alcohol consumption.

Self Image

Self reporting by the elderly needs to be examined; the elderly are likely to forget or not be too concerned with their past, particularly if it interferes with their self image.

> Over the past decade, there has been growing acceptance that alcoholism in the elderly is a significant public health problem (Atkinson and Kofoed 1982) Cited in Kofoed et al. 1987, p. 47).

This observation was made approximately eighteen years ago. Today, the problem is greater; the aged is a growing minority (Barnes et al. 1980, p. ix) who places a tremendous burden on the health care system. Countries all over the world are struggling with this stark reality. Smaller, less developed countries with fragile economies, would best adopt a behavioral approach to understanding alcohol intake by the elderly. One aspect of this is peer socialization, bringing alcoholics together and developing a program for them.

Special Treatment Considerations

Further, in treating the elderly alcoholic one may be dealing with a number of other problems, such as cognitive impairment, some aspects of psychological dysfunction and social dislocation, (that is, some elderly alcoholics might be forced to live with relatives, a prospect which the elderly never become entirely adjusted to in the first instance.) In this respect, they may turn to alcohol to cope with their "loneliness," anxieties and failing health. According to Madden (1984, p. 92) "elderly people constitute in many countries a rapidly expanding age group," and this could be translated into additional costs to the state. Old age is one thing; dealing with old age and alcoholism is another.

Graham and Schmidt (1999) report that poorer psychological well-being was highly correlated with heavy drinking among people 65 and older, but not related to frequency of drinking. This indicates that what is important to the old is not so much loneliness per se but how often it occurs. For when it does it may precipitate heavy bouts of drinking.

Physiological Changes

Take into consideration also that the aged undergo physical changes which might make them more vulnerable to the effects of alcohol and other drugs (Barnes et al. 1980, p. ix). Under these circumstances, the aged unwittingly can fall victim to what might otherwise be "non-risk" drinking. Alternatively, increased tolerance can lead to serious problems among the aged. It might simply mean that the aged must consume more alcohol to obtain a desired effect. This could be a problematic situation, for aging itself carries certain constraints such as the slowing of reflexes and changes in the metabolic rate. These can and do become exacerbated when the aged engage in alcohol consumption, particularly, heavy alcohol consumption. In addition, excessive alcohol consumption can lead to personality deterioration and anti-social behaviors (Glatt and Hills 1968).

These types of behaviors persist even though, under normal circumstances, the elderly are not likely to drink, and those who used to, may stop doing so altogether. However, it is interesting to observe what condition carries more weight in predicting alcohol consumption of the elderly: the "normal conditions," that is, physiological, psychological, and the like, or the effects of aging, such as, loneliness, increased stresses, strains, and isolation. The literature is inconclusive as to why some healthy elderly drink and why others do not. In one study (Neve et al. 1997), it was reported that when compared to younger alcoholics (age 35-44), older alcoholics (age 50+) "presented an image of chronic addiction." It was determined that older alcoholics' addiction began in their youthful years and continued right through their older years. Still, others developed drinking at later stages of their lives, albeit at lower consumption levels than those who started in their youth.

Special Group of Persons

It would appear, therefore, that older alcoholics are a group of persons who either had started their drinking careers in their youth and never looked back, or were normal drinkers, who, because of a particular event in their lives, began to use alcohol with increased frequency, though not necessarily with intensity. The elderly alcoholics may very well be people who are unable to handle the losses associated with aging and retirement (Levin 1990, p. 94). As far back as 1988, the National Institute on Alcohol Abuse and Alcoholism in the United States observed that the problem of alcohol abuse among the elderly had been overlooked, in the alcohol literature. The problem had to do with surveys among the general population and clinical studies. The latter, more than the former found that problems with alcohol do not necessarily decrease with age. According to the institute, the reason why we may have been led to believe this is that these problems were not readily identifiable outside a treatment setting.

Physiological State

When food is taken into the stomach, different digestive rates take place. When there is very little or no food, digestion is speeded up to the brain, the kidney and the liver. Other tissues receive a supply of alcohol but not in such large amounts as the previously mentioned areas. What this means for the elderly is still unclear. We do now know however, that there is a decreased resilience in almost all body systems (Barnes et al. 1980). Added to this is that many elderly alcoholics might have given up drinking simply because of reduced tolerance, or that they ran the risk of losing friends, whom they desperately needed. In short, it became "socially unacceptable" or "intolerable." But there are other possibilities supporting the alcoholic habit among the elderly.

> Elderly patients may be admitted to a treatment facility for a particular physical or psychiatric disorder for which alcohol abuse may in fact be the primary etiological factor...several studies indicate that among elderly psychiatric patients...the proportion of persons with alcoholism is high—often as high as 50 percent of all elderly patients (Barnes et al. 1980, p. xvi).

It is clear that poor health and physical discomfort increase with age: (Brody 1985) and these are real factors we have to deal with when assessing the use of alcohol among the elderly. However, it is noted that the elderly alcoholic is easier to treat than their younger counterpart since they tend to be "more faithful in attendance" (Brody 1985, p. 8). There is also the possibility that more sedentary activities than active solitary ones can be associated with increased mortality risks (Berkman 1985).

If the risk of alcoholism among the elderly is due to isolation caused by depression, bereavement, retirement, loneliness, physical illness and the like, then we have to agree with Droller (1964) "the most important therapy is social" (p. 35). This factor should be taken into consideration when interviewing the elderly. It has also been pointed out that in circumstances where the elderly invites the researcher to stay, "the elderly might be quite motivated to give responses that he or she thinks would be pleasing or interesting to the interviewer" Mishara and Kastenbaum (1980, p. 46). Observation therefore, is the key when collecting primary data from the elderly alcoholics.

Summary

Alcohol abuse has been identified as a major response to stresses related to aging. At least 10-15 percent of persons over fifty-five years of age use alcohol. The Gerontology Alcohol Project (GAP) assessed individuals on their physical and mental health, family and social adjustment and financial and legal status as it related to their drinking.

One of the problems with aging is that the aged are likely to forget or not to be too concerned with their past, particularly if it brings back uncomfortable memories. Besides, the aged are a growing minority and they have a significant impact on the health care system. It is therefore of tremendous interest that alcoholism, which is seen as behavioral here, should be determined by the health care givers in order to assess alcoholics seeking care for other health disorders. This is especially significant for small developing economies which can least carry the increased burden of health care cost, far less the burgeoning cost of alcohol abuse.

Elderly alcoholics also have to face decreased participation in social activities and failing health and they may turn to alcohol to cope. These two factors may also be coupled with poor psychological well-being. In addition, the poor undergo physical deficits; changes take place in their physiology and this can be directly related to levels of alcohol consumption. The effects of all of these are personality deterioration and antisocial behaviors.

The literature is inconclusive about why the elderly drink. One theory is that older alcoholics began drinking in their youthful years and continued right into older life; another theory holds that elderly alcoholics developed drinking later in their lives. This may very well be the case of people facing aging and retirement. These are real factors which must be taken into consideration when treating elderly alcoholics. However, it has been advanced that the elderly alcoholics are easier to treat than their younger counterparts because they are more responsive and regularly go for counseling.

Since the elderly alcoholic suffers from depression, bereavement, retirement, loneliness, physical ailments and the like, it is believed that the best therapy is social. Increased socialization could facilitate greater information and understanding as to why the elderly drink and this could redound to greater scientific explanation or outcomes regarding their drinking.

Suggested Readings

Beresford, Thomas; and Edith Gomberg. 1997. Alcohol and Aging. New York: Oxford University Press.

Golding, Jacqueline M.; Victor E. Leino; Catherine R. Ager; Heidi Ferrer; Kaye Fillmore; Middleton. 1994. "Demographic and Methodological Characteristics Associated with Changes in Frequency of Alcohol Use: A Meta-Analysis from the Collaborative Alcohol-Related Longitudinal Project." Addiction Research 2, no. 2:155-70.

Graham, Kathryn 1998. "Alcohol Abstention among Older Adults: Reasons for Abstaining and Characteristics of Abstainers." Addiction Research 6: 473-87.

Maddox, George; Lee N. Robins; Nathan Rosenberg, eds. 1986. Nature and Extent of Alcohol Problems Among the Elderly. New York: Springer Publishing Company Inc.

Rogers, John D.; and Thomas K. Greenfield. 1999. " Beer Drinking Accounts for Most of the Hazardous Alcohol Consumption Reported in the United States." Journal of Studies on Alcohol 60, no. 6:732-39.

Zimberg, Sheldon. 1979. "Alcohol and the Elderly." In Drugs and the Elderly: Social and Pharmacological Issues, edited by David Petersen, Frank Whittington and Barbara Payne. Illinois: Charles C. Thomas.

CHAPTER 12

Workplace Drinking

Introduction

Drinking in the workplace is a common feature of almost all societies which consume alcohol on a sufficiently large scale to cause alcohol problems. Research has shown that people drink in the workplace for a number of reasons, chief among them being the need to cope with stresses within the environment. Bennett and Lehman (1998) examined the relationship between on-the-job drinking and its effects on co-workers and found that the drinking climate correlated with stress and withdrawal.

Stress, Alcohol and Productivity

The above suggests that stress in the society can be mirrored in the workplace. Again, the drinking climate and stress on the job were negatively associated with cohesion. Literally put, teamwork could act as a buffer against alcohol consumption and thus have little or no adverse effects on productivity. In further research, they examined the relationship between individual exposure to co-worker substance use and work group membership (Bennett and Lehman 1999). They report a significant relationship between exposure and consequences. Again, there was a greater degree of significance, the higher the climate of drinking. For example, "employees who work in groups where more individuals work with machinery...are more likely to experience consequences..." when they are exposed to co-worker substance use "than employees who work in groups with less occupational risk" (p. 314).

Still, it might be difficult in modern society to build cohesive units within the workplace, except through unionization and other forms of associations. One of the reasons for this is that modern society has brought with it a certain degree of alienation and competitiveness in the workplace, in addition to the breaking up of workers along status lines. Different work carries different status. As a result, a proliferation of rules, role-playing and expectations are acted out on a day-to-day basis. As Bennett and Lehman (1999) discovered, it is not so much drinking but with which groups one is associated that predisposes one to drink.

Some employees may insist that they do not drink in the workplace but the effects they have on the work, nonetheless, have implications for them and their co-workers. Leigh (1995) found a positive relationship between alcohol use and occupational fatality rates. On the other hand, Ames et al. (1997), in examining drinking patterns and workplace problems, reported that drinking was related to the number of problems in the workplace.

These particular findings reflect growing concerns of managers, industrial relations experts and human resource managers in that the workplace needs to be a place which provides job contentment, job enrichment and fulfillment.

Some workplace problems may have their etiology contingent upon their location. Marshall and Tang (1998) found significant relations between drinking and family problems ($r = .55$, $p. <.000$), but insignificant relationship between geographic location of business and alcohol consumption. The researchers called for the "duality" type Employees Assistance programs, to identify mental health problems as co-factors in alcohol-related problems.

Mother Loss

Some problems may have their etiology from a mental health perspective, namely schizophrenia. In one study (Hilgard and Newman 1963), the researchers compared schizophrenic patients and alcoholic patients with controls from a nearby representative urban community. They reported that mother loss was a feature in both diagnostic groups when compared to the control group. However, "schizophrenic women showed loss of both mother and father at a significantly earlier age than the control subjects" (p. 409).

Data Contamination

The slow pace of research in the workplace is compounded by data contamination and tardiness in areas where there are temporary workers, such as those engaged in seasonal work, part-time work, and when workers come down or are diagnosed with other work-related problems. Also, some firms may consider it too costly to maintain records on part-time or seasonal workers, thereby compromising the data collection procedures when they are required.

On the other hand, lack of available data in the workplace may stem from the health care system in the country as a whole. The importance and significance of alcohol abuse in the workplace is relevant for developing countries like Trinidad and Tobago which has a high amount of alcohol-related social ills. It remains one of the Caribbean countries, if not the only one, to have an inordinate amount of Alcoholics Anonymous (AA) organizations.

Good data collection methods in the behavioral and social sciences mode, applied to workplaces, can deepen our understanding of how workplace conditions and dynamics impact alcohol abuse among workers and by extension, the family. There are two scenarios associated with this: the first is that individuals can enter the work environment already predisposed to drinking, where the workplace further drives the would-be alcoholic into the welcoming arms of his co-workers, themselves abusers. The second is that the stresses and strains in the workplace could propel individuals to alter or make "manageable" their situation by drinking. Therefore, in order to understand workplace drinking one must be aware of, not only the culture of the organization but, the behavior of individuals as well.

Confounding Variables

In the first instance, the individual might have dealt with his problem if left alone without being influenced by co-workers. In the second instance, newcomers

may not be able to resist the influence of workplace drinking. At the workplace, dynamic sociological and psychological forces are at work: the need to be accepted, rewarded, attached to a group, fully understanding the social structure within the organization, that is, subordination and superordination; there is also the anticipation of self-actualization, that is, becoming "someone" within the organization and reaching the top. All these factors impact on workplace behavior and they can lead to drinking, especially in the early stages of employment.

The issue of leadership comes to the fore also. Erstwhile members and friends often send the message that they understand the organization "better than anyone else" and that drinking is part of the culture. Older workers too might view alcohol consumption as the only way to deal with the frustrations of a dead-end job that has no promotion; no motivation; lack of respect for employees by management; poor working conditions and low staff morale; poor planning and working under the threat of dismissal. Thus, workplace drinking must be contextualized; each situation can be different and can hold different hazards to the abuser. Therefore, both individual personal factors and environmental ones will form part of the equation in understanding work place drinking.

The workplace can be considered the home away from home; the issue of social support is therefore an important factor in alcohol prevention. To the extent that individuals can receive a satisfactory outlet for their problems, either through problem-solving techniques, human resource manpower strategies, or trade union affiliation, then alcohol problems in the workplace could be considerably reduced.

Prejudice in the Workplace

In multiethnic societies of the Caribbean, for example, Trinidad, Guyana and Suriname, there is the real possibility of heightened perception of prejudice when it comes to the issue of landing jobs, projects, or contracts, not to mention promotion and higher status positions within organizations. Since management styles may be perceived to be tied to race, ethnicity or class, the organization can produce subtle, sometimes open ethnic prejudices that have embarrassing outcomes, leaving employees with a lack of commitment to the workplace and alienated. These perceptions may be translated into actual or imagined unfair work practices: unnecessary pay increases, additional duties without compensation and other issues.

This sets the stage for vertical and horizontal conflict and group rivalry in the workplace. As a result productivity is affected. This could be followed by heavy drinking which may already form part of the cultural landscape.

On the other side of the coin, work-related drinking may come about by the size of the firm and the nature of contacts made (Shore 1997). This researcher calls for more research "to provide empirical evidence of the effect of workplace culture and to examine the relative impact of various risk factors on workers in different situations" (p. 297).

Notwithstanding, the very composition of the workplace in terms of ratio of men to women, the nature of the work involved and the size of the firm could well determine the level of drinking. When this is compounded by home problems, attitude and lack of professionalism, their drinking can become deep-seated within the workplace.

Productive Alcoholics

The vast majority of these alcoholics are in their productive years, late thirties to mid-forties, and married with children. However, absenteeism reduces potential, resulting in a wastage which may run into millions of dollars worth of goods and man-hours lost. According to Glatt (1969), there are huge losses when we pull together the wastage in loss of efficiency, absenteeism, accidents and loss of years of training.

According to the author, a survey carried out on male alcoholics showed that 40 per cent had been found to be drinking excessively for at least ten years. What was interesting was that half of these patients knew they had a problem, and that they needed treatment from as far back as five years. During that time, some of them had slipped down the occupational ladder.

> Top executives are not immune to the risks of alcoholism than other occupational groups... such a man moves in circles where drink is widely accepted as a social and business lubricant; under such circumstances even a personality who is emotionally fairly well adjusted, and psychologically not particularly "vulnerable" may be tempted, and learn to drink heavily as a result of social pressures (Glatt 1968, p. 86).

The author suggests that factors such as personality make up, environmental strain and stresses and accepted group customs may make alcoholism an occupational hazard among top business executives.

A common feature of workplace drinking may come from high expectations in the workplace and family background, that is, pressures and problems with spouse, financial situations at home and the behavior of children.

Ames and Grube (1999), using ethnographic analyses through on-site observations and unstructured interviews and survey data reported that the availability of alcohol on the premises of the workplace is a major factor in alcohol problems. They report that the work culture plays a supportive role in the encouragement of drinking. Managers, union leaders and others find it "relatively easy to obtain and drink alcohol at or near work" (p. 391). It could be assumed therefore, that not only the workers are responsible.

Detecting Alcoholism in the Workplace

It has been said that "prevention is better than cure" and that a lot of alcoholics hide their habit in the workplace for fear of loss of promotion, or loss of job for that matter. Glatt (1969) points to a list of signs prepared by H.M. Trice informing how to detect alcoholism in the workplace. Here are some of them:

(a) Leaving one's post temporarily, absenteeism, unusual excuses for absences, lower quality of work, mood changes after lunch, red bleary eyes, increased nervousness and hand tremors

(b) Spasmodic work pace and hangovers on job... and avoiding the boss and associates

(c) Loud talking... longer lunch periods, arriving late at work and leaving early

(d) Flushed face, increase in minor illnesses, use of breath purifiers and lower quality and quantity of work (Glatt 1969, p. 87-88)

Glatt advises that there should be a greater amount of understanding of the alcoholic at work. Employers and managers should actively engage in the rehabilitation of their alcoholic employees. This would encourage the alcoholic to ask for help at an early stage of his condition. "Here is...ample scope and need for a program of research and education...in the problem of alcoholism in industry" (p. 88).

Employee Assistance Programs (EAPs) may be introduced in the workplace to deal with employee substance abuse and personal problems. These programs are sponsored by either the employers or the union, or both. They offer a distressed employee an opportunity to find solutions to his personal problems (Schlesinger and Horberg 1988), and represent one form in which both employer and employee can work together to deal with employee health and well-being, and falling productivity.

Summary

Workplace drinking is a feature of almost all societies which have problems with alcohol. One factor implicated in workplace drinking is stress. Researchers Bennett and Lehman (1998; 1999) found that drinking was associated with stress and withdrawal and that teamwork acted as a buffer against alcohol consumption. Again, a relationship was also found between exposure and consequence, depending on the level of occupational risk of the persons to whose indulgence they were exposed. Those groups working under risky conditions tended to influence the drinking of other workers more readily than other groups working under less risky conditions.

Modern society has brought in its train alienation and competition and the breaking up or classification of workers along status lines, thus precipitating a set of rules and role playing among employees and this leads to drinking in the workplace. As a result, the workplace reflects growing concerns of managers and industrial relations experts.

Mental health problems and biases are some of the factors that must be addressed when undertaking research into alcohol.

Data collection with precision can deepen our understanding of how workplace dynamics operate. One scenario is that workers can come to the workplace already having a drinking problem and this, compounded with abuses, adds to the likelihood of imbibing. Another scenario is that the workplace itself throws up these stresses.

One has to understand the workplace as an environment which not only affords employment and self-actualization, but which can impact workplace behavior and lead to the drinking of alcohol. However, there is also the possibility of landing in a dead-end job with no prospects for advancement and job enrichment. Thus workplace drinking takes place because of a multiplicity of factors. In this regard workers should find a satisfactory outlet for their problems.

In multiethnic societies the problem may be a bit more complex. Vertical and horizontal conflicts in racial, ethnic and other factors may converge. Shore (1997) calls for more research into workplace culture and risk factors associated with different situations. It is suggested here that age, role playing, and role strain can interact with domestic problems and provide fertile ground for workplace drinking.

Prevention is the best cure. Glatt (1969) points to several types of observation to detect alcohol in the workplace.

(1) Temporary absences, absenteeism, excuses for absences, lower quality of work, mood changes after lunch, red bleary eyes, increased nervousness

(2) Hangovers and spasmodic workpace, avoidance of authority

(3) Loud talking, late arrivals for work; early exit from work

(4) Increase in minor illnesses and use of breath purifiers

Finally, there needs to be greater cooperation between managers and union members, in order to reap the benefits of Employee Assistance Programs (EAPs).

Suggested Readings

Moggi, Franz; Paige Crosby Ouimette; John W. Finney; H. Rudolf. 1999. "Effectiveness of Treatment for Substance Abuse and Dependence for Dual Diagnosis Patients: A Model of Treatment Factors Associated with One-Year Outcomes." Journal of Studies on Alcohol 60, no. 6:856-66.

Trice, H.M.; and W.J. Sonnenstuhl. 1988. "Drinking Behavior and Risk Factors Related to the Workplace: Implications for Research and Prevention." Journal of Applied Behavioral Science 24:327-46.

CHAPTER 13

Reducing Alcohol Consumption among Certain Populations

Introduction

Prevention should be the key; this Olson and Gerstein (1985) believe should be directed at persons who are not only likely to become alcoholics, but those who are already alcoholics. Prevention becomes more appropriate particularly in the manner in which it is implemented. For example, it should be non-personalized and seek to change the incentives, opportunities, risks, and expectations of drinkers in society (Olson and Gerstein 1985, p. 24-25).

Role of Communities

Communities also have a role to play in reducing alcohol consumption: regular meetings should be held to educate members about the dangers and social consequences of alcohol consumption, "alcohol awareness" weeks should be mounted; seminars and forums should be held to deal with emergent alcohol-related problems and to foster community support for those at risk and those wishing to return to sobriety.

In fact, research shows that community residential care for substance abusers can produce better outcomes (Moos et al. 1995). In this respect women may also remit more readily than men. In addition, they tend to have higher quality friendships and extended families (Humphreys et al. 1997). Again, patients who relapse tend to have less family cohesion and organization (Finney and Moos 1991). This may suggest that the alcoholic by himself cannot aid his own recovery (Esser 1968).

Still, families may not feel that confident in the face of alcohol's terrible consequences (Schlesinger and Horberg 1988). It is estimated that approximately 1 in 3 heavy drinkers develop scars on the liver, loss of cells in different regions of the brain, inflamed lining of the stomach and hypertension, or high blood pressure (Mackey 1988).

Student-Friendly Schools

Again, children should have a social environment which could steer them away from situations which are deleterious to their well-being. Research has shown that children who drop out of school are four times more likely to abuse alcohol than those who complete school (Crum et al. 1998). It would seem therefore, that part of the strategy is to make the school environment and curricula more student friendly so as to encourage children's completion, especially at a period of their lives when they might be exposed to peer and societal pressures. Alcohol education in schools has not achieved its desired goals, particularly its out-of-school effects during the course of a person's lifetime (Olson and Gerstein 1985).

Dialogue between Management and Unions

Preventative methods against alcoholism should also place great emphasis on what is considered to be safe levels of drinking, the provision of dialogue between management and union, and employers and working staff. In addition, there should be a strict code of advertising (Krasner et al. 1984) where teenagers and women are eliminated from the tube. Thus prevention of alcohol must utilize the social approach, for in the final analysis, it is a societal problem and we should assemble all the experts on society and social interaction.

Drinkers seem to have a problem with the real world, but drinking does not provide the tools to deal with reality; it only gives one an illusion of mastery.

> Beyond the .15 percent BAC level, one's ability to navigate in the real world plummets steeply. At .20 percent the drinker is...dazed, confused...uncoordinated. At .30 percent concentration, any response to the stimuli of the outside world becomes an almost insurmountable chore... At the .40 level most people pass out, losing consciousness... At .50 percent...he or she has entered a coma. At .60 percent...death comes about as a result of the inhibition and paralysis of one's respiratory centers (Goode 1984, p. 128).

Legislatively speaking, an alcohol concentration of 0.10 percent reflects evidence of intoxication. Drinkers are advised therefore to stay below these levels.

Counseling for those at Risk

There are a number of measures by which we can reduce alcohol consumption and bring it down to tolerable levels. One can organize individual, group, or family counseling, depending on the needs of the individual. This is the short-term approach. One can undertake community surveys or longitudinal research designs all with a view to better understanding alcoholism and uncovering the various treatment modes.

Longitudinal Research Designs

Longitudinal research has the advantage of identifying factors that take time to develop. Yet, the basis for the increase in alcohol problems particularly among the young, is due, in part, to rapid social change and the growth of the alcohol industry (Bennett 1983, p. 221). It would be important therefore to understand the ongoing effects of these two factors across time. Initially, these two factors have led to more and more children being exposed to alcoholism, either directly or indirectly in their homes. As such, the need for "alcohol interpretation" through longitudinal research must be recognized as another strategy to be employed in reducing its unwelcomed effects. Schools and the workplaces provide some areas in which prevention could start the former for the young persons, the latter for the adults (Niven. Cited in Browne, 1983).

Mood Changes

Jin et al. (1998) suggest that mood changes could predict short-term outcome whereas more enduring personality traits are factors to be considered in long-term abstinence. However, the accent appears to be in the schools:

> Many persons believe that health and school personnel need to improve their diagnostic capabilities to better recognize children with an alcoholic parent and thereby promote the breakdown of the family's denial. Others...believe the focus should remain on the effects on children or on improving community resources for children (Brown 1983, p. 216).

Reducing Biases and Barriers

As far as research is concerned, Brown (1983) advises on the need for controlled studies while at the same time holding constant biases, such as selection of subjects, over-selection of acute case, over-reporting and lack of focus of the relationship between childhood problems and adult drinking. Other barriers to seeking help stem from persons' attitudes, namely that they feel that they could control their own drinking, or the fear they have for what their boss or family might say (Grant 1997, p.370). It should be noted however, that among other things, the probability of recovery from alcoholism lies in the relationship to social class and social stability. In fact, if one has a steady income and belongs to a high social class, and if one receives social approval, the victim is likely to recover (Humphreys et al. 1997, p. 231).

On the other hand, Employee Assistance Programs (EAPs) can be instrumental in "catching" or treating people where they work, or where they spend the majority of their waking hours. A large proportion of work-site problem drinkers, together with the attendant safety consequence of alcohol abuse can be dealt with in this manner (Kenkel 1997, p. 211).

Experiencing Caution in Alcohol Problems

One author (Heather 1995) cautions about the need to take a more careful look at the problems. She recommends (1) the need to spend more time understanding important differences within the family, (2) brief interventions among treatment seekers and non-treatment seekers should be identified, and (3) the need for findings to be more cautious, that is, without being too over-optimistic (p. 287). But there remains a plethora of techniques which people can use to control alcohol consumption, for example, warning displays about alcohol and its effects on alcohol containers (Marshall 1992). Also, the effects of the media control on alcohol (Baillie 1996), and the effects on outcomes by Alcoholics Anonymous (AA) meetings (Pisani et al. 1993).

Legislative Impact

As previously mentioned, legislation and social norms may act as buffers in containing alcohol consumption. For example, in a telephone survey conducted in New York, it was determined that the amount of alcohol consumed by 17 and 18 year olds had decreased significantly after the introduction of a minimum age (19) for the purchase of alcohol. Does the media fuel sales and influence demand? It was reported that persons who were shown a film followed by questionnaires before and after, developed a capacity to refrain from drinking (Sobell et al. 1993).

> The study of drinking practices can be undertaken to identify the patterns of beverage alcohol consumption in a community, to describe changes in consumption over time, and to extract social or personal correlates of various patterns of consumption.... The data should also be analyzed in light of cultural and social variables such as historical drinking practices and preferences, urbanization, and statutory changes over time, (e.g. taxation, control over outlets) (Haglund and Schuckit 1982, p. 34).

A group of authors, namely Dennison et al. (1980), have put forward a brilliant idea: that "instructional procedures and strategies that involve the affective domain must be incorporated in alcohol education" (p. 77). The authors argue that unlike cognitive instruction, instruction in the affective aspect of alcohol consumption will sensitize individuals to "a continuum of attitudes toward alcohol." The idea is to tap into the subjective aspects of alcohol's attitudinal and personal responses.

Clearly, a program of this nature ought to allow persons to be more in touch with their own behavior and experiences when they have to make a decision to drink. However, it is not as simple a matter as it seems. When someone consumes alcohol his mental state is altered and he is subject to cues, particularly from his immediate environment. The question of rewards and punishment can provide the impetus to behave or not behave in a particular manner. The question is this: since alcohol has been established as an inhibitory-reducing substance, how do we identify the factors which will increase or reduce this inhibiting response?

This question was answered by Fillmore and Vogel-Sprott (2000) when, under experimental conditions, they tested the effect of conflict (both from a cognitive and motivational response). The objective was to determine whether "greater disinhibition was indicated by a more intense or extensive response [cognitive or motivational] on various social behaviors (aggression, self-disclosure, risk taking)" (p. 239).

Where there was a cognitive conflict situation, that is, where reinforcement was presented for both inhibition and response, alcohol impaired or reduced inhibitory control. In short, where the individual has to make a choice, the choice would come down on the side of reduced inhibition. The researchers reported that once the conflict was resolved, inhibition increased for both the experimental group and the control group, suggesting that alcohol consumption has implications for conflict situations, that is, it can reduce inhibitions and may lead the drinker to "lose control."

Reviewing the Symbol of Alcoholism

Thus, the symbolism of alcohol as the drug of sociable and acceptable pleasure should seriously come under review, particularly from governments' policies on alcohol consumption. However, the teaching should start in the home as well. In this respect, warnings should be instituted where they do not exist and more should be done in terms of monitoring to determine effects on levels of drinking.

One study, Malouff et al. (1993), examined the impact of televised warnings on belief change and found that, after testing four of the warnings recommended in the United States Senate, repeated exposure to such warnings had the tendency to produce negative reactions to beer advertisements.

The above is just one of the many behavioral approaches to alcohol consumption which indicates no simple direct relationship (Wilson 1978), yet by no means takes away from the many experiments demonstrating the link between expectations and outcomes. Bates et al. (1993) recommend a saliva test based on the alcohol oxidase methodology as a useful and convenient technique for measuring alcohol intoxication.

From a review of the related literature, this chapter has shown that the various approaches to excessive alcohol consumption reflect the multi-causal nature of the problem. At the same time, solutions point to the salience and reliance of the behavioral mode. We must recognize that because of the nature of alcoholism, as far as treatment is concerned, we should not leave any stone unturned. The efficacy of certain treatments come up for review time and time again, not only by professionals but by lay persons as well. Further, treatments are administered based on one's own perspective or confidence about an outcome.

How to Beat the Alcohol Habit

To beat the alcohol habit, different approaches must be undertaken since at any one point in time, some social factors might explain a greater proportion of the outcome variance than others. This was the new thinking in 1975 when "doubts were surfacing about the efficacy of alcoholism interventions and treatments" (Walsh 1989). The author explains that it was around that time that scholars recommended the redefinition of the alcohol problem in public health terms. For one, large-scale alcohol problems were not really situated in a small group of alcoholics; rather, drinking problems for which there were many, were found throughout the general population. For another, although the heaviest drinking created the greatest risk of developing problems, these problems tended to cluster among the group of less heavy drinkers. Clearly then, a policy shift will allow us to zero in, not only on alcohol, but where the greater or larger concentration of drinking takes place.

Problem Drinkers not the Heaviest Drinkers

This revelation is not new. Long ago it was recognized that the vast majority of problem drinkers were not the heaviest of drinkers. We were led to believe that this was indeed the case under the disease model which basically absolved the drinker from his/her responsibility. This move was followed by the establishment of Alcoholics Anonymous in 1935 which recruited a group of recovering alcoholics in order to promote the image of alcoholism as a disease which could be cured, if not contained (Walsh 1989).

Curbing the alcohol problem may have implications for the new public health measures across the globe, but such measures can only be successfully evaluated by the degree to which they are facilitated by the respective culture. Different countries have different norms and value systems which tap into the levels of compliance or efficacy for that matter. Under these circumstances, officials must tailor their policies to suit not only the prevailing sentiments surrounding alcohol, but also the perception which is driven by a long history of the country's drinking culture.

Walsh (1989) points out that the fear of alcohol can make some countries develop taboos to deal with the problem. She points to Italians, the affluent countries, the French and those who had a temperance tradition like United States, England, and the Scandinavian countries which all reacted to alcohol problems by adopting measures consistent with its cultural image.

Devaluing Social and Cultural Beliefs

It is because we tend to devalue our social and cultural factors of alcoholism that some treatment programs and their impact on special populations are not factored into the equation of cost, recovery, and efficacy. Beauvis and La Boueff (1985) suggest that the problem of dealing with alcoholism among the American Indians had to do with the naïve conception by officials that Indians shared the same cultural goals as everyone else.

For indeed, there are two faces of alcohol consumption: the appearance of relaxed social drinking as opposed to the appearance of excessive, sometimes explosive encounters.

> Alcohol, then is a double-edged sword. On the one hand, it can be a positive social force, acting to promote conviviality and social cohesion.... On the other hand, alcohol when used excessively can cause misery and suffering of the greatest magnitude for the abusers and their loved ones (Jung 1994, p. 4).

Blaming the victims will not work; invoking sanctions and making them responsible will. Victims need to be counseled with behavior therapy and other related techniques. Above all, the diversity of counseling techniques in various fields needs to be brought together to bear on the problem.

> For prevention...to make progress, the diverse range of groups and individuals with a stake in prevention need to cooperate and coordinate their efforts. Because prevention is a comprehensive concept, many different initiatives will be going on simultaneously. Information about the effectiveness of these initiatives, and about the practical difficulties of implementing them, must be shared if the initiatives are to survive and prosper (Olson and Gerstein 1985, p. 31).

Also, we have to remove politics from alcoholism. Casswell (1985) reiterates that different countries obtain different results, depending on the policies they adopt towards alcohol consumption. She observes that there is a direct relationship between "increases in per capita consumption... [which] have been accompanied by significant increases in...alcohol-related problems" (p. 157). Countries identified as limiting alcohol consumption are Sweden, Norway and Finland.

Suggestions to Counter Situational Vulnerability

Here are some additional tips, particularly for those who accept that, under certain conditions, they are vulnerable to excessive alcohol consumption:

- Circulate at social events slowly, and with a clear head; one of the most frequent reasons for drinking is to ease self-consciousness, and a sense of loneliness

- Get others to converse with you, while you yourself keep quiet
- Avoid discussion of your own activities; avoid broadcasting your own opinion (Terhune 1968, p. 107-109).

It would appear also that AA, in spite of what has been said of them, could help people gain sobriety. One thing which this group has in common is that members all have a problem with drinking, and by coming together, they form a social bond with a cohesive purpose in mind. Members reinforce their commitment to each other, a further powerful indication of the effects of group behavior on alcohol consumption. An alcoholic may learn on entry into the program that there is no cure for alcoholism, but that he can never drink again (Milt 1976, p. 115). After being presented with the guidelines of AA, the new member must eventually take the responsibility for doing something about himself/herself.

> The Alcoholics Anonymous group serves as a microcosm of the patient's broader social universe and reflects his basic interpersonal problems. In a setting in which he is accepted uncritically, it is possible for him to work through his problems, and with the help of the therapist, to cultivate more suitable and satisfying kinds of interpersonal behavior. Even if he is rebuffed in this experiment, he learns in this accepting environment that he can experience rejection without falling apart and without needing to resort to alcohol (Milt 1976, p. 118).

Drinking as Behavioral

Drinking remains undeniably behavioral, although some of the factors leading up to relapse may be affective, psychological, even spiritual (Katz and Ney 1995). These authors outline a series of common factors that one can observe among alcoholics. Here are some of them:

Behavioral

- Decreasing recovery-oriented activities
- Isolating oneself from others
- Avoiding support system in recovery
- Avoiding talking about alcoholism and recovery

Cognitive

- Preoccupation with thoughts of drinking
- Believing that one can control drinking
- Focusing on everything but recovery
- Questioning one's identity as an alcoholic

Social/Interpersonal

- Withdrawing/distancing from social relationships
- Experiencing peer/cultural pressure to drink
- Making recovery contingent on other people
- Lacking family or peer support
- Blaming family/friends for problems
- Openly rejecting help

Affective

- Experiencing heightened anxiety
- Judging oneself harshly
- Feeling ashamed
- Feeling overwhelmed/helpless
- Losing confidence in oneself
- Experiencing ambivalence and doubt

Psychological

- Denying the need for a program
- Feeling inflated, i.e., that one is cured
- Projecting onto/blaming others
- Distancing reality

Physiological

- Having cravings
- Sleeping or eating irregularly
- Experiencing difficulties in physical coordination

Spiritual

- Depending on willpower to stay sober
- Feeling unable to relinquish control
- Letting go of hope, faith

(Katz and Ney 1995, p. 236-39).

Should Alcohol be Banned?

The answer is no, but there should be some effective policy measures put in place. The reasons for this approach are towering. According to Brecher (1985), the untold damage which has been done can be found in the number of first admissions of males to state mental hospitals, medical-surgical wards, public drunkenness, homicides, suicides, damage to unborn babies, college students' behavior, spousal abuse, child abuse, vehicular accidents and loss of productivity. In addition, the effects of other drug use on alcohol can be disastrous. But why will prohibition work now when it did not work before? In the period 1920-1933, the United States Congress banned alcohol. However, this was unsuccessful. The move did not find favor mainly because the United States failed to prohibit other drugs at the same time alcohol was prohibited (Brecher 1985).

The argument goes this way: banning alcohol increases the use of other drugs like marijuana and barbiturates. When drug users cannot get alcohol they turn to other drugs. On the other hand, if they cannot get other drugs, they turn to alcohol. Banning other drugs becomes useless without banning alcohol, for more would be gained by making alcohol unavailable than by making any other drug unavailable (Brecher 1985, p. 266).

The general opinion of those who want to reduce alcohol consumption says alcohol should be banned but this is easier said than done for reasons advanced. The claim is that it has the same deleterious effects as any other mind altering drug, but it is difficult to assess since so many cases never come to social or medical attention (Hanlon and Pickett 1984, p. 461).

When all is said and done, there is no need to detoxify those who have slipped through the social net and put back onto the road of recovery and responsibility.

Detoxification Centers

We would undoubtedly need the services of a detoxification center with the object of the relief of subjective symptoms with the end result being prevention and treatment. According to Beshai (1990), detoxification straddles a three-part process: (1) drying out, (2) fully assessing the patients' problems against the backdrop of his/her lifestyle and attitude, (3) the development of rehabilitation. Beshai (1990) identifies four types of detoxification services, namely, (1) the medical model—involving hospitalization, (2) the non-medical model—involving non-hospitalization, but needing medical support, (3) out-patient model—receiving treatment from private practitioner, and (4) social model—involving the use of a supportive environment.

After examining the related literature, Beshai (1990) is of the view that the majority of alcoholics can be safely treated in a social model program where they can benefit from a reliable environment, one which could lead to cost efficiency and a greater pledge to entertain treatment:

> To ensure the safety of patients treated at social model programs, the staff members in these programs should have knowledge of medical problems and physical

symptoms that signal the need for evaluation by a physician. In addition, social model detoxification programs should be closely linked with medical programs and hospitals so that medical services are readily available when they are necessary (Beshai 1990, p. 480).

The Importance of the Social Model

The use of the social model was seen at the emergency wards in New York city hospitals where "at least 60 percent of all emergency rooms admissions were alcohol-related" (Beshai 1990, p. 480).

In addition, we will have to pay particular attention to the variation in "sex, educational attainment, age, cigarette use and problem alcohol use" when employing preventive interventions for alcohol abuse by primary care providers (Volk et al. 1996).

Summary

Prevention is the key to curbing alcohol abuse. This becomes necessary not only to reduce abuse but also to prevent the materialization of the condition called alcoholism particularly for those at risk.

Communities, where quality of friendship and extended families are fostered, can produce better outcomes. Also, children should have a student-friendly environment as they spend most of their time in school appreciating norms and acquiring values. This is the time when they are heavily influenced by peer pressures and society's influence.

Safe levels of drinking should also be seen as an option to be acquired. In this respect management and union need to sit down and work things out. Responsible advertising should eliminate children and women as symbols of drinking success. Group and individual counseling, community surveys to develop what is termed the "social-problem approach" need to be implemented.

We also need to examine the salience of longitudinal studies in alcohol prevention and the significance in mood changes in these studies. Mood changes could predict short term alcohol consumption effects.

From a methodological viewpoint, it is suggested that we hold constant, biases such as, subjects selection, over-selection of acute cases, over-reporting and look more closely at the relationship between childhood problems and adult drinking. Not to be discounted in the list of preventive measures is to determine how the individual feels about reducing his risk and what others might say about him.

The Employee Assistance Program can be viewed as one instrument which can be used very effectively for treating people in the workplace. It should be noted that a combination of legislative and social norms may act as buffers in containing alcohol consumption as was shown by a survey of alcohol use by 17 and 18-year-olds.

Other preventive areas include: tapping into the affective domain of alcoholics' attitudinal and subjective responses, using experiments such as a saliva test (Bates et al. 1993), the use of a multidisciplinary approach, and the redefinition of alcohol problems from a public health perspective.

There are two aspects of alcohol consumption: relaxed drinking and explosive drinking. Blaming the victim may not work; prevention is a comprehensive concept comprising different initiatives. Politics need to be kept out, if not removed from alcoholism.

Some tips for situational vulnerability: circulate at social events, converse with others, keep your drinking opinion to yourself. Drinking remains undeniably behavioral: this is why there might be strong opinion to ban alcohol. The negative effects of alcohol evidence is towering: a large number of first admissions to state mental hospitals, medical-surgical wards, public drunkenness, homicides, suicides, damage to unborn babies (fetal and otherwise), use of hard drugs, spousal abuse, child abuse, vehicular accidents, loss of productivity, college students' deviant behaviors.

Prohibition did not work before but according to one writer, it can work now (Brecher 1985). In the past when attempts were made to ban alcohol, the use of other drugs was not prohibited.

The establishment of detoxification centers is also significant in preventing alcohol abuse. It helps the alcoholic to dry out, to fully assess the patients' problems, and promotes rehabilitation.

It is believed that a social model program where alcoholics can be treated in a socially supportive environment will bring good results (Beshai 1990). Overall, the best policy is seen as the development of national alcohol policies (WHO 1995).

Suggested Readings

Collins, Lorraine R.; William M. Lapp; and Charles V. Izzo. 1994. "Affective and Behavioral Reactions to the Violation of Limits on Alcohol Consumption." Journal of Studies on Alcohol 55, no. 4:475-86.

Collins, Lorraine R.; Gernot Gollnisch; and Charles V. Izzo. 1996. "Drinking Restraint and Alcohol-Related Outcomes: Exploring the Contributions of Beverage Content and Self-Monitoring." Journal of Studies on Alcohol 57, no. 5: 563-71.

Gual, Antoni; Anna Lligoña; and Joan Colom. 1999. "Five-Year Outcome in Alcohol Dependence. A Naturalistic Study of 850 Patients in Catalonia." Alcohol and Alcoholism 34, no. 2:183-92.

Klijnsma, Marinus P.; Mary L. Cameron; Tom P. Burns; Sean M. McGuigan. 1995. "Out-Patient Alcohol Detoxification-Outcome After 2 Months." Alcohol and Alcoholism 30, no. 5:669-73.

Lipscomb, Thomas R.; and Peter E. Nathan. 1980. "Blood Alcohol Level Discrimination: The Effects of Family History of Alcoholism, Drinking Pattern and Tolerance." Archives of General Psychiatry 37, no. 5:571-76.

McCoy, David G.; and Kristine Napier. 1985/86. "Alcohol and Tobacco Consumption as Risk Factors for Cancer." Alcohol Health and Research World 10, no. 3:28-33.

McGinnis, Michael J. "Prevention in 1989: The State of the Nation." American Journal of Preventive Medicine 6, no. 1:1-5.

Morgenstern, Jon; and Marsha E. Bates. 1999. " Effects of Executive Function Impairment on Change Processes and Substance Use Outcomes in 12-Step Treatment." Journal of Studies on Alcohol 60, no. 6:846-55

Murphy, George E. 1992. Suicide in Alcoholism. U.K.: Oxford University Press.

Rimmer, John; and R. Reich. 1971. "Alcoholism II. Sex, Socioeconomic Status and Race in Two Hospitalized Samples." Quarterly Journal Studies on Alcohol 32:942-52.

Roth, Dee; and Jerry Bean. 1985/86. "Alcohol Problems and Homelessness: Findings from the Ohio Study." Alcohol Health and Research World 10, no. 2 :14-15.

Sinyor, David; Tom Brown; Lorain Rostant; and Peter Seraganian. 1982. "The Role of a Physical Fitness Program in the Treatment of Alcoholism." Journal of Studies on Alcohol 43, no. 3:380-86.

Slater, Michael D.; and Melanie M. Domenech. 1995. "Alcohol Warnings in TV Beer Advertisements." Journal of Studies on Alcohol 56, no. 3:361-67.

CHAPTER 14

Enough is Enough!

Introduction

If alcoholics are so much out of control, it certainly "does not help anyone understand why heredity drinkers sometimes go on binges" (Fingarette 1988). Thus when researchers are talking about "loss of control," they are basically speaking about the inability of drinkers to stay within the bounds of social norms of behavior, not necessarily going on sporadic or unrestrained drinking. That should be left for the non-problem drinker.

> Drinking starts a reaction which is subjectively experienced as a deep need for alcohol and results in continued drinking to the point of being either too intoxicated or too sick to ingest more alcohol. The episode may last hours or weeks. At this juncture the drinker can apparently still regulate the situations in which he will drink, but if he starts he cannot always regulate the quantity he will consume, although this inability may be immediately rationalized (Snyder 1958, p. 184).

The Assessment of Alcoholism

Alcohol is used around the world and it may mean different things to different people. It may be considered a tranquilizer, an aphrodisiac or simply sinful (Hanson 1995).

Hanson continues to outline various patterns of alcohol consumption, which take place in diverse cultures, excesses that is regarded as normal and which do not lead to problems in drinking or alcoholism. Some of these examples will be cited here:

The Yuruna people in the Xingu River region of the South American tropical forest consume large amounts of alcohol, but do not become disinhibited; so too are the residents of Vicas in the Peruvian Andes who have engaged in ceremonial drinking since pre-Columbian days. In Eastern Bolivia, the Camba drink, undiluted distillate of cane sugar produces 89 percent ethyl alcohol, yet the inhabitants' intoxication with it is considered normal. The same can be said of the Aritama in Northern Columbia. They do not outwardly display disinhibition (Hanson 1995, p. 22).

The author makes the point that it is "one's belief," which is of the utmost importance when studying the "effects" of alcohol. While the pharmacological effects of alcohol are quite noticeable in people who drink, as opposed to those who do not, it is the meaning given to these experiences by virtue of the particular culture to which one belongs, that is significant (Hanson 1995).

If, on the one hand, the cultural tradition suggests that the drinker ought to feel aggressive and sexually aroused and, further more, will not be held accountable if he acts upon these impulses, then aggression and overt sexual advances are likely to result from drinking. Thus, alcohol as a drug can be viewed as an enabler or a facilitator of certain culturally-driven inebriate states, but it cannot be seen as producing a specific response pattern among all human beings who ingest it (Hanson 1995).

It is quite clear then that while the properties of alcohol can produce certain changes in the individuals' physiology, and in varying degrees may be more pronounced in some than in others, it does not necessarily lead to "destructive" or problem-behaviors as is evident in studies of different cultures. Thus, behaviors under certain cultures can have a degree of legitimization, no matter how "problematic" they are. In short, one can blame the alcohol and the culture; the drinker may be considered the unwitting pawn in the whole scenario.

According to Hanson (1995), the Italians drink a lot, but they have few abusers. Chinese drink but have few alcoholics.

It should become very clear to us by now that alcohol per se is not the problem. Man has been drinking for quite a long time. However, it is how alcohol is used or rather misused that creates problems worldwide. At best, factors which are learned either from the culture, or from social interaction with a particular group or groups imbibing, may lead to the self-fulfilling prophecy of becoming an alcoholic because one's parents, (presumably one's father) was an alcoholic. Even as this point is made, from a practical aspect there are some individuals who will continue to respond to their drinking habits as long as alcohol remains readily available to them.

And while there are few alcoholics in the class of abstinent and moderate drinkers, the vast majority of problems caused by these few are still sufficient to affect entire societies (National Institute of Mental Health 1969, p. 5).

Modernization and urbanization, although they may represent some of the greatest facilitators for drinking, can be brought under control by social factors. One effective control against alcohol consumption is the culture. But to change cultural patterns takes some time for those changes to develop and once the culture has been handed down through socialization, then it becomes all the more powerful—too difficult to alter in mid stream. Carried to extremes, culture can be interpreted as "human rights." Basic human rights such as the right to the enjoyment of life and "individual freedom" are interpreted also as a right to alcohol consumption and the right to "lose control."

It has been suggested that a client's social, psychological and socio-economic condition, taken together, is the best single predictor of long-term remission, that is, for levels of abuse and stability (Cooper 1983). In looking at teenage drinking on the other hand, Maddox (1962), believes that "no attempts have been made to verify" what teenagers report on their drinking behavior (p. 231). In some countries, like the Caribbean island of Trinidad, youths drinking and smoking is seen as a form of manliness; "to hold" one's liquor is a sign of maturity. In addition, national celebrations like carnival create long-term attitudes and the cultivation of a mentality structured upon the use of drinks "for any occasion."

One also has to take into account the "physical and emotional setting within which drinking occurs" (Tarter and Schneider 1976, p. 491). Thus, we can see that the debate between genetic culpability and social issues is varied and contentious. Even when we wish to scientifically isolate the social factors, we must take into consideration the problem of unraveling the psychological ones, for many social issues have psychological outcomes, and not necessarily the other way around. When social encounters have their outcomes in psychological effects it may reflect inability to deal with these social problems and this may lead to heavy drinking.

In addition, and with specific reference to multiethnic societies, we note that ethnic differences in alcoholism had long been established (Caetano 1984; Muhlin 1985). In an exploratory study of treatment outcomes following a 12-year follow-up of Black and White female alcoholics, it was found that "White females tended to abstain and Black females tended to be uncontrolled drinkers" (Idleburg 1982, p. 96).

Social Irresponsibility—Personal and Social Responses

In examining "social irresponsibility" we are looking at it from two (2) angles: (1) that is, "the social response," or the lack of policies or mechanisms put in place to limit the further development and spread of alcoholism, and (2), personal response or "personal irresponsibility," meaning that individuals willingly and deliberately choose alcohol for certain reasons and under certain circumstances. They can decide not to drink; it becomes their choice. But they do not take into consideration a priori their previous use of alcohol and the consequences thereof. These same individuals may more likely than not, work satisfactorily for years, although if they persist in their alcoholic habit, their physical and mental deterioration in the workplace will become manifest. In effect then, these individuals know that if they do not work (at least most of them), they will not earn a living and will lose a whole lot more than just a drink. As a matter of fact, "approximately 80 percent of adult alcoholics are regularly employed up to the point of disability," with three-fourths of them being professionals, or skilled laborers (Hanlon and Pickett 1984, p. 461).

The literature may show that alcoholics indeed have poor work attitudes and suffer consequently from poor work relationships, family relationships, and other socially unacceptable behaviors. However, what the literature hardly mentions is the large number of alcoholics who are "functional." They report to work, they maintain their professions or their daily routine, and most of all, they manage to avoid social opprobrium. Under different circumstances, when they are among friends and family members, (on weekends, or vacation) these individuals take on a different personality. They become "saints" in their socially respected circles, but "devils" in other settings, away from public glare and scrutiny, where large crowds of persons congregate, and where drinking is accepted. This is where the frequency and intensity of drinking shoot off into higher gear.

Another area to be addressed is the concentration of alcohol within the various classifications, that is, light drinkers, frequent drinkers and heavy drinkers. Arguably, it may make little difference if one drinks "lightly," once or twice a month in heavy amounts or "frequently," once or twice a week in small amounts. The question is what it may lead the individual to become, since concentrations and types may vary on different occasions.

Another area of immediate concern is the chicken and egg syndrome: which comes first nurture or nature? Is the alcoholic born or is he/she a product of the environment? Studies on the proposed genetic predisposition to alcohol consumption assume that alcoholics are born (that is, offspring of alcoholics, particularly males, have a greater risk to becoming alcoholics themselves). However, very little, if any, attempt is made to determine how these alcoholic parents became alcoholics themselves, that is, whether they developed alcoholism as a result of environmental factors. In this respect, retrospective studies would unravel a lot of the uncertainty. It will also identify in no uncertain manner where the salient features lie, that is, whether socially driven alcoholism is a precursor to the perceived genetically-proned fathers of alcoholics. In fact, Vogel-Sprott (1997) notes that tolerance does not develop when favorable outcomes follow intoxicated behavior. In short, there is no development of alcoholism taking place when persons who drink experience a good outcome; that is, they do not have behaviors that are socially, mentally and physiologically unacceptable.

In effect, we come back full circle to whether "social irresponsibility" encompasses and overrides the genetically predisposed one. According to Makela and Room (1989, p. 173):

> Social response to alcohol problems may be thought of in two areas: policies aimed at the control of alcohol, which we will call public control strategies, and policies aimed at deviant drinkers, which we will call personal control policies.... There is controversy over whether laws aimed at reducing overall consumption of alcohol will reduce alcohol problems. Opponents argue that the demand of addicted drinkers...is inelastic. Since addicts will not reduce their drinking, the non-problem drinker will bear the burden of higher prices for alcohol or restricted outlets or hours for purchasing alcohol, and all to no avail so far as reducing the number of addicts. Critics also note the costs of such programs in terms of added administrative needs and job losses in the alcohol industry itself and in related industries such as tourism and restaurants.... On both sides of the arguments are questions about cost benefit ratios and infringement of human rights (Makela and Room 1985, Cited in Bucholz and Robins 1989, p. 173).

The above argument however, does not take into consideration the at-risk drinkers. It looks at the two extremes, the alcoholic (addict) and the non-problem drinker, if by non-problem drinker we do not include the at-risk ones. It also presumes once an alcoholic, always an alcoholic (the thrust of the genetic argument).

In addition, it presupposes that there is one body of alcoholics, that is, one large cohort group that does not succumb to societal pressure, peer pressure, or receive clinical treatment, or is assessable in any way. Opponents of laws to reduce alcohol consumption should take into consideration that laws can impact on demand no matter how inelastic that demand.

Furthermore, we must decide what we want: more responsible behavior reflected in reduced motor vehicle accidents, violence and spousal abuse on the one hand or job losses in the tourist industry on the other.

Again, if extricating the alcoholics from the alcohol industry is so damaging why not reduce the alcohol content by law, without reducing quality. For example, the alcohol content for beers, rums or whiskies could be reduced by fiat, proportionately speaking. Culturally and nationally, different tastes will now be cultivated, if not remain the same. In the same way an alcoholic or any drinker will now have to cultivate a taste for one drink or class of drinks as opposed to another. Clearly then, it would take more than the usual number of drinks for the alcoholic to reach the point where he/she will commence his/her "irresponsible behavior," a behavior which will eventually assist the alcohol industry, nevertheless, since demand will increase. All societies recognize when alcoholic beverages are consumed but these alterations are always "within limits...and these limits are more lax than those for sober persons in the same situations" (Marshall 1979, p. 24).

Culturally and situationally speaking it explains why the Irish drink heavily and have alcohol problems; the Jews drink but do not have these problems (suggesting that the attitudes and ritual play a part); Italians drink, yet have low levels of alcohol abuse; Chinese drink but have very few drinking problems and Mormons drink and have a drinking problem (Hanson 1995).

Thus, the question may be, does the whole alcohol debate, consist of methodological flaws and misconceptions? Perhaps, it may be unwittingly so.

Summary

When researchers talk about "loss of control" they mean the inability of drinkers to stay within what is considered "normal behavior." Different countries may have different problems with alcohol consumption. In this respect, alcohol may be perceived differently from one culture to the next. Some view it as an aphrodisiac; others see it as simply sinful, yet others may perceive it as a tranquilizer.

For example, one's belief might be an important factor in studying the effects of alcohol, although we cannot discount the pharmacological effects. Under these considerations, alcohol cannot be seen as producing a particular response among all human beings; the drinker may be trapped between the culture and the alcoholic drink. Alcohol per se is not the problem; it is how alcohol is used that constitutes a problem. Yet, there are those among us who will continue to respond to alcohol because alcohol remains fully available.

Factors responsible for this are modernization and urbanization, which set up demonstration effects on different people depending on their age, social class or religious upbringing. Drinking is correlated with socio-economic status, ethnicity, age and religion (Skolnick 1980). These factors are compounded in their effects by a client's social and psychological state, as well as other factors such as national celebrations.

Social irresponsibility is constructed on two levels, at the individual/personal level and at the national level. It is to be noted that almost 80 percent of adult alcoholics are regularly employed (Hanlon and Pickett 1984).

Another area for consideration is to determine how alcoholic parents themselves became alcoholics, that is, whether alcoholism was developed from their social environment, in the first instance. There is a school of thought which tells us that laws aimed at reducing alcohol consumption do not work since the demand of addicted drinkers is inelastic, and that those who will bear the brunt of high cost will be the non-problem drinkers. However one has to look at the at-risk drinkers. It is the opinion of the author of this book that at-risk drinkers who are targeted can help reduce the growth of alcohol addicts. In this respect social responsibility-specific policies must be put in place.

If removing alcoholics from society is very difficult, then efforts to reduce alcohol content by law, depending on the type of alcoholic beverage, should be introduced. When this approach is coupled with culture and situation, we may understand why Chinese drink but have few problems; why Jews drink and have very little alcohol problems. On the other hand, the Mormons and the Irish drink but have problems.

The point is we are not aware that laws have been enacted to deal with the level of alcohol content. We know that if this is followed by the "right" attitude and the "right" culture, then alcohol abuse will be reduced significantly.

Suggested Readings

Erickson, Carlton K. 1992. "A Pharmacologist's Opinion- Alcoholism: The Disease Debate Needs to Stop." Alcohol and Alcoholism 27, no. 4:325-28.

George, William H.; Gail L. Lehman; Kelly L. Cue; Lorraine J. Martinez; Peter A. Lopez; and Jeanette Norris. 1997. "Postdrinking Sexual Inferences: Evidence for Linear Rather Than Curvilinear Dosage Effects." Journal of Applied Social Psychology 27, no. 7:629-48.

Isaacs, Morton. 1977. "Stereotyping by Children of the Effects of Drinking on Adults." Journal of Studies on Alcohol 38:913-21.

CHAPTER 15

Alcoholism: The Interdisciplinary Approach

Introduction

A real possibility is to embrace alcoholism from an interdisciplinary perspective.

It is quite clear that based on the evidence before us and the arguments which abound, alcoholism could be "understood" in all its variations by bringing together various perspectives to bear on it. Given that an interdisciplinary framework to address outcome and efficacy may be a long way off, it nevertheless remains an idea worth debating. A number of studies have courted the idea of an interdisciplinary approach to alcoholism; and these will be examined here.

The Interplay of Physiological and Other Factors

In examining the multi-causal nature of alcoholism, one appreciates the interplay of physiological, sociological, cultural and psychological factors. Thus, what is specifically being addressed is the interaction of hereditary and environmental factors.

In looking at the etiology of alcoholism, one study suggests that there may be many pathways leading to alcoholism. McCord (1988) in a paper titled: "Toward Understanding Genetic and Social Factors," believes that:

> Differences between alcoholics whose fathers were alcoholic and whose fathers were not alcoholic in terms of mother's impact suggest that there may be alternative

> paths toward alcoholism. Along one, the probability that a man will follow his alcoholic father's footsteps appear to be particularly augmented by mother's showing respect for the alcoholic father. Along the other, the probability that a father will become an alcoholic is augmented by lack of maternal control. The one path might represent imitation or expectation coupled with genetic impact and the other might represent inhibited impulsiveness (McCord 1988, p. 138, p. 568).

Non-Addictive Pathological Drinking

Again, it has been shown by Strauss (1988) that there is what is called "non-addictive pathological drinking." It was reported that some homeless persons studied, exhibited "powerful needs to drink heavily." Apparently, these needs were not driven by physical addiction or loss of control. The researcher surmised that it was due to their social situations and their lifestyles. Interestingly their behavior changed when their circumstances were altered, that is, after they found jobs and accommodation (Strauss 1988).

Strauss, elaborates on the developmental process of dependency where it starts with a perception, but ends with a psychological and physical dependence.

Williams (1947) also identifies the link between environment and genetics, while dismissing the etiology of alcoholism by psychological factors. He contends that although the literature on the psychology of alcoholism is voluminous, it leads to no "completely satisfactory answers" (p. 567).

> [T]he idea that the addictive use of alcohol is an "escape" from the troubles of living is, itself, hardly adequate since the environmental difficulties of the alcoholic-to-be are not with certainty greater than those of people who resist alcoholism (Williams 1947, p. 567).

Williams goes on to explain that once a person becomes an alcoholic he/she either continues to be an alcoholic or becomes a total abstainer. These individuals never become moderate drinkers. He adds that when people who suffer from stress take alcohol, they never cease drinking when the stress disappears. He believes that the same scenario takes place with members of Alcoholics Anonymous (AA): though they become psychologically adjusted to non-drinking they cannot afford to be moderate drinkers.

According to Williams (1947), the evidence for the hereditary thesis has shortcomings because addiction takes place when the individual is in an environment which is favorable to the development of alcoholism:

> If a potential alcoholic with a susceptible metabolic individuality is reared in an atmosphere where drinking is common and relatively unrestrained, where money to purchase liquor is available and there is abundant leisure time in which to

> indulge, the chances of escaping addiction is very small... On the other hand, if the potential alcoholic is reared and lives continuously under conditions which discouraged the use of liquor, his chances of escape is good. According to the best information, it usually requires several years of relatively heavy drinking to develop serious addiction. If the potential addict could be forwarded, avoidance of alcoholism would be made relatively easy (p. 581).

Interdisciplinary Approach—A Concession

It is my contention that the interdisciplinary approach does not impact positively on the body of research seeking an adequate explanation for alcohol consumption; it merely is a concession that alcoholism is "both a genetic disorder and an environmental one." However, the idea that the two factors may be operating simultaneously, still has to be addressed by the literature. The reason for the almost total absence of interdisciplinary studies may be that there are so few "genetically driven alcoholics" in the first place with which the culturally-induced ones interact to bring about an alcoholic outcome.

Separating the Environment

How then, do we separate the heredity and the environment? Susser (1985) argues that there are designs that aim to do just this, namely, twin studies, fixed clusters involving family, the family set design, and the comparison of relatives reared separately. But these particular approaches are fraught with problems.

> [T]he method of heritability estimates fail to cope with either biological interaction, or with confounding that arises from co-variation between genotype and environment. Genotypes interact with their environments and alter them, and environment in turn may alter the manifestation of a genotype (Susser 1985, p. 9).

This point seems to be particularly important for those calling for an interdisciplinary approach. For one, all genetic studies on environmental strain are not so convincing as they are made out to be. Male offspring of hospitalized alcoholics were followed and compared with the adoptive offspring of two groups of controls without a history of alcoholism, and the risk of alcoholism in the offspring of alcoholics was about four-fold.

However, when the analysis was restructured to take into consideration moderate drinking, problem-drinking, and heavy drinking, there were little differences in drinking between the offspring of alcoholics and the controls. The author (Susser 1985) concludes that genetically predisposed alcoholics remain a minority within "the clinical diagnostic entity of alcoholism."

Problems in Methodology

Problems of design and control therefore, remain critical features in separating heredity and environment"... the picture of the child's genetic background... and social experience is often incomplete" (Susser 1985, p. 20). But there is no easy retreat for the geneticists. They have grudgingly "accepted" that even when they locate persons who are at risk to alcoholism, they cannot generalize their findings to the wider population of alcoholics. Their design and their controls are further questionable so that in fact, the geneticists have to cross two major hurdles: (1) develop a rigorous research design that will take into consideration memory lapses, social and environmental control, and (2) convince or show by demonstration that the vast majority of alcoholics are driven by both genetic and environmental factors. Until they can do this, they will have to adopt the combination of genetic and environmental perspectives to strengthen their claim.

It must be pointed out further, that as the sun sets on the arguments of the genetic origins of alcoholism, it is believed that there may be attempts to provide a clearer picture. When interdisciplinarians from the genetic camp champion the call for a multidisciplinary approach, they tend to use the word "social environment," rather than simply "environment." Social environment conjures images of physical, social, psychological, and situational factors, all of which may impact the individual simultaneously.

To conduct a study on genotype and environment assumes independence between both, which may not necessarily prove true. Some genotypes select certain environments (Susser 1985, p. 9).

In sum, the interdisciplinary approach throws very little light on solving the alcohol problem which runs the gamut from the young to the aged. We have to look elsewhere for the solutions to this problem.

Strauss (1988, p. 33), on the other hand, advises that there is a need to train scientists who would be willing to participate in research that requires interdisciplinary collaboration based mainly on drinking patterns.

Community Approaches

Additionally, public health authorities through the Department of Health and Human Services in the United States have called for communities to be instrumental in fighting alcohol and drug use by developing coping skills through peer groups instruction and culturally appropriate strategies.

> There is an urgent need to obtain base line data within the black population, with follow-up studies to include interracial studies that address age, regional and occupational differences and socio-cultural consequences (legal employment, family problems, etc.) of alcohol use and misuse (Benjamin and Benjamin 1981, p. 243).

The suggestion of an interdisciplinary or multidisciplinary approach to alcoholism was set out in great detail twenty four years ago. Keller (1975) writing on the multidisciplinary perspectives on alcoholism and "the need for integration" points to a history of interdisciplinary maneuvers such as the founding of "the

Center for Alcohol Studies, first formed at Yale University beginning in 1940-41 and subsequently continued at Rutgers University" (p. 134). He also recognizes that the idea of multidisciplinary is one to which "lip service is readily given." Noting that there are inherent difficulties in conceptualizing "the fundamental holism of alcoholism," Keller suggests that we begin with our history on alcoholism to find out how it became partitioned by various perspectives.

Temperance and Anti-alcoholism

Keller identifies the classic Temperance movement which he regards as an anti-alcoholic movement, skittling any "broad perspective on alcohol problems." Their tactic failed, he recalls, since most alcoholics had become so during Prohibition.

He concludes:

> Not enough has been said about the necessary integration. Frankly, I do not have a clear conception of how the disciplines can be truly integrated in performing the studies required to verify the holistic etiological perspective, nor exactly how the professions can be integrated for the first experimental programs of prevention (Keller 1975, p. 146).

Still, he advises that teaching of the holistic perspective, and support emanating from research centers will put us on the road to integration.

The call for a multidisciplinary approach to alcohol dependency might have fallen on deaf ears since the Temperance Movement days, but it might have been the result of an already hardened interest-driven research with political and economic agendas backed by research grants by some of the more prominent institutions. These actions have significant symbolic effects on an already unsuspecting alcohol-preoccupied population harboring images of a genetic etiology of this "disease."

The Present Focus

The present preoccupation is the increased consumption of alcohol among teenagers, especially females. Officials are caught between genetic etiology and behavioral irresponsibility. Teenagers lie about their age to purchase alcohol, but what is driving the new craze? Is it a world of growing hypocrisy; a world of adults who warn about drinking but make excuses why they themselves must have a drink? Or is it a new-found individual liberty that is sweeping cultures the world over, following on the heels of the fall of the Soviet Union and the collapse of the Berlin Wall? It is instructive to note that the Soviet Union is now reported to be having high incidences of alcoholism and alcohol-related problems.

The call for a multidisciplinary approach will have to turn around a tremendous amount of resources, not to mention the dislocation and accommodation of interests. I know of no professional who is prepared to sacrifice or share his discipline's interests at the risk of it being subsumed by another, in this instance, for example, the genetic one. I agree with Keller (1975), that the call for a multidisciplinary approach to alcoholism will remain just that—a call. Still, it is a responsible position, but I hear very little, if any response resonating from officials and researchers.

Summary

One option for understanding alcoholism is by embracing the interdisciplinary perspective. In this respect, a multidisciplinary framework may be worth debating. A number of studies have focussed on a multidisciplinary approach to understanding the full etiology of alcoholism.

This will necessarily mean an interplay of physiological, sociological, cultural and psychological factors. In short, it addresses the interaction of hereditary and environmental factors.

The "loss of control" thesis advanced by the geneticists has been further questioned when Strauss (1988) found "not-addictive pathological drinking." Homeless men's drinking habit was driven by a "powerful need" emanating from their social situations and their lifestyles. To further support his findings the researcher reported that when these men's social situation changed, that is, when they found jobs and accommodation, their behavior changed as well.

Strauss (1988) argues on the developmental process of dependency, commencing with a perception. At the same time Williams (1947) discusses the link between environment and genetics, while dismissing the psychological etiology of alcoholism. He argues that there are two options which present themselves with those who drink heavily: they either become alcoholics or they become abstainers. Further, those who "drink for stress," never cease to drink when their stress disappears.

It is Williams' contention that addiction takes place when an individual is in an environment which is favorable to its development.

It is this author's suggestion that there is a paucity of studies on the interdisciplinary approach to the adequate understanding of alcoholism and this may be due, in part, to the lack of match between "genetically driven alcoholics" and culturally driven ones.

It is Susser's (1985) position that even when we control genetic influence, little difference is found between offspring of alcoholics and their controls. One reason for this is the problem of separating heredity and environment.

The interdisciplinary approach throws very little light on understanding the etiology of alcoholism, and the idea of a multidisciplinary approach is one to which lip service is readily given (Keller 1976).

Any attempt to go the interdisciplinary way must take into consideration the redeployment of a tremendous amount of resources and the risk of dislocation of interests.

Suggested Readings

Johnston, Richard D.; and Roger Williams. 1985. "Genetic and Environmental Factors in the Individual Susceptibility to the Development of Alcoholic Liver Disease." Alcohol and Alcoholism 20, no. 2:137-60.

Prescott, Carol A.; John K. Hewitt; Andrew C. Heath; Kim R. Truett; Michael C. Neale; and Lindon J. Eaves. 1994. "Environmental and Genetic Influences on Alcohol Use in a Volunteer Sample of Older Twins." Journal of Studies on Alcohol 55, no. 1:18-33.

CHAPTER 16

THE ECONOMIC COST OF ALCOHOL CONSUMPTION

Introduction

The cost of alcohol consumption must not be overlooked. It is staggering. The alcohol industry rakes in billions per year, just like the tobacco industry, and this is good news for governments in terms of taxation and employment. Like most other commercial entities, alcohol consumption must be seen as being caught in a quagmire of social contradictions. To control the use and abuse of alcohol consumption would, of necessity, affect the industry's profits and consequently the government's share of the spoils. At the same time, it denies its recreational benefits to a vast majority of individuals.

The Real Cost of Doing Nothing

The question which remains to be answered is: what will the continued and unabated influence of alcohol on the minds of young children and younger adults have on families and society. Also, to what extent does alcohol consumption produce the first step toward hard-drug usage and sicknesses such as schizophrenia, depression, and other related diseases? What is the total cost of alcohol consumption to societies around the world? It seems that on the one hand income is generated, but on the other hand, the amount which is exacted, not by the alcohol industry per se, but by human suffering, and the consequent loss to the society, is greater.

> In 1979, the total United Kingdom consumer expenditure on all items amounted to about $115,000 million.... Nearly $9,000 million were spent on alcohol, representing almost 8 percent of all consumer spending. In the same year, 1979,

> Custom and Excise Duty plus Value Added Tax (VAT) on that alcohol provided the government with an income of £2,928.1 million (Brewers' Statistical Handbook 1980. Cited in Eastman 1984, p. 34).

Social Cost of Alcohol Consumption

We need to be aware of the financial cost of drinking to the society and the number of alcohol-related deaths by social categories. Most of all, we need to know the loss of man-hours which is reflected in the Gross National Product (GNP) of the country. Some costs, such as failed business ventures, bankruptcies, and foreclosures, loss of customer service and faulty decision-making, never come to the fore. It is now ten years since Walsh (1990) revealed the economic state of affairs of American drinking. Writing on "the shifting boundaries of alcohol policy" she noted that "the economics of alcohol use and abuse was estimated in 1983 at over $100 billion," $71 billion in lost productivity; $18 billion in mortality; $14 billion in health care costs; and $12 billion relating to losses in property and crime. She predicted that the costs will continue to rise.

Pearlin and Radabaugh (1976) agree that social and economic factors heavily influence distressed persons. Their overall premise is that the "consumption of alcohol may serve as a mechanism for coping with anxiety aroused by economic conditions" (p. 652). In their research titled "Economic Strains and the Coping Functions of Alcohol," the researchers discovered that people who were lacking control of their lives as reflected in attitudes, were more predisposed to use alcohol as a form of coping mechanism and, as mastery declined, economic strain rose. However, this economic strain was not tied to money, per se, but on how economic resources were managed in seeking out opportunities and realizing goals.

The Poor Drunkard

In large measure therefore, the poor are the ones who are identified as likely to drink more than their resource-endowed counterparts. The circularity of their position is quite evident. They drink to ease their problems which carries an economic cost. To deal with the stresses of their economic cost, they must in turn drink; a condition brought on by drinking in the first instance.

> Thus, it is the poor who are most likely to have to bear the burdens of anxiety that result from economic threat, and it is also the poor who are least likely to have the experiences and opportunities that contribute to a sense of mastery, a characteristic that serves to reduce potential reliance on alcohol as a distress management device (Pearlin and Radabaugh 1976, p. 659).

On the other hand, some authors (Heien and Pittman 1993) seek to categorize the cost of alcohol consumption into external and private costs, suggesting that in many cases of alcohol-related incidents, the victims or their families accept the risk and eventual costs.

> Whether or not some activity result in an external cost depends on who is affected. Consider activities such as eating, drinking, playing sports, having children, etc. Those activities often result in negative outcomes. Consider the case of overeating. First of all, the cost of food is a private cost. This is true for the family as well as the individual since the household is considered the primary decision making unit in society. Even if it is not well known that overeating causes health problems, the costs are still private since they fall only on the individual (Heien and Pittman 1993, p. 303).

This is indeed a simple economic look at something that wreaks havoc in people's lives and it fits squarely into the realm of individualism and privacy. It also hints unabashedly of ignorance of the spillover effects of private and individual costs, into public ones, considering the purview of modern governments and the public at large who are asked to pay high (external) costs.

Relative Cost of Alcohol Consumption

More sobering contributions on the cost of alcohol consumption can be found in the comments of Fox et al. (1995); McKenna et al. (1996); Goodman et al. (1997). They all point to the relative costs of alcohol consumption vis-à-vis other drugs, including substance abuse and treatment costs. Fox et al. (1995), state that more than 60 medical conditions out of 1,100 diagnoses are identified as attributable to substance abuse, representing 4 million days in abuse-related care. As far as quality of life is concerned McKenna et al. (1996) report that chronic alcoholics appropriate greater alcohol costs and experience poorer life quality than the normal population.

Still, it was determined that alcohol consumption has significant effect on income. Heien (1996) using regression model estimates the effects of alcohol consumption on earnings. The researcher found, among others, that "moderate drinkers have greater earnings than either abstainers or abusers."

Jones et al. (1995) report that in New Zealand alone, $57 million is lost per year. They arrived at this estimate by measuring the cost of absenteeism and reduced work efficiency, "between the top 10 percent and the bottom 10 percent drinkers."

Alcohol's Substantial Contribution to the Economy

It must also be remembered that "alcoholic beverages make a substantial contribution to the nation's economy" (Olson and Gerstein 1985, p. 18). This fact, perhaps, more than any other, may be responsible for the ambivalent attitude towards alcohol at the policy and administrative levels.

> The alcoholic beverage industry consists of three tiers; the distillers, vintners, and brewers; the distribution and importation companies; and the bars, taverns, liquor stores, groceries, restaurants, and other outlets depend on the sale of alcohol for their profit margins. Also, many spectator and participant sports have become closely linked with alcohol sales (Olson and Gerstein 1985, p. 18).

World Production of Alcohol

It is reported that the world's output of alcohol is tremendous. World production grew from 823.9 million hectoliters in 1965 to 1295.2 million hectoliters in 1980 (Walsh 1985) and continues to grow, beer being the favorite alcoholic beverage. World wine production alone is dominated by a few countries, namely France, Italy, and Spain (Walsh 1985). Yet, it becomes difficult to offer any support for alcohol as a great economic benefit when there are so many social costs involved. The problem is that alcohol has unique characteristics. Simply put, alcohol is not a commodity like any other (Walsh 1985). However, we must recognize that the alcohol industry is a complex commercial entity with branches reaching across the globe and having "the power to influence national control legislation" (Iwaarden 1985, p. 45).

Powerful Interests Behind Alcohol

The current lobbying of interest groups to influence the passing of legislation has implications for the levels and social costs of drinking. Alcohol is caught between powerful economic interests and a great many who imbibe out of recreational, occasional and irresponsible behaviors. Specifically, alcohol has friends and foes; and this is so because of its very nature and appeal.

In a seminar held in November 1977 and published by the Commission of the European Communities, one commentator noted that "in many circles...alcoholism is not seen as a problem since its damaging effect is never truly realized" (p.75). The author gave the reasons for this as "the very long periods" over which its effects become known and "in all countries the manufacturers of alcoholic drinks were well represented by powerful pressure groups..." (de Vita 1977, p. 83).

Alcohol's Contribution to Health

Current trends indicate that alcohol, particularly wine, is good for one's health:

> [A]lcohol is related to health, and it is even viewed as beneficial and is widely used even in infancy and adolescence. Hence, the scientific underevaluation of the problem is supported and substantiates an "opinion" widely held by the population. This is a result of misguided health education and widespread stereotype beliefs which attribute to urine...a fundamental role in the treatment of

> various diseases and physical disorders, a source of energy and therapy (de Vita 1977, p. 75. Cited in Seminar of the Medico-Social Risks of Alcohol Consumption 1977).

Even when we stop or reduce the levels of alcoholism, we will still have to bear the costs of detoxification and rehabilitation (Goodman et al. 1997). The latter, however, is more costly than we may perceive it to be.

In the final analysis it is a social cost, sapping human energy, which is used for economic and social purposes, not to mention the cost of accidents or diseases, lower productivity and higher mortality. In short, alcoholism represents an attack on the individual's mental and physical health which is really an attack on the community (de Vita 1977).

However, no one wants to address directly the alcohol costs; the issue is too tied up with ideological, cultural and economic interests. Whenever one questions the cost of alcohol consumption, one is tinkering with the cultural foundation of many societies which have an "on-and-off" love affair with this drug. They will argue, and rightly so, that alcohol is not the problem; people have been drinking for years and the symbol of alcohol has found its rightful place both as a lift at social functions and celebrations, and as a companion to the lonely.

The Heavy Weight of Indirect Cost

If we want to make any serious impression on the economic cost of alcohol consumption, it is perhaps better to start looking at the indirect costs. One suggestion

which comes to mind is to reduce the need to abuse alcohol without limiting the supply, since the vast amount of alcohol is used not by the alcoholics who are relatively few compared to the large majority of recreational and moderate drinkers. If anyone is to be discouraged from drinking it would be light to problem drinkers.[1]

In addition, it is widely regarded in some circles that we should develop some ethical method to deal with the relationship between sponsors and researchers. The suspicion here is that sponsors may, as in the case of the tobacco industry, direct and influence opinion in a positive light, while underplaying the ill-effects of their commodity, in this case, alcohol.

The National Institute on Alcohol Abuse and Alcoholism in the United States laments the problem in attaching a cost to alcohol abuse. "First, researchers attempt to identify costs that are caused by, and not merely associated with, alcohol abuse, yet it is often hard to establish causation..." and secondly, "many costs resulting from alcohol abuse cannot be measured directly." Yet, "estimates of costs give us an idea of the dimensions of the problem..." (p. 1).

In making a commentary, Gordis, Director of the Institute (1990) suggests that when different methodologies produce similar results, one gets a stronger indication of the relationship between alcohol-related problems and damage to society.

Summary

The economic cost of alcohol consumption warrants investigation. It is a staggering billion-dollar industry. This revenue assists government and aids in employment, just like the tobacco industry. Therefore any attempt to control alcohol will have an effect upon the industry's profits and government's share as well.

We must measure the real cost of alcohol consumption: how it affects young and adult minds, how it produces the first step toward hard drugs and other illnesses such as schizophrenia, depression and the like, the total cost of human suffering. We can appreciate therefore, that alcohol consumption makes its greatest cost felt in social, rather than economic terms.

However, we can translate total social costs to economic costs. In this way we will be able to place a dollar value on some of the violence which can be laid at the doorstep of alcohol consumption or alcohol abuse.

It all comes down to mastery or social responsibility. Two researchers (Pearlin and Radabaugh 1976) reported that lack of social and economic control translates into increased economic strain, that is, how one spends money, and seizes opportunities when they arise.

Alcohol is not a product like any other. It is a complex commercial entity, having universal branches and universal appeal in various nations (Iwaarden 1985). This makes friends and foes of alcohol.

To attempt to deal directly with alcohol cost one risks the possibility of tinkering with ideological and cultural foundations and economic interests, many of which may have a peculiar "love affair" with the drug.

One approach is to identify the light to problem drinkers in society, since a vast amount of drinking does not take place among the alcoholics per se, but those most likely to become alcoholics.

Methodologically speaking, it can be established that there is a relationship between alcohol-related problems and social costs to society.

Suggested Readings

Bauer, H.; and R. Baab. 1995. "The Self-Concept and Personality Structure of Alcohol Intoxicated Drivers: How Do They See Themselves, and How They Are Judged by Others?" Blutal Kohol 32, no. 1:8-25.

Caces, Fe; and Thomas Harford. 1998. "Time Series Analysis of Alcohol Consumption and Suicide Mortality in the United States, 1934-1987." Journal of Studies on Alcohol 59:455-61.

Devlin, N. J.; P. A. Scuffham; and L. J Bunt. 1997. "The Social Costs of Alcohol Abuse in New Zealand." Addiction 92, no. 11:1491-1505.

Humphreys, K.; and R. A. Moos. 1996. "Reduced Substance-Abuse-Related Health Care Costs among Voluntary Participants in Alcoholics Anonymous." Psychiatric Services 47, no.7:709-13.

Neumann, M.; and J. Toepffer. 1995. "Alcohol Drinking Problems in Assessing the Public Economic Impact." Fortschritte der Medizin 113, no. 33:476-79.

O'Farrell, T. J.; K. A. Choquette; H. S. Cutter; F. J. Floyd; R. Bayoog; E. D. Brown; J. Lowe; A. Chan; and P. Deneault. 1996. "Cost-Benefit and Cost-Effectiveness Analyses of Behavioral Marital Therapy as an Addition to Outpatient Alcoholism Treatment." Journal of Substance Abuse 8, no. 2:145-66.

Pirzada, S. R.; R. Ries; and J. P. LoGergo. 1997. "Cost of Co-Morbid Alcohol and Drug Problems." American Journal on Addictions 6, no. 3: 193-204.

Plant, M.; and B.Vernon. 1996. "Ethics, Funding and Alcohol Research." Alcohol and Alcoholism 31, no. 1:17-25.

Smart, R. G.; R. E. Mann; and S. L Lee. 1996. "Does Increased Spending on Alcoholism Treatment Lead to Lower Cirrhosis Death Rates?" Alcohol and Alcoholism 31, no. 5: 487-91.

---

1 Problem drinkers here mean, qualitatively those who have grown accustomed to using alcohol "for every occasion."

CHAPTER 17

The Measurement of Alcoholism: Methodological Flaws and Misconceptions?

Introduction

Frankfort-Nachmias and Nachmias (1996) view the role of methodology as the cement which unites or binds the sciences. The social scientist's aim is to provide general explanations for "why?" questions.

> A scientific methodology is a system of explicit rules and procedures upon which research is based and against which claims for knowledge are evaluated. This system is neither unchangeable nor infallible. Rather, the rules and procedures are constantly being improved; scientists look for new means of observation, analysis, logical inference, and generalization. As these are developed and found to be congruent with the underlying assumptions of the scientific approach, they are incorporated into the system of rules that govern the scientific methodology (Frankfort-Nachmias and Nachmias 1996, p. 13).

While a preponderance of alcohol studies has been forthcoming, observers and researchers have used various definitions of alcoholism. In addition to those already given, there are others. The American Psychiatric Association, identifies an alcoholic as:

- Remaining intoxicated for at least two days
- Becoming tolerant of alcohol, needing markedly increased amounts to achieve the same effects

These two features are extremely important when attempting to describe alcoholism. As such the methodology should at least incorporate duration and tolerance in assessing this condition. In this chapter, "methods" mean the tools used in the research process either to generate data or to collect and analyze it. According to Sarantakos (1993) "methods" are guided by the underlying paradigm of the study.

In the first instance therefore, I will examine some of the measuring instruments associated with alcohol consumption and following this, I will comment upon them.

Internal Consistency

The SMAST has been popular, particularly in the mid-seventies. According to Selzer et al. (1975), the Short Michigan Alcoholism Screening Test (SMAST) has internal consistency as determined by alpha coefficients, that is, 83, 89 and 95. Scores were validated by using a product-moment correlation coefficient and a Goodman's gamma. As such, it is claimed to be very reliable, being able to capture the variance on alcoholism with a certain degree of efficiency.

> The mast scores were calculated by adding up the points assigned to each item for which the subject gave a response indicating alcoholism... Those in group G were scored 1 and those in group A were scored 2. This computation yielded a validity co-efficient of r=.79 (gamma =.95), indicating that the alcoholics scored higher than . . . others (Selzer et al. 1975).

The authors were able to construct a measuring instrument which allowed them to make quantitative assessments among different categories of responses. For example, those ongoing general social questions were:

- Has drinking ever created problems between you and your wife, husband, a parent, or other near relative? (Yes, 2 points)
- Have you ever gone to anyone for help about your drinking? (Yes, 5 points)
- Have you ever been in a hospital because of drinking? (Yes, 5 points)

Further, a stepwise regression was used to select "MAST,"[1] items which only significantly improved the outcome of the dependent variable, that is, whether one was alcoholic or non-alcoholic (Selzer et al. 1975, p. 117).

It should be remembered, however that this Short Michigan Alcoholism Screening Test (SMAST) is an abridged version of the MAST which was criticized on grounds that the definitions in it were too broad, and was therefore restricted to persons who were grossly alcoholic (Selzer 1971, p. 1653). In addition, MAST has higher rates in detecting people who may have alcohol-use disorder (Teitelbaum and Mullen 2000). In response, therefore, the SMAST version (MAST) attempts to deal with not only the "grossly alcoholic," but also lays claim to capturing a greater measure of alcoholism by attending to the methodological shortcomings of its parent scale. Overall, the MAST provides a good measure of consistency in determining the types of alcoholics in certain populations (Selzer 1971; Yersin et al. 1989).

Quantity, Aggregate versus Occasional

In measuring drinking patterns as they relate to quantity and frequency, there are certain concerns which should be highlighted. One has to look at quantity both from "an occasion" perspective, and from aggregate time period perspective.

In this respect, the revisiting of alcohol concepts or measurements for that matter gives the researcher the golden opportunity to improve on past research and come up with a better measuring instrument. Consistent with this approach, a number of developments have taken place, all with a view to capturing the validity of a measurement for alcoholism in varying degrees. These range from the development of an entire scale to the construction of an internal scale for the measurement of impaired control over the consumption of alcohol (Cornel et al. 1994; Tracy and Bates 1994; Kennedy et al. 1994; Hennessy and Saltz 1993; Polich et al. 1981; Weed et al. 1994; Heather et al. 1993).

Quantity-Frequency, Basic

Most of these researchers and authors tried to build on the foundation of the quantity-frequency-variation (q-f-v) by focussing on measurements to capture severity of drinking problems, namely, the detection of cognitive defects; standardized field sobriety tests; combining qualitative index with quantitative data; index construction; and the development of the Minnesota Multiphasic Personality Inventory-Adolescent (MMPI-A) scales, respectively.

Importance of Methodological Issues

Other measures have been more or less consistent in providing outcomes. Our main purpose therefore in presenting this chapter, is to highlight some of these methodologies to give a clearer picture to the reader and to showcase the importance of methodological issues in arriving at a fuller understanding of alcoholism in "all its forms."

CAGE Measurement

One such methodology is the CAGE which is the acronym for a four-item questionnaire intended as an instrument to screen for alcohol-related problems. The four items are:

- Feeling the need to cut down on your drinking

- Becoming annoyed at criticism of your drinking
- Feeling guilty about your drinking
- Needing a drink first thing in the morning to get going.

However, the CAGE questionnaire has raised some concerns as to its suitability for certain populations. One study (Liskow et al. 1995) supported the CAGE methodology in detecting substantial sensitivity to alcoholism; another study identified some shortcomings in special populations, namely, college populations and women. The researchers noted that the CAGE demonstrated its effectiveness as a screening instrument by separating those with a lifetime of alcoholism and those who are not so dependent. It is reported that the researchers found a sensitivity of 86 percent and a specificity of 93 percent when used with one or more "yes" responses. In the final analysis, the investigators recommended a CAGE score of 1 to be used in most clinical settings because of the likelihood in these settings that prevalence will be relatively high. Where low levels of alcoholism were found in the population, a CAGE score of 2 was suggested.

Reliability of CAGE

Another study by Heck and Williams (1995) using the CAGE to screen for drinking-related problems in college students, found that when it came to screening women for alcohol-related problems, the instrument was less accurate. Some of the reasons given were: there was no standardized definition of problem drinking in the literature (p. 284) and the relatively low frequency of problem drinking among the samples of students, particularly as it related to women.

Bongers and Van Oers (1998) contest the need for one specific measurement in data collection. They report that there is essentially no difference between mail survey method and personal interview method. The two researchers were responding to the inconsistencies of findings in the alcohol literature generally. Their recommendation, they noted would go a long way in solving the methodological problems associated with measuring alcohol consumption.

Methodology and Family Studies

Riskin (1963, p. 343) observed that "much of clinical psychiatric research and therapy has been traditionally oriented towards the individual patient." However, researchers are now moving towards "an individual's behavior," particularly as it relates to the family. One focus of attention lies in the family's "manner of communicating or their underlying interactional pattern of behavior" (p. 344).

> Analysis of family communication also leads to insights concerning family "laws" or "rules". The laws are more or less consciously held values which are related to the values of the family's cultural environment. Rules are hypothetical constructs

formulated by the observer to account for observable behavior in the family. The family may be totally unaware of them (p. 345).

Interviewing families can take the form of meetings with the spouses or the entire family (Riskin 1963, p. 346). Questions can relate to how parents met, their expectations of the marriage, relationship with in-laws and birth of children and how long each family member talks (p. 346). All these factors, it is observed, impact on alcoholism.

Family Studies and Analysis of Interaction

Therefore, an analysis of the interaction and the quality of the interaction is what is recommended for family studies. The aim is to capture the relevant measure depending on the particular area of investigation. However, Room (1990, p. 49), believes that confusion abounds over "the failure to distinguish between methods of questioning and methods of aggregation, ...because of confused terminology and designations."

The point remains that there can be no uniformity in terms of measuring alcohol consumption, particularly when it comes to identifying differences in personalities, situations and outcomes. It is felt by this author that the main concern must be to examine the various aspects of alcoholism and to obtain as clear a consensus as possible over similar situations, circumstances and populations.

Family Bonds Can Override Effects of Alcoholism

Notwithstanding, the extent of family treatment, the effectiveness of family bonds as instruments which can stem the tide of alcohol abuse or alcoholism must receive due consideration.

In looking at alcoholism within families, one also has to take into consideration the accuracy of the information gleaned from family members since family bonding has implications for the "transmission"/ "non-transmission" of alcoholism to offspring, and its prevalence among adults.

> Use of patient interviews done or in combination with data from patient records or questionnaires does not control for possible distortion, omission or ignorance. Although patient records can be used as a check on data obtained during interviews of relatives, the nature of patient records—retrospective data compiled by many people over a number of years, and unclear as to the definition of alcoholism used—imposes limits to their usefulness (Cotton 1979, p. 106).

Cotton (1979) distinguishes a number of areas in which variability in family drinking can occur, and what measures could be taken to avoid them. Areas to look for are:

(i) The source of the information

(ii) The nature of the sample

(iii) An emphasis on disease, rather than health

(iv) The failure to exclude infants and other relatives too young to become alcoholics

(v) An absence of comparable control groups. Errors which could be reduced by controlling for the likelihood of denial by the patient; and

(vi) Taking cognizance of a family history of alcoholism, using specific definitions of alcoholism, using comparative data from patients and relatives' help, in addition to "carefully designed questions" (Cotton 1979, p. 106-107)

"Whatever method of asking about amount of drinking is used, most studies move to aggregate the data from the different questions..." (Room 1990). The researcher sees this as the source of all confusion regarding family studies.

Time of Alcohol Consumption

Cahalan and Cisin (1968) emphasize the quantity-frequency-variability index (q-f-v) and the volume-variability (v-v) measure. On the other hand, Knupfer (1966, p. 937) observes that one of the methodological problems in alcohol research is time of "alcohol consumption" . In examining two groups of drinkers, whose total weekly intake was roughly the same, there were some observed differences. Daily light drinkers were represented more heavily by women and the poor, the older, and the less well educated.

> More of them are engaged in white collar occupations, and more of them grew up in either rural areas or very small towns.... The sociability patterns of the two groups also differ. More of the weekly heavy drinkers visit friends, go to parties, frequent taverns, while more of the daily light drinkers attend church services and socialize with church members (Knupfer 1966, pp. 239-240).

MAST

> The Michigan Alcoholism Screening Test (MAST) was devised to provide a consistent, quantifiable, structured interview instrument for the detection of alcoholism that could be rapidly administered by non-professional as well as professional personnel. The MAST consists of 25 questions, many of which have also been used by other investigators in surveys of alcoholism...some of the questions are sufficiently neutral that persons reluctant to see themselves as problem drinkers may reveal their alcoholic affliction. Questions relating to

amounts of alcohol consumed were not used because of the vague responses they evoke. Where MAST is used for screening purposes, clinical confirmation may occasionally be required (Selzer 1971, p. 1653).

Time of Life, Type of Alcohol

Bowman et al. (1975, p. 1155) explained that there are some aspects of alcohol consumption which are not taken into account when measuring this phenomenon.

They are: the time period in the individual's life when drinking takes place, and the type of alcoholic beverages which were consumed within that period. Not considered also, are the frequency of drinking occasions, the point in time or the occasions when each beverage was drunk, and the quantity of each beverage consumed on each occasion.

Confusion over the Meaning of Frequency

Most of the disagreement between systems of measuring drinking patterns relates to the dimensions of quantity and frequency. This is due in part to the fact that quantity has two meanings—quantity per occasion, and aggregate quantity over the time period examined, which is arrived at by some combination of quantity per occasion and frequency. Furthermore, quantity per occasion may be measured

as a variable rather than an average or modal quantity, making it possible to index the degree to which this quantity varies from one occasion to another. Thus, in the quantity-frequency data there are implicit four interrelated dimensions:

i. Quantity per occasion
ii. Variability of quantity per occasion;
iii. Frequency of occasions; and
iv. Aggregate quantity for the entire time period (Bowman et al. 1975, p. 1155)

MASS

Another alcoholism scale, The Missouri Alcoholism Severity Scale (MASS), possesses less validity particularly as it relates to "years of problem drinking and number of hospitalizations" (Evenson 1986, p. 382). But by and large, drinking has been associated with socio-cultural variables as studies by Mulford and Miller (1960) and others have indicated.

Haglund and Schuckit (1982) have suggested that one way of examining drinking practices is to review alcohol consumption through industry and government-regulating industries, but these were unreliable, since as the authors explained, they do not control the amount of free income spent on alcohol, "which may be very important in comparing two groups or the same group over time" (p. 35).

The Use of Professionals as Measuring Instruments

Other measurement methods include key informant, namely doctors, social workers, clergymen, or community surveys, but these have limitations when it comes to "comparability between studies" (p. 33). Haglund and Schuckit identify five (5) reasons for separating the alcoholic from the problem drinker to the normal drinker:

(i) Quantity-frequency-variability
(ii) Psychologically driven drinking
(iii) Socially driven drinking
(iv) Medical (negative) outcome for drinking
(v) Physical addiction

The authors contend that once one understands the survey methods used, the diagnostic criteria, and the sample characteristics, one will be able to relate the findings to particular subject areas.

Finding the "Right Method"

Still, one cannot get away from the fact that the continuous use of various methods mean that there is an increasing attempt to develop the "right" instrument to capture as much variance as possible in various settings. In this regard, different methodological approaches tend to bring about new insights into patterns of drinking. One study (Sitharthan et al. 1996) reports that the strategy of cognitive-behavioral treatment goes a long way in reducing alcohol consumption, and may record "a 50% fall in consumption." For example, a causal model looking into the relationship between personal and family characteristics and well-being reported a .97 "goodness of fit" index. However, strictly speaking, there is no one "right" method.

CAST

Other authors (Hodgins and Shimp 1995; Yamazaki 1996), went the route of the Children of Alcoholics Screening Test (CAST), "a 3-item screening instrument developed to identify children who are either living with or have lived with alcoholic parents." Both authors report high reliability for this test having "shown to be internally reliable," and having demonstrated "good retest reliability."

Sourcing the Community

Community surveys represent another way of unearthing factors relating to the prevalence of alcoholism. Manis and Hunt, as far back as 1957, examined 2 percent of households in a city. Using a geographically stratified list of dwellings, the researchers were able to uncover and predict alcoholic deaths of persons over the age of 20. In addition, it was reported that a "comparatively large number of problem drinkers" spoke about their own experiences suggesting that under-reporting due to fear of stigmatization can be overcome by this method.

Convergent Validity, Longitudinal Stability

Again, Windle (1996) undertook a study "to evaluate the convergent validity and longitudinal stability of a five-group drinker typology (abstainer, light, moderate, heavy and problem drinkers)." That research which tracked 10th and 11th graders was able to distinguish their particular behavioral patterns as regards percentage of their friends who participated in drug-taking, including illicit drugs, the exhibition of coping skills, and the like. The researcher revealed that his was a specific kind of typology aimed at bringing adolescent drinking under control and for establishing treatment modes.

CARTA

Rhea et al. (1993) found "good concordance" when comparing sibling reports of parents problem-drinking symptoms. The researchers used questionnaire data from the Colorado Alcohol Research on Twins and Adoptees (CARTA). In comparing 142 pairs of male and female twin and non-twin siblings, they located a significant gender difference. Male offspring agreed with mother's drinking behavior, and female offspring supported father's drinking behavior. However, there was greater evidence of reliability on objective items, rather than subjective ones. The above has implications for the type of questions asked and the gender of the respondents.

Touch-Tone Method

In addition, the use of touch-tone as a form of data collection significantly validates the use of technology as another method to overcome structural hurdles of inconvenience and costs. Searles et al. (1995) in their attempt to daily monitor alcohol consumption, invited fifty- one respondents ($N = 51$) to use an Interactive Voice Response system where they answered, on a daily basis, 11 questions related to quantity and stress levels. The response rate was 93 percent as compared to the use of traditional quantity-frequency (q-f) measurement of alcohol consumption.

"Heavier drinking" subjects retrospectively under-reported their consumption significantly more than lighter drinking subjects ($F = 11.95$, $p<.005$), although both had linear inclinations. Yet, the same individuals had the tendency to report "high daily consumption," even when under-reporting consumption aggregately.

Methodological Adaptability

The above study clearly indicates that respondents may be more comfortable using one type of method than the other. It also shows that as researchers, we must be ever mindful of the changing realities of the research field and attempt to understand the respondents' role and how they are influenced by these technologies as they respond to research questions. One method may or may not be "acceptable" to a group of respondents as a reliable instrument in attempting to understand a particular phenomenon.

Conventionally, large-scale studies on alcohol consumption have taken the form of description and trends. For example, Midanik and Clark (1995) studied "two national alcohol surveys to assess rates of drinking patterns." The objective was to determine, if any, demographic variables on a comparison basis and this certainly must be regarded as another innovative measure in charting new courses in the fight against alcohol consumption. Notwithstanding, we must be ever mindful that there are ethnic differences in the use of alcohol consumption. Many researchers are of the view that these differences are significant, and not merely transient. Nonetheless, they have implications for measuring instruments.

Measuring Ethnic Drinking

Cherpitel (1998) reports that a number of screening instruments used for understanding alcohol abuse by Blacks, Hispanics and Whites in an emergency room setting did not perform "equally well", by ethnicity or gender. The conclusion was that researchers need to place these measuring instruments in different settings to understand or evaluate the need for brief intervention, or referral for problem drinking. In this regard, it is to be noted that Horn et al. (1992) suggest the need for us to understand the characteristics of cultural drinking following a study in which they compared MAST- positive and MAST- negative patients from a general hospital in Switzerland.

This underscores the significance that some measuring instruments may be situation specific; others culturally and nationally so.

Controlling Error

In spite of the above, it should be pointed out that in undertaking rigorous methodological scrutiny and cutting-edge research in alcohol consumption, attempts must be made to hold at minimum "the normal errors" ever present in data collection. These errors, namely under-reporting and memory, have been shown to have significance in impacting and altering outcomes. It would be better to use large samples to overcome these errors. And this is a fundamental statistical and methodological approach emanating from the central limit theory, that is, the more one's sample approximates the total population, the smaller the variability.

Drinking Behavior—Most Frequently Used Outcome

According to Bowman et al. (1975) "drinking behavior remains the most frequently used outcome measure in studies of alcoholism..." (p. 1154). He was responding to work done by Emrick (1974) who had completed a review to examine the relationship between outcome criteria and drinking behavior following treatment. However, he was not too sure that the methods currently in use were taking other relevant issues into consideration.

Khavari and Farber (1978) writing about the assessment of alcohol consumption described behavior as "the simple most important variable in defining and measuring alcohol-related problems." They observed that "major reviews of alcoholism treatment evaluations" were consistent in their indication "that of all the dependent measures available, the level of drinking" was the preferred measurement of outcome for alcoholism.

Most attempts to measure alcohol consumption have to do with the quantity-frequency measure, which is arrived at by multiplying the amount drunk on a given occasion by "their usual frequency of drinking over a given period of time." However, Khavari and Farber (1978) found that "one major criticism of the Q-F index has been that measuring frequency and quantity gives no indication as to the variability of an individual's drinking behavior." This statement came in the late 1970s. Since then there have been numerous attempts to measure variability.

Ledermann's Theory of Drinking Distribution

In the 1980s, Ledermann's theory of alcohol consumption took center stage. According to Skog (1985), the Ledermann's theory of the distribution of alcohol consumption consists of two hypotheses. Firstly, it proposed "that the annual intake of alcoholic beverages varies tremendously within populations and that these variations can be described mathematically by a so-called lognormal distribution function." Secondly,... "the two parameters of the lognormal distribution are closely related to each other," implying "that the variance of the distribution can be predicted from the mean." The argument basically points out that the number of drinkers at any consumption level can be calculated since the variance (how drinking patterns vary) is in close association to the mean.

> Ledermann's theory has been severely criticized by several authors. It has been argued that the hypothesis of lognormal, and in particular the hypothesis implying an exact relation between the average and the variance, is neither founded on rational arguments, nor is supported by Ledermann's own data... (Skog 1985, p. 84).

Granovetter (1973. Cited in Skog 1985), advises that we look at weak alcoholic ties and not so much strong ones since strong ties "are fairly inefficient transmitters of different types of influences between people, while networks of weak ties...are extremely efficient"(p. 88).

The Limitations of Methodology

Methodologies are employed based on the nature of the study, and the peculiar circumstances, including resources, which constrain the researcher. The second point to remember is that all methodologies have some limitation inherent in their capacity or in their construct, to uncover the total level of alcohol consumption. It follows to a great extent, therefore, that alcohol abuse will be with us for quite sometime, particularly as it is subject to changing circumstances. For example, when we think we understand the drinking patterns of a subpopulation of alcohol abusers, another subpopulation appears on the horizon, moving in another direction and revealing different consumption patterns, most likely responding to a different set of circumstances or values.

Room (1979) notes that there have been many approaches to the study of alcohol consumption, namely, attitudes toward drinking, attitudes toward treatment and reactions to aspects of others' drinking, but that the real problem seems to be the low standing which drinking studies have among social problems. One of the reasons for this is that "social scientists working in alcohol studies have failed so far to communicate to their fellow social scientists the strategic usefulness of alcohol-related phenomena as a focus for analysis of many social issues" (p. 251).

Three Commonly Used Methods

Seppa et al. (1999) identifies three commonly used methods to determine heavy drinking namely: (1) interviews, (2) structured questionnaires, and (3) the use of laboratory markers to detect heavy drinking. Using these three methods, the researchers undertook a study of middle-aged men who were heavy drinkers in order "to compare aggregate measures of heavy or problem drinking, and their variations across time among the same subjects" (p. 66).

Mm-MAST and CDT

When the Malmö-modified Michigan Alcoholism Screening Test (Mm-Mast) and serum carbohydrate-deficient transferrin (CDT were used), Seppa et al. found that alcohol-drinking habits were not stable in middle age. However, while Mm-Mast detected heavy drinkers, CDTs or carbohydrate-deficient transferrins and positive self-reports decreased. In effect the Mm-Mast measured the relationship between social consequences and advancing age, "even at smaller consumption levels" (p. 65).

The results indicate that in using the two methods, namely the self-report Malmö-modified Michigan Alcoholism Screening Test and the CDT the researchers were able to better understand the variation in alcohol consumption over time.

Importance of Epidemiology as a Method

The United States National Institute of Alcohol and Alcoholism recommends screening for emerging alcoholics. According to the institute, the screening of patients for alcohol problems is a medical necessity.

In fact, the Institute was identifying a growing trend towards epidemiological studies investigating alcohol-related problems among groups over periods of time. "These studies," the Institute explains "can tell us how many people suffer from alcohol-related problems" and "what groups...are at greater risks, thereby providing information for developing treatment and prevention programs." However, it is the opinion of the Institute that surveys, although having limitations, can capture some of the concerns surrounding reliability and validity in drinking behavior, when their questionnaires are well prepared.

Children of Alcoholics

Children of Alcoholics (COAs) must be mentioned in any methodological discussion. The United States National Institute of Alcohol and Alcoholism accuses many studies on children of having methodological shortcomings. Noting that "many COA studies use a biased sample selection of children in treatment or in trouble," there were some studies which carried no controls at all, making generalization from treatment to non-treatment populations difficult. Of specific concern to the Institute was the effect of the development process among different age groups all lumped together, the effect of marital conflict and the extent of parental drinking in longitudinal studies. Interestingly, the Institute continues to show that not all children exposed to parental alcoholism become alcoholics. Some of the factors responsible for this turnaround are "the ability to obtain positive attention from other people, adequate communication skills, average intelligence, a caring attitude, a desire to achieve, and a belief in self-help."

MAST and Q-F—Basic Tools

In spite of the plethora of methodological excursions into alcoholism, the conventional tests, namely the MAST and the Quantity-Frequency Scale seem to hold considerable methodological sway in explaining alcohol-related behaviors. These tests are used by many in some of the latest studies as criteria for assessing validity and reliability of new instruments. This means that some measures are stable having been tested in the crucible of research over the years, all in an effort to validate these measuring instruments, notwithstanding that increased respondent burden (Cunningham et al. 1999) may thwart the best of efforts.

> The good news is that alcohol-related data are getting better and better. Refined data collection methodology and analysis and better reporting continue to increase information validity and reliability. Alcohol epidemiological research also has raised important questions for future alcohol research—questions that will help us to better prevent and treat alcohol abuse, alcoholism, and related consequences. For example, epidemiological research findings show that only a minority of alcoholics develop cirrhosis. Thus, a need has been identified for research on risk factors other than alcohol (e.g., genetic, nutritional, viral) that may be involved in cirrhosis development (The United States National Institute on Alcohol Abuse and Alcoholism, a p. 3).

The World Health Organisation (WHO) in focussing on drug-classification of alcohol-related problems, pointed out that in order to establish a valid basis for alcohol classification there must be international cooperation. Of concern for the likely occurrence of this was, one the low priority given to alcohol problems in some countries and, two the struggles of medical services with the first stages of development in some countries (Edwards, Arif and Hodgson 1982).

Summary

The role of methodology in the social sciences is to unite or bind that is, to use a system of connecting rules and procedures in the research process. These two factors are very important when attempting to describe alcoholism or alcohol abuse. Basically, "method" is guided by the philosophy of the study, the basic aim being to achieve significant outcomes.

The Short Michigan Alcoholism Screening Test (SMAST) is a reliable test for measuring assessments among different categories of responses. SMAST is a shortened version of MAST which does not restrict itself to measuring only those who are grossly alcoholic.

However, "quantity" in order for it to be measured reliably, has to be approached from "an occasion" perspective to an "aggregate" figure (over a time period) perspective. The vast majority of researchers on alcohol build on the foundation of the quantity - frequency variation, whether they are specifically looking at cognitive defects in individuals or combining quality with quantity data.

A number of methods have been identified in this chapter in order to showcase their importance. The CAGE method attempts to screen for alcohol-related problems. Overall, researchers report that the CAGE measurement is a valid instrument and that slight adjustments may be necessary for clinical and other special populations.

Another methodological approach is to understand the manner of communication which takes place within families, especially as it relates to values that they hold dear to themselves. Insights can take the form of how parents met, their expectations and relationship with in-laws.

However, it should be pointed out that there can be no uniformity in measuring alcoholism or alcohol abuse for that matter. Of particular concern is the reliability of information gleaned from in-laws. One has to be particularly careful about the source of the information, the nature of the sample, the setting up of control and experimental groups, and family history of alcoholism. In fact, it has been observed that confused terminology and designation about alcoholism lies at the heart of inconsistencies surrounding alcoholism. On the other hand, Knupfer (1966) believes that one of the methodological problems has to do with the time alcohol is drunk. He observed that daily light drinkers were more heavily represented by women, the poor, the old and the less educated. In addition the type of alcohol drunk had to be taken into consideration (Bowman et al. 1975).

On the other hand, The Missouri Alcoholism Severity Scale (MASS) has less validity in assessing problem drinking and the extent to which alcohol consumption leads to hospitalization (Evenson 1986).

Another method suggested for assessing alcohol consumption is the investigation of records of doctors, social workers, clergymen and the use of community surveys.

Children of Alcoholics Screening Test (CAST) attempts to assess the risk of alcoholism among children who are either living with an alcoholic parent or lived with one. These children can act as informants.

One interesting method is to identify a particular pattern of behavior, that is, who you hang with. In short, developing a kind of typology of behavior (Windle

1996). Also, the touch-tone method attempts to collect data using telephone technology. Respondents collect their own data by recording their responses to questions posed on a questionnaire.

In using a variety of methods one must take into consideration that ethnicity may play a factor in data collection response rates. The bottom line remains that one should control for as many errors as possible for in the end it comes down to behavior and how much you drink.

No one method is better that the other. However, when different methods are used together and interpreted as a "methodological construct", it may contribute to a greater amount of validity and reliability. What is important, notwithstanding, is the relevance of the method to the problem at hand.

Three commonly used methods to determine heavy drinking are interviews, structured questionnaires, and markers. The National Institute on Alcohol Abuse and Alcoholism adds more: surveys and epidemiological studies.

In the end, the Michigan Alcoholism Severity Scale (MAST) and the Quantity-Frequency scale seem to hold considerable methodological leverage as data collection instruments.

Suggested Readings

Bohn, Michael J.; Thomas F. Babor; and Henry R. Kranzler. 1995. "The Alcohol Use Disorders Identification Test (AUDIT): Validation of a Screening Instrument for Use in Medical Settings." Journal of Studies on Alcohol 56, no. 4:423-32.

Collins, Lorraine R.; Gernot Gollnisch; and Charles V. Izzo. 1996. "Drinking Restraint and Alcohol-Related Outcomes: Exploring the Contributions of Beverage Instructions, Beverage Content and Self-Monitoring." Journal of Studies on Alcohol 57, no. 5:563-71.

Kozlowski, Lynn T.; Helen M. Annis; Howard D. Cappell; Frederick B. Glaser; Michael S. Goodstadt; Yedi Israel; Harold Kalant; Edward M. Sellers; and Evelyn R. Vingilis. 1990. Research Advances in Alcohol and Drug Problems. Vol. 10. New York: Plenum Press.

Mancino, Michael; Michael R. Cunningham; Pattie Davidson; and Robert L. Fulton. 1996. "Identification of the Motor Vehicle Accident Victim who Abuses Alcohol: An Opportunity to Reduce Trauma." Journal of Studies on Alcohol 57, no. 6:652-58.

Martin, Christopher S.; Nancy A. Kaczynski; Stephen A. Maisto; Oscar M Bukstein; and Howard B. Moss. 1995. "Patterns of DSM-IV Alcohol Abuse and

Dependence Symptoms in Adolescent Drinkers." Journal of Studies on Alcohol 56, no. 6:672-80.

Miller-Tutzauer, Carol; and Neil Agnew. 1974. "The Ledermann Model of Alcohol Consumption: Description, Implications and Assessment." Quarterly Journal of Studies on Alcohol 35:877-98.

Mulford, Harold A.; and Donald E. Miller. 1960. "Drinking in Iowa: iv. Preoccupation with Alcohol and Definitions of Alcohol, Heavy Drinking and Trouble Due to Drinking." Quarterly Journal of Studies in Alcohol 21, no. 2:279-91.

______.1963. "Preoccupation with Alcohol and Definitions of Alcohol: A Replication Study of Two Cumulative Scales." Quarterly Journal Studies in Alcohol 24, no. 4:682-96.

Murray, David M.; and Brian Short. "Intraclass Correlation among Measures Related to Alcohol Use by Young Adults: Estimates, Correlates and Applications in Intervention Studies." Journal of Studies on Alcohol. 56, no. 6:681-94.

Neff, James Alan; and Keir Sue Hoppe. 1992. "Acculturation and Drinking Patterns among U.S., Anglos, Blacks, and Mexican Americans." Alcohol and Alcoholism 27, no. 3:293-308.

Pedersen, Willy; and Anders Skrondal. 1998. "Alcohol Consumption Debut: Predictors and Consequences." Journal of Studies on Alcohol 59, no. 1:32-42.

Pinsky, Ilana. 1999. "A Frequency and Content Analysis of Alcohol Advertising on Brazilian Television." Journal of Studies on Alcohol 60, no. 3:394-99.

Raistrick, Duncan; Geoff Dunbar; and Robin Davidson. 1983. "Development of a Questionnaire to Measure Alcohol Dependence." British Journal of Addiction 78:89-95.

Rehm, Jürgen; Ulrich Frick; and Susan Boudy. 1999. "A Reliability and Validity Analysis of an Alcohol-Related Harm Scale for Surveys." Journal of Studies on Alcohol 60, no. 2:203-208.

Schmidt, Wolfgang; and Jan de Lint. 1970. "Estimating the Prevalence of Alcoholism from Alcohol Consumption and Mortality Data." Quarterly Journal of Studies on Alcohol 31:957-64.

Timko, Christine; John W. Finney; Rudolf F. Moos; and Bernice S. Moos, 1995. "Short-Term Treatment Careers and Outcomes of Previously Untreated Alcoholics." 56, no. 6:597-610.

Tonigan, Scott J.; Radka Toscova; and William R. Miller. 1996. "Meta-Analysis of the Literature on Alcoholics Anonymous: Sample and Study Characteristics Moderate Findings." Journal of Studies on Alcohol 57, no. 1:65-72.

Uitenbroek, Daan G. 1996. "Seasonal Variation in Alcohol Use." Journal of Studies on Alcohol 57, no. 1:47-52.

Zimmerman, Mark; Bruce Pfohl; Dalene Stangl; and William Coryell. 1985. "The Validity of DSM - 111 Axis IV (Severity of Psychosocial Stressors)." American Journal of Psychiatry 142, no. 12:1437-41.

---

1 MAST means Michigan Alcohol Screening Test; it is from this scale that the SMAST scale was developed.

CHAPTER 18

Social Irresponsibility

No review of sociological approaches to alcohol can ignore the substantial and heated protests of some sociologists against the disease concept of alcoholism. Arguments mustered against treating alcoholism as a disease include the following...

> Alcoholism does not meet the traditional medical concept of a disease because of the voluntary ingestion of the causal agent. Second, there is no natural cutting point that divides drinkers into "cases" and "noncases", forms a continuous distribution. Third, there is stigma associated with labeling a person as an alcoholic. Lastly, defining excessive alcohol intake as a disease gives a jurisdictional claim over drinking behavior and makes an unvalidated claim that medical professionals enjoy special skills in treating it (Bucholz and Robins 1989, p. 165).

Social Irresponsibility

Social irresponsibility, is, in its broadest sense, behavior for which someone can be held responsible. Such behavior carries significant implications for the personal and social life of the individual and the behavior of governments. In other words, irresponsible behavior can directly or indirectly impact negatively on others, not to mention the socializing effect it tends to have on young minds seeking out role models.

It has also been observed that irresponsible behavior can be brought about by conditions which do not support normal behavior (Reber 1985).

In both these definitions, alcohol is the element which is present and it is interacting with conditions which produces 'at risk' behaviors. 'At risk' behaviors can be classified "irresponsible" by altering behaviors considered normal in an unaltered situation or environment, as well as an altered situation or environment.

Irresponsibility Operationalized

Traditionally, "irresponsibility" has come to mean something someone does with negative implications and who is well aware that "better" behavior is an attainable goal. In contrast to this position is the concept of "loss of control." This is the central argument of the disease model which argues that persons who lose control in variable degrees are in truth and in fact, not responsible for their actions.

Relieving People of Responsibility

Loss of control as defined by the geneticists therefore absolves the individual from irresponsible behavior. If there were no successful challenges to the "loss of control" thesis, one would have to accept grudgingly the disease model. However, the disease model, along with its "loss of control" thesis has been challenged by social scientists in the following areas: laboratory studies, clinical research, longitudinal studies, and cross-ethnic and cultural studies. Further, individuals can stop drinking but continue their anti-social behavior anyway, for "alcohol problems are often interrelated with other problems of life functioning" (Sobell and Sobell 1978, p. 11).

Irresponsibility Magnified

Irresponsible behavior for some individuals may become a feature of normal life due to their inability to deal with other mundane issues. Alcohol use by these individuals merely compounds the problem as irresponsibility is transferred from one situation to another. This is accomplished with a certain degree of ease since irresponsible behavior was already manifest in the individual's social interactional and networking life, a fact which allowed him to imbibe as much and as frequently as he wanted. Also, his significant others and those within the wider circle of social contact would have already grown accustomed to his peculiar behavioral patterns.

> Designating alcoholism a disease also buffered the drinker from blame and admitted the logical possibility of treatment. Advocates of the disease model began campaigning in the 1930s for optimism about cure and for the creation of therapeutic programs. Alcoholics Anonymous (AA) was founded in 1935 and recruited a loyal membership of "recovering alcoholics" determined to promote the image of alcoholism as a treatable disease and the alcoholic as a sick person worthy of help (Walsh 1989, p. 132).

Irresponsibility versus Moral Failing

One can quickly fall into the conceptual trap that suggests that morality is associated with irresponsible behavior. In some respects morality has to do with right or wrong behavior, or adhering to the principles of it. As such, it hints at making people conform to what society deems "acceptable," and for members of society to act in accordance with those standards.

Where "irresponsibility" is concerned, there are some individuals who can demonstrate "irresponsible" behavior, yet stay within the bounds of morality. Both immorality and irresponsibility carry sanctions. There are variations of immorality as well as variations of irresponsibility. Free choice is another common feature of both. However, morality in large measure has to do with religious and spiritual aspects. Irresponsibility carries a more pragmatic and mundane aspect. Also, irresponsibility carries within it the kernel of "responsibility," that is, that the person knows of the effects or outcomes of his behavior through past experiences. He also knows that he is engaging in alcohol abuse temporarily (a person is hardly likely to be abusing alcohol 24 hours a day). The "irresponsibility" thesis therefore recognizes the quality of reflection/introspection as a necessary feature of all human beings. In short, cognitive processes kick in when the individual returns to soberness.

One has to be careful, however, that one does not get carried away into believing that the individual is able to effect immediate attitude change following his drunken state. It is to be noted "that attitudes and subjective norms are not sufficient determinants of intentions, and that intentions are not sufficient determinants for action..." (Bagozzi 1992). There is no guarantee that the individual will change to a permanent state of what is called "responsible" behavior.

The Moral and the Irresponsible

As mentioned above, the moral model of alcoholism shares boundaries with the irresponsible thesis such as having the option to "freely choose a drink" and taking responsibility for one's actions. However, as pointed out by Tarter and Schneider (1976), the moralists feel that alcohol is "not the product of physical, psychological, or social factors" (1976, p. 80) as the author of this book points out.

> Because abusive drinking cannot be objectively defined within the context of the moral model, there remains both ambivalence and vagueness as to what constitutes alcoholism. For example, in cultures where drinking is totally prohibited one is likely to be identified as an alcoholic more readily than in cultures where drinking is tolerated and sanctioned in both religious and secular occasions. Moralists tend to adopt an "all or none" attitude viewing the beverage itself as evil (Tarter and Schneider 1976, pp. 80-81).

The Drunk and Responsible Thinking

The alcoholic does not think rationally; at least not as well as he is expected to. This does not mean he cannot think cognitively, but there could be cognitive relapse (Parsons and Nixon 1998). Yet, even when he can think cognitively, he sometimes refuses to make decisions. His entire orientation towards alcohol is that it is more rewarding to get drunk than to make a "responsible move." And this is supported in varying degrees by the culture. The social, political and even the cultural environment allow him a free rein to imbibe.

The alcoholic notes that alcohol is not given the type of negative stigma as other hard drugs. He observes that he is not "breaking any law" as other hard drugs do, and he notices that those who say they "don't drink," often drink on special occasions, sometimes in amounts that are equal to or exceed his drinking at one sitting. Further, some of his friends and associates who find him "socially unacceptable," will offer him a drink on occasions that they define as "appropriate": parties, weddings or on some other "significant occasion." In large measure, the alcoholic deals with ambivalence towards him in the social environment from which persons send him conflicting messages.

Reasons for Drinking

Deep within the socio-emotional state of the individual, resides the reason why he will drink and continues to drink. The alcoholic may have given up on life's struggles, and "irresponsible" behavior offers him a permanent respite from those encounters. He may have subjective states as any other individual, but this will hardly allow him to drink for longer than the average person. Even when we observe that the alcoholic may have personal problems, we might ask, how permanent are these personal problems. His drinking might start as a "personal problem," but is certainly not sustained by those problems. It, however, provides a "cop out" to life's continuing challenges, uncertainties and expectancies. In short, it provides an opportunity to abandon one's social responsibility to one's self, one's family and one's society. The social environment connects with government's policies and the individual connects with the society.

Social Abandonment

This social abandonment of principles could start in one's early years and, together with custom, habit and modeling, could leave teenagers without strong social and coping mechanisms themselves making them vulnerable to the condition called alcoholism (Bradizza et al. 1999). Since at any point in time we are bombarded by a number of factors, some more negative than others, we must be cognizant of the fact that some home environments may be more harmful than others. Penick et al. (1999) discovered that alcoholism can be scientifically predicted from a number of factors namely, alcoholic severity, psychiatric suffering and/or social impairment.

It must be pointed out though, that although there is no alcoholic personality, there still exists in large measure, a number of individuals whose social situations produce psychological, irresponsibility sequelae. Levin (1990) admits that "there are few empirical psychological findings in alcoholic populations..." with "a few holding up across studies and populations" (p. 84). Many of these studies, he observed, were about male alcoholism, which focussed on the alcoholic after he had already become an alcoholic, not the pre-alcoholic personality, as is debated in the literature. This observation is made particularly against the background that the gender differences in alcoholism appear to be lessening (Friedman and Humphrey 1985).

A Different Social Problem

Clearly, "Alcoholism is not one of those social problems which will get better if we leave it alone," (Kane 1981, p. 23), or for that matter, ignore it.

When it comes to the genetic model, notwithstanding the issue of standardization and methodological issues surrounding twin studies, we must ask the question of behavior's role in the "transmission" of alcoholism from parent to child and further, what is it that is actually transmitted? An appetite for alcohol? Enjoyment of alcohol? Relief of some dysfunctional or dysphoria by alcohol? Or, in terms of learning theory, more than normal reinforcement by alcohol? (Levin 1990, p. 73-74).

Socially Unacceptable Behavior

Social irresponsibility as mentioned earlier, carries two components: social irresponsibility at the personal level and social irresponsibility at the societal level. And we have control over both, but more so the former than the latter.

> The disease model is being applied to any socially unacceptable behavior as a means of absolving people of responsibility for their actions, criminal or otherwise. The practice is justified on this basis: Drug use constitutes an addiction. Addiction is a disease. Acts stemming from the disease are called symptoms. Since the symptoms of a disease are involuntary, the symptoms of drug addiction disease are likewise involuntary. Addicts are thus not responsible for their actions (Wekesser 1994, p. 35).

Anyone can become an alcoholic; all you have to do is drink when you want, how you want, and in whatsoever amounts you feel like drinking. It's as simple as that! You don't have to be particularly genetically predisposed to become an alcoholic. Social and environmental factors will take care of that.

Scientific Confirmation Yet to Come

As yet, no scientific study has confirmed that alcohol consumption is a disease. To this end, therefore, the debate about what causes alcoholism must be placed into perspective. It is into this void that my arguments are placed. In short, I intend to put alcohol on trial. A central theme in this book is that there are two, and only two, concerns which ought to engage the attention of alcohologists (sociologists who study alcohol) and social scientists. This theme is whether alcoholics are genetically predisposed or socially predisposed. I will argue, then, that it is "social irresponsibility," a negative social act which is responsible for alcoholism.

Significance of Sociology

Sociology is concerned with understanding actions rather than observing behavior. Action arises out of meanings which define social reality. Meanings are given to men by their society. Shared orientations become institutionalized and are experienced by generations as social facts. It follows that explanations of human actions must take account of meanings which those concerned assign to their acts, the manner in which the everyday world is socially constructed, yet perceived as real and becomes routine (Silverman 1971; Weiner 1981, p. 12).

That social irresponsibility is the cause of alcohol consumption can be viewed from both the individual and societal level. We have already discussed individual irresponsibility, and it is now important to focus on irresponsibility at the societal level, and in particular, governments' inadequate policy responses to the alcohol problem. Few governments, apart from England and the United States, have raised serious concerns over the use of alcohol by various population, particularly adolescents and teenagers.

National Responsibility

Very few have taken sufficiently strong measures to combat the growing menace of alcohol consumption. The reason for this is that people are "free" to engage in alcohol consumption. They believe that because they are adults, they can exercise good judgment in imbibing. Political leaders also encourage the free consumption of alcohol by not instituting tough measures against its inordinate consumption. For many, the political risk may be too high.

Alcohol consumption rakes in large amounts of revenue for many countries. Therefore, it is not in the economic interest of many governments to ban alcohol consumption altogether.

Yet, in as much as alcohol consumption affects the productivity levels of a country, national policies should be adopted to track levels of drinking within the society. In so doing, countries which have a culture that "encourage" people to drink can determine the amount of alcohol's damage (costs) to the society, in relation to its revenue-earning aspect. In this way we will be in a position to quantify and monitor the amount of damage that is inflicted on society. It makes little sense to ask all individuals to "exercise caution" when drinking. Caution in relation to alcohol consumption is never advertised, except in respect to driving. But then, how many drivers respond to these cues, as opposed to the amount who do not respond? How many people can be cautious when faced with the excitement that gratification brings?

How many resources are placed into the "abstinence" advertisements, as opposed to the "drink, drink and be merry" advertisements.

> Countries in which the alcohol producers and distributors are not major profit-making industries have been most ready to enact and enforce control measures. In Sweden...a government bill which came into force in 1978 defines the overriding policy as one to limit total consumption...in Norway in 1980 a white paper stated the major objectives of alcohol policies to be the reduction of total consumption of alcoholic beverages. Finland's state alcohol monopoly comes under the jurisdiction of the Ministry of social Welfare and Health (Casswell 1985, p. 357).

Like the above, more governments should have policies reflecting attempts to control this substance, in its various forms, notwithstanding cultural and political constraints. In short, they should be displaying a greater sense of responsibility.

Curbing Social Values

How do you curb social values that are counter productive? Barring or limiting alcohol consumption may raise a hue and a cry from quarters that champion "freedom to choose," and "rights of the individual," not to mention the political price some governments may have to pay, and threats to the "survival of the tourist industry." Hence, where does the "responsibility" for alcohol consumption lie? Social responsibility brings into question the prevalence of social norms and lifestyles of drinkers; but "responsibility" must be seen as being able to override any negative effects caused by alcohol consumption. Of course, as mentioned before, there are other risk factors—situational, nutritional, viral that may be involved in alcoholism.

Notwithstanding, research has shown that the social setting brings into focus the tightly knit social bond of persons who eventually rely on, and cannot do without, the group-a group which incidentally may nurture drinking habits. Equally important also, is that research has shown that some people drink excessively when in isolation, suggesting that the "bottle" becomes their companion. This is a cause for concern, for the risk of overdose is ever present. Further, social dysfunction of alcohol consumption can be located by examining the literature on who gets married, who gets separated or divorced, and the type of marriage and onset of alcoholism. There appears to be a greater degree of separation and divorce among alcoholics than non-alcoholics.

The issue of social irresponsibility, therefore, must take into consideration the effects of norms, values, perceptions and ideologies, and how they impact on what is herein called "social irresponsibility," and the individual's ability to repel or inculcate these values. In sum, he must have the ability to discriminate between "good" behavior and "at-risk" (bad) behavior.

Locating the Problem

The task is to locate the problem, or put another way, show where the highest rates of alcohol consumption lie that is, whether in behavioral, social and psychological factors, or in medical ones. Once we have determined this, we can adopt strategies both at the individual and the public level to put controls in place and bring about some measure of "social responsibility" to this seemingly intractable problem.

According to Diana Chapman Walsh:

> The first step in preventing a problem is to locate it, and the shifts now taking place in alcohol policy began with redefining where the problem lies. Two influential documents shaped that new understanding, the first issued in 1975 by the World Health Organization (WHO) and produced by a distinguished international group of eleven alcohol experts. The second, by a panel convened in 1978 by the National Academy of Sciences (NAS), expanded on the first and applied it to the United States. The model of breadth, depth, and lucidity, the NAS report has helped recast U.S. alcohol policy into preventive terms. In part, this involved relocating the problem by adducing evidence that "heavy drinkers typically account for less than half of the people with problems". Because "alcohol problems occur throughout the drinking population...at lower rates but among much greater numbers" in moderate drinking groups (in no sense "alcoholics"), a de facto policy of identifying and treating alcoholics misses the mark (Walsh 1990, p. 50).

Thus, for Walsh (1990) reduction in average consumption of alcohol in the United States taking place at that time may have reflected increasing number of abstainers rather than fewer heavy or moderate drinkers.

Noteworthy also in the "irresponsibility thesis," is the "positive relationship between anomie and heavy drinking (Jessor et al. 1974).

This theory of deviant behavior suggests that an individual has a tendency to commit deviant acts based on his position within the socio-cultural, socialization, and personality systems. The authors explain that it has to do with rejection of the norms of society, the doubting of one's beliefs together with the weakening of the personal belief structure, in addition to the deficiency of the personal control structure reflected in impulses to engage in deviant acts.

Using two areas of the Houston Standard Metropolitan Statistical Area with census characteristics, except for ethnicity, the hypothesis "that there will be a positive relationship between anomie and use of alcohol among urban working-class, Mexican Americans and Anglos was tested" (Jessor et al., p.895). Accordingly, the survey instrument was pretested in neighborhoods similar to those from which the final sample was to be drawn and then revised.

The Spearman-Brown split-half reliability co-efficient for the 11-item anomie scale was VH = .746. An anomie scale found that the two groups were similar in their normlessness, but the Mexican Americans were more likely than Anglos to condone heavy drinking at social functions, and to apply restrictive standards on women's drinking. Those ethnic differences remained even when occupational status and religious beliefs were statistically controlled (p. 899). It was found that "the norms of the two groups were similar" yet "both groups showed differences in behavior, suggesting some act of responsibility/irresponsibility in varying degrees, perchance from their social environment or culture.

Brecher (1985, p. 260) puts the argument forcefully:

> It is commonly known/supposed that alcohol addicts are weak willed and that it is their weakness of will that led them to become-and to remain-addicts. The evidence is superficially plausible: even though two people may drink alcohol...in precisely the same pattern, it is said, only one of them may become addicted. The difference between the two may not be in the strength of will, however... The preponderance of the evidence currently available favors the view that the difference lies in the childhood of the two drinkers, in their social environment, and in the stress to which they are exposed as adults.

Alcohol Addiction

It is Brecher's view that "alcohol addiction was second only to nicotine addiction in incidence and prevalence in the United States." Further, the fact that

there were about seven to nine million alcoholics or problem drinkers in America, was a great cause for concern.

As have been mentioned before, the evidence points to several consequences of alcohol consumption—drunken-driving leading to accidents, suicides, "battered child syndrome," homicides, domestic abuse, rape, arson, drowning, airplane crashes, among numerous others. In addition, we do not know how much crime is committed where alcohol might have been the predisposing factor, but which was "camouflaged" by a more recent drug use, that is, if other drugs were involved.

One has to realize that the matter cannot simply rest here. The problem with alcohol consumption needs to be appreciated by virtue of the kinds of images and stigmatization, in addition to the extent of research, it has been subjected to from the 19th century to the present. Bucholz and Robins (1989, p. 163) argue that alcohol intersects with religious and ethnic studies, social change and social movements, theories of social control, criminology and social deviance, media research and analysis of social organizations; age, gender roles, medical sociology and sociology of the workplace.

Powerful Sociological Forces

It is Bucholz and Robins' (1989) view that there are powerful sociological underpinnings to alcohol consumption.

In spite of its shortcomings, credit must be given to Alcoholics Anonymous (AA) as one of the several voluntary or self help groups which became active during the post-depression era because of non-involvement by professions with individuals suffering from alcohol problems (Sobell and Sobell, 1978, p. 2). In further support of the behavioral social/ psychological thesis Hanlon and Pickett (1984, p. 460) have this to say:

> In addition to communicable and organic disorders to which we are subject and which we often share with other creatures, another group of conditions exist that is peculiar to our own invention. These are behavioral disorders that involve the unreasoned compulsive consumption of certain chemical substances, some natural, some man made to our ultimate, physical, psycho, and social detriment.

The Historical Significance

Hanlon and Pickett point to the historical significance of alcohol in the history of mankind. They observe that it was one of our earliest discoveries, and it was a discovery that some persons when they consumed it, developed a kind of craving which defied the consequences. Looking at alcoholism from an epidemiological standpoint, Hanlon and Pickett (1984, p. 461) conclude that it is "an acquired chronic progressive disease involving the compulsive intake of excessive amounts of alcohol and leading to its more advanced stage..." The authors cite what appeared to be concentrations of alcoholics. These were found in pressure or non-routine jobs; urban settings, and among Scandinavian, Nordic, Celtic and Polish nationalities. They also point to the magnitude of the problem which was difficult to determine because of non-reporting of cases of alcoholism, and due to the amount of persons bordering between problem drinker and alcoholic.

Quoting a 1964-1965 survey conducted by Rutgers Center of Alcohol Studies, the researchers revealed that 12 percent of a national sample of adults were heavy drinkers with the greatest number being men as opposed to women. But the picture does not end there. The implication is that alcohol consumption is related to a wide variety of problems (including diseases), reflected in growing absenteeism in the workplace and many man hours lost, child physical and sexual abuse, the latter of which has contributed to the problems of vagrancy and street children, as abused children develop psychological problems affecting their normal pattern of interaction and socialization, and their ability to develop intellectually. Still others have become problem drinkers or alcoholics themselves, and continue the vicious cycle of abuse with concomitant psychological and social consequences. The cost to society is great!

Responsibility versus the Illness Model

When we talk about responsibility, whose responsibility are we talking about? Is it personal responsibility or societies' responsibility or both? We maintain that once we start talking about the drinkers' responsibility, we come face to face with the illness or medical model. But that is exactly what we want to do! For when a person is ill, he or she is not responsible for his or her subsequent behavior, if only because one is placed in the sick role. In other words, proponents of the medical model feel that a sick man should not be responsible for his illness. Where alcoholism is concerned, we think he is responsible! What is disturbing though, is that if we extend the sick role concept to alcoholics and they do not recognize that they are sick and submit themselves for treatment, a condition of the sick role, then we arrive at another position, and that is, that they are roving about committing "deviant" acts considered to be "unlawful," by breaking the norms.

On the other hand, if they are considered ill and are largely allowed to behave as normal, then someone in authority is allowing these "ill people" to think they are "healthy." Either way someone is abdicating his/her "responsibility," the patient or the caregiver, or both. Sick role theory holds that a person must present himself/herself under the care of physician or health professional, for the purpose of recovering his/her health. This ensures that they return to society after having been certified fit. The person who certifies his/her healthy condition is a caregiver, most likely a physician.

Alcoholic/Non-Alcoholic

There are real situations where individuals can be "alcoholic" on some occasions and can be "normal" at other times, sometimes through their own volition.

It would seem to us therefore that the occasion is the defining element in producing the "sometimes-off, sometimes-on" alcoholics. But since situations can be avoided, the alcoholic-to-be can know when to keep away from a situation, since he/she would have learned that to do otherwise would make him do things he would be sorry for later.

It is argued that as far as the individual is concerned, unless he is non-functional, that is, unless he cannot work, he reaches to work late, does sloppy work, runs away at every opportunity; has family problems-beats his wife and children, and has regular altercations with the law, then he cannot be considered an alcoholic, for by definition, an alcoholic is socially and medically, "dysfunctional."

Positive Attitude as a Predictor of Alcohol Consumption

When an alcoholic is "functional" he displays a sense of responsibility and by the same token, when he engages in actions which suggest that he is "out of control," then he displays a sense of "irresponsibility." When the society supports him, (either his work or his family, friends and significant others; weak government policies) in his behavior, then we arrive at a point of "social irresponsibility." Few studies have focused on "social irresponsibility" as an explanatory variable in alcoholism. In one such study, Rule and Phillips (1973), found that there were more positive attitudes towards a patient with a behavior problem called "alcoholism," particularly when it was seen that alcoholism (medically so) was the causal agent for such behavior. On the other hand, when the individual's behavior was seen as being responsible for "alcoholism,"(socially so) a less positive attitude was seen. In sum, alcoholism defined medically evoked positive and sympathetic attitudes because it was felt that the individual was affected by something over which he had little or no control. On the other hand, where the individual's behavior was not so defined, he received negative reactions.

The Mask of Responsibility

In short, alcoholism as a predictor variable and as a medical condition evokes more positive responses. People are more understanding when "alcoholism" is an independent variable impacting on behavior. When it is the other way around, when it is seen as a dependent variable caused by behavior, it evokes less sympathy. In large measure therefore, this suggests that when an alcoholic is medically diagnosed he receives more tolerance. This tolerance, we suspect masks the "responsibility" or any inclination to act responsibly. It is therefore more convenient for the alcoholic to medically accept his/her condition and escape social opprobrium.

According to Butts and Chotlos (1973), a number of researchers have been identified in looking for "responsibility of behavior" in terms of alcohol consumption, or alcoholism for that matter. Thus, the issue of "loss of control" is conceptualized in such a manner that individuals believe their behavior is beyond control. Belief in an external "loss of control could be a method of evading the responsibility for anticipated negative reinforcements" (Phares, Richie and Davis 1973).

The "Weakness" of Comparison Studies

Previous studies (Goss and Morosko 1970), comparing alcoholics with non-alcoholics had certain weaknesses (that is, the groups differed considerably in age and social class). However, when two different groups of excessive drinkers from a Veterans Administration hospital in the United States were studied (Butts and Chotlos 1973), alcoholics showed more external loss of control than non-alcoholics who were of the same socio-economic status, and age. Further, Arbuckle et al. (1994) argue that alcohol consumption affects "the cognitive functioning of sober social drinkers."

Specifically, those who drink on social occasions or for recreational purposes, do not have impaired cognitive functioning. This suggests that drinkers at one of the lowest categories (that is, social drinkers) respond well to social cues when sober. In effect, therefore, irresponsible behavior resides both with the alcoholic and the non-alcoholic. However, a greater amount of "irresponsibility" is displayed at the lower drinking continuum. The vast array of social problems caused by alcoholics are not caused by heavy drinkers. They are caused by the abstainers and social drinkers (Walsh 1990). This says a lot for where the heaviest concentration of irresponsibility lies.

It is important to show that when sober, heavy drinkers can do likewise. This finding is supported by Sobell et al. (1993), who argue that alcoholics become more dependent on cues, including cues to sexual behavior (Neff and Burge 1995), or criminal activities, thus placing them in a position where suggestions can be made or accepted readily. Hence, it is not strange, to have social drinkers' responding to cues when sober and heavy drinkers responding to cues when heavily intoxicated. Agostinelli and Miller (1994) report inverse relations between self reported behavior and riskiness of drinking. In essence, when people drink, they do not assess their behavior in line with how they drink, for the drinker always underestimates the outcome of his/her drinking, making him liable to "irresponsible" behavior.

Simple cues may not do much, however. It may work for the social drinker and the heavy drinker, on occasions. It is interesting to see how cues will work, if at all, when an alcoholic meets a significant other, a loved one, when in the act of imbibing, one whose negative position on alcohol consumption he is quite familiar with.

The Loss of Control Thesis

The loss of control thesis has been assailed on many fronts. It would be opportune to identify one of them. In 1962 an alcohol researcher demonstrated how male alcoholics "exhibited a pattern of normal drinking" and that the expected physiological differences reportedly found in alcoholics seemed not to "affect their ability to control drinking" (Wekesser 1994, p. 38). The writer goes on to cite an instance where a psychologist and a physician reportedly found that alcoholics "bought and stockpiled alcohol" all with the intention to get as drunk as they wished, "even while undergoing withdrawal from previous binges." In short, their drinking behavior could not be explained "by a physiologically uncontrollable force, sparked by the use of alcohol" (p. 39).

But why does the model of alcohol as a disease refuse to go away, in the face of mounting evidence?

> One leading alcohol researcher asserts that alcoholism is a disease simply because people go to doctors for it. Undoubtedly, addicts seek help from doctors for two reasons. Addicts have a significant psychological investment in maintaining this view, having learned that their sobriety depends on believing they have a disease. And treatment professionals have a significant economic investment at stake. The more behaviors are diagnosed as diseases, the more they will be paid by health insurance companies for treating these diseases (Wekesser 1994, p. 42-43).

Social Irresponsibility and the Social Environment

There is no doubt in my mind that the large body of alcohol abusers use the cover of disease to continue to drink and feel sorry for themselves as if afflicted by some unseen element while they continue to wreak havoc within their homes and society. We have already noted the societal constraints such as economic benefits to the country; the issue of "freedom" and "democracy" and the argument that the alcoholic needs medical care and attention.

The social irresponsibility thesis posits that although individuals may "not be able to control" their drinking, they are aided and abetted by their behavior in their social environment. Social environment is an enabler. The alcohol abuser, by habit, continues to frequent the very places where alcohol is available and at once compromises himself.

The majority of individuals with alcohol use disorders do not enter treatment (Grant 1997), and roam around in society either being regarded as "responsible" or encouraged to drink because they may be better off drinking than committing some "other deviant act." It never occurs to the alcoholic that "social irresponsibility" can be a deviant act for which sanctions may be meted out. In an age where increasingly "responsibility" is identified for a number of diseases it is only a matter of time when tougher "sanctions" will be handed out to "offenders."

Constellation of Social Factors

All this points to the fact that "alcoholism" has been dropped from the Diagnostic and Statistical Manual (DSM-3r) in favor of "alcohol abuse" and "alcohol dependence" (Wekesser 1994, p. 50) suggesting that alcoholism is not a disease, but one that is subject to a host of social factors.

> I use the term "alcoholic" to refer to people who believe they are powerless over their addictions and act accordingly, and to those who call themselves "alcoholics". They are practising the philosophy of "alcohol-ism", just as Catholics practise the philosophy of Catholicism (Wekesser 1994, p. 50).

Alcohol is frequently used as an agent or an excuse for deviant behavior (Goode 1984, p. 124). As such, alcoholism is everyone's responsibility (Robinson 1979). We have no choice but to be responsible for the "irresponsible behavior" of the abuser. It has been argued that once a person loses control over his drinking, it does not mean that he cannot exercise future control over it. Robinson (1979) argues that it all comes down to the psychological state of the individual at the time, and the particular situation (p. 58):

> The idea of responsibility must be played out further. If we accept the disease concept of alcoholism as put forward by Jellinek, it would be difficult for a alcohol abuser or an alcoholic to accept the advice of his doctor in terms of persuading the alcoholic to change his drinking habits, since the alcoholic by definition will himself be incapable to do so (Robinson 1979, p. 66).

Still, the AA model advocates the removal of personal responsibility from the shoulders of the alcoholic. Yet, according to Robinson (1979), the alcoholic is asked to adopt some sort of "motivation" before he embarks on a treatment program. This suggests a kind of double standard. On the one hand, it means, that the alcoholic is not responsible for his actions, but on the other hand he is asked to display "motivational responsibility." Therefore, even the AA is displaying a sense of irresponsibility in dealing with the matter.

The fact is that neither chemicals in beverages, nor physiological, nutritional, metabolic, nor genetic defects have been found to explain alcoholic drinking (US National Institute on Alcohol Abuse and Alcoholism (1979. Cited in David Robinson, Alcohol Problems). There is a small group of individuals who are genetically predisposed to alcohol (Beauchamp 1980) but these may be the people who are the cause of much of the social ills. I say this for a number of reasons: Ledermann, a French demographer demonstrated that:

> alcohol consumption cannot be normally distributed since this would imply that the dispersion around the mean could only range from zero to about twice the mean. However, in all the countries from which alcohol consumption data are available...drinking well in excess of twice the national average occurs (Beauchamp 1980, p. 103).

Further, "loss of control" by alcoholics is contradicted by research which shows that alcoholics can in some instances return to a lower intake of alcohol (Beauchamp 1980, p. 79).

Again, Beauchamp (1980) citing Mello (1972) observes that "alcoholics can manipulate or control their drinking to a rather surprising extent" (p. 79). Thus, the stereotype that the alcoholic is predictable in his drinking habits is shattered.

In light of the above, Beauchamp (1980) argues that if "loss of control" has to be retained as a concept, it should simply mean that there will be predictable drinking behavior of the alcoholic because he has found himself in a similar position to which drinking has previously resulted in undesirable consequences.

> [N]o study has indicated that genetic factors control 100 percent of the risk for alcoholism in any individual, a finding that highlights the importance of environmental events interacting with genetic influences in contributing to the alcoholism risk... For those studies that administer populations at high risk have their own liabilities. Different results can be expected when the subjects chosen for different studies are dissimilar on demographic characteristics such as sex, age, race or ethnic backgrounds...(Schuckit, Klein and Twitchell 1995, p. 47).

The challenge to the disease theorists is this: determine, just like cancer or hypertension, when a person is at risk from "the disease" called alcoholism, and determine what measures one will take to prevent its manifestation, as in the case of any other major disease. The storm over the disease model has come from Jellinek's analysis (1946) of ninety-eight questionnaires from a mailing sent to

about 1,600 AA members (Peele 1985, p. 29). But this storm will be abated by rational, logical and "responsible" research on "irresponsible" behavior.

Obviously, there might have been too much emotion caused by alcohol dependence in the past. The evidence before us suggests that the alcoholic should be held accountable for his actions and to do so we must first remove the last vestiges of cover used to carry out his activities—the loss of control thesis. Here is where the intellectual battle will take place as we head into the new millennium, and the possibility of not getting very far with removing this social malaise from societies around the world looms over our heads, if we continue with the present approaches to investigating this problem.

One Unanswered Question

Mendelson and Mello (1979, p. 11) explain that there is one unanswered question remaining about alcoholism and that is, what factors combine to maintain alcohol abuse once a pattern of excessive drinking has become established?

The answer may not be forthcoming in the foreseeable future, unless we develop innovative methods to determine final outcomes between genetic culpability and social irresponsibility.

> All the newer approaches emphasize that the drinker must accept responsibility and play an active role in bringing about the desired change.... No longer is the heavy drinker viewed as a victim of disease, a passive patient who will be treated by an expert (Sitomer 1988, p. 2).

It is fair to say skid row has failed, psychology has failed, genetics has failed, and prohibition has failed. Indeed, the general public must understand that alcohol consumption in its varying forms is a social malaise carrying a heavy responsibility—a responsibility that has nothing to do with morality or sinfulness. It is largely a matter of behavior, a vast array of normal individual and organizational behaviors called social irresponsibility.

Summary

No review of sociological approaches to alcohol can stay away from the heated arguments over the disease concept. Some identify with the argument that alcohol does not really meet the criteria for a disease because of the voluntary ingestion of the substance. It also sends a false message that alcoholism can be treated by a physician, giving them special skills in treating this behavior.

In truth and in fact alcoholism is a negative social behavior exhibited by both the individual and organizations particularly governments. But such behavior, as stated by Reber (1985) can be brought about by conditions which do not support normal behavior.

Basically, it is the individual's interaction with this substance called alcohol, which creates the risk to alcoholism.

The loss of control thesis allows people to be absolved from their behavior since this concept is tied to the disease model. However, on closer examination one finds that when drinking is controlled, the "diseased" individual usually carries on with other types of anti-social behavior prompting speculation that the individual really has a social problem rather than a medical one. One may exhibit alcohol behavior merely as a reflection of inability to deal with other issues in one's life.

Morality has to do with "rightness" or "wrongness" from a religious point of view. It sees the individual as a "sinner" and it is very contextual. However the moral model like the irresponsibility thesis ascribes a certain amount of freedom of choice to drinking. In this respect there is a certain amount of responsibility exhibited by the two theses.

The similarity between the two ends there, for whereas the moralists believe that drinking carries no physical, psychological or social factors impacting on behavior, the behaviorist does.

Alcoholics do not think rationally. Contextually he is allowed a free passage to imbibe for he breaks no law by drinking. Interestingly, using the cloak of irresponsibility gives him a shelter just as the disease model, one being an extension of the other. The difference is that, with the social irresponsibility thesis the individual can be held accountable for his actions. With the disease model he is absolved of responsibility. This is where we part ways with the disease model for it offers the alcoholic a permanent cop out and leaves little or no hope of recovery.

Social abandonment of principles leading to social irresponsibility can start early in one's life or it could be due to some traumatic event which the individual was unable to overcome.

There is nothing called an alcoholic personality. There are few empirical psychological findings on alcoholic personalities and most of them are about men. What is needed to be asked is the role of behavior in the transmission of alcohol from parent to offspring.

Deep within the individual's socio-economic state may lie the reason/s for his drinking and becoming an alcoholic. It therefore becomes untenable for the disease model to absolve people from responsibility due to their socially unacceptable behavior. The fact of the matter is that anyone can become an alcoholic; some may not have to try as hard as others.

No scientific study has confirmed that alcohol consumption or any variation of it, is a disease. Sociology is concerned with understanding actions rather than observing behavior. We must understand that social irresponsibility, shared by governments and by individuals, has a certain rationale. Governments rake in large amounts of revenue from the sale of alcoholic beverages, including its use by hoteliers and others attached to the tourist industry. In large measure, therefore, if we understand or appreciate this, we will understand the position of most governments towards alcohol consumption.

Symbolically then, messages are transmitted from those within government circles to those outside that drinking carries with it "legitimate" reasons. In this manner free choice finds explanation within one's "democratic right to enjoyment of life..."

If this is the case, then it is the responsibility of governments around the world to institute alcohol surveillance and tracking methods to monitor levels of drinking in the population. It is imperative that we understand the causes of abuse and use that understanding to intervene in ways that will reduce or prevent the development of a pattern of substance abuse and the consequences which may follow (Kaplan 1987, p. 40). A few countries, namely Sweden, Norway and Finland, in addition to the United States and England have taken measures and have demonstrated commitment at the national level to deal with the growing menace of alcoholism.

By so doing, they are demonstrating a sense of social responsibility and sending a message to citizens who freely imbibe to clean up their act, that is, their socially irresponsible behavior.

Social irresponsibility clashes with established norms and cultural values. However, the author of this book believes that norms and values can be changed by legislative and symbolic actions and meanings. Most of all, individual responsibility has the power to repel those values considered detrimental to individual health and development.

Authorities have to zero in on the problem or miss the mark entirely. For example, it has been pointed out that the people who cause problems are not really the alcoholics per se; they are too few compared to the vast majority of problem drinkers who drink less but whose numbers are greater (than the number of alcoholics). The measures to be adopted therefore should be preventive. The best form of prevention is responsibility.

Alcohol addiction is second only to nicotine in incidence and prevalence in the United States. There are approximately seven to nine million alcoholics or problem drinkers in America, a huge population by any demographic count when we realize that a population of drinkers that size is greater than the population of many a country. Alcohol intersects with religious and ethnic studies, social change and social movements, social deviance: age, gender, and the sociology within the workplace.

Is it consumption preference, metabolism, sensitivity, or reaction to tolerance? Why do many sick alcoholics not present themselves for treatment as any other sick person is the question to be asked of the proponents of the disease model of alcoholism.

Some individuals are alcoholics on one occasion and on other occasions they are normal individuals. The ambivalence can take place both at the societal and individual levels.

Few studies have focussed on the irresponsibility thesis. One particular study Rule and Phillips (1973) found that more positive attitudes were elicited from persons depending on what they thought about alcoholism. Those who were more sympathetic towards the alcoholic felt that alcoholism was the cause of their (alcoholics) behavior; those who thought it was the individual's behavioral attitude were less tolerant of the alcoholic. Behavior brought about by illness therefore is more tolerant than behavior which brings about illness.

Most findings comparing alcoholics with non-alcoholics report that alcoholics seem to have more loss of control in terms of their behaviors, although those who drink on social occasions or for recreational purposes are not so affected (Arbuckle et al. 1994). Again, the vast majority of individuals with alcohol use disorders do not enter treatment (Grant 1997) and some even stock alcoholic beverages when they are sober, so that they can become highly intoxicated once more. Take into consideration also that the word "alcoholism" has been dropped from the Diagnostic and Statistical Manual (DSM-3r) in favor of "alcohol abuse" and "alcohol dependence" (Wekesser 1994, p. 50) suggesting that alcoholism is not a disease. In this respect alcoholism is everyone's (social) responsibility (Robinson 1979).

Why would an alcoholic who will not learn to behave or exercise responsibility go to a physician who will advise him to take his medication? Will he take it? Will he follow his physician's advice to change his drinking habits? According to (Robinson 1979) he is incapable of doing so.

If "loss of control" is to be retained as a concept, it should simply mean that there will be predictable drinking behavior of the alcoholic because he has found himself in a similar position to which drinking has previously resulted in undesirable consequences (Beauchamp 1980).

The challenge issued by this author to the proponents of the disease concept is firstly to determine when someone called an alcoholic and about to "lose control" is at risk (just like any other disease) and takes corrective measure. Secondly, to tell the general public what measures the physician is using to reduce its manifestation in order to prevent the alcoholic from raving "out of control," as he (the alcoholic) is about to become progressively worse as any other untreated patient with a serious disease. Thirdly, to give the general public the overall statistics for the number of alcoholics "cured," "not cured," or who have "slipped into recidivism" for the past ten to fifteen years.

As we head into the new millennium a major battle looms between the proponents of unabated alcohol consumption and controlled alcohol consumption and who should be the referee. Amidst all the suggestions and recommendations there remains one unanswered question: what factors combine to maintain alcohol abuse once a pattern of excessive drinking has been established? (Mendelson and Mello 1979).

This question may be answered decisively by developing innovative methods to determine final outcomes. In this respect, "responsibility" must be a major factor and must play an active role in bringing about the desired change.

Suggested Readings

Dupont, Robert L. 1984. Getting Tough on Gateway Drugs: A Guide for the Family. Washington: American Psychiatric Press.

Mancino, Michael; Michael R. Cunningham; Pattie Davidson; and Robert L Fulton. 1996. "Identification of the Motor Vehicle Accident Victim who Abuses Alcohol: An Opportunity to Reduce Trauma." Journal of Studies on Alcohol 57, no. 6:652-59.

Mann, Robert E.; Reginald G. Smart; and Lise Anglin. 1996. "Alcohol-Related Measures as Factors in Traffic Fatalities." 57:646-51.

Uttenbroek, Daan G. 1996. "Seasonal Variation in Alcohol Use." Journal of Studies on Alcohol 57, no. 1:47-52.

REFERENCES

Aas, Henrik; Knut-Inge Klepp; Christian Jón La Berg; and Edvard Aarø Leif. 1995. "Predicting Adolescents' Intentions to Drink Alcohol: Outcome Expectancies and Self-Efficacy." *Journal of Studies on Alcohol* 56, no. 3:293-99.

Agostinelli, Gina; and William R. Miller 1994. "Drinking and Thinking: How Does Personal Drinking Affect Judgments of Prevalence and Risk? *Journal of Studies on Alcohol* 55, no. 3:327-37.

Allman, Lawrence R.; H. Augustus Taylor; and Peter E. Nathan. 1972. "Group Drinking During Stress: Effects on Drinking, Behavior, Affect, and Psychopathology." *American Journal of Psychiatry* 129, no. 6:669-78.

Alterman, Arthur I.; Jeffrey Bedrick; John S. Cacciola; Megan J. Rutherford; John S. Searles; James R. McKay; and Terry G. Cook. 1998. "Personality Pathology and Drinking in Young Men at High and Low Familial Risk for Alcoholism." *Journal of Studies on Alcohol* 59, no. 5:495-502.

Ames, Genevieve M.; and Joel W. Grube. 1999. "Alcohol Availability and Workplace Drinking: Mixed Method Analyses." *Journal of Studies on Alcohol* 60, no. 3:383-93.

Ames, Genevieve M.; Joel W. Grube; and Roland S. Moore. 1997. "The Relationship of Drinking and Hangovers to Workplace Problems: An Empirical Study." *Journal of Studies on Alcohol* 58, no. 1:37-47.

Arbuckle, Tannis Y.; June S. Chaikelson; and Dolores Pushkar Gold. 1994. "Social Drinking and Cognitive Functioning Revisited: The Role of Intellectual Endowment and Psychological Distress." *Journal of Studies on Alcohol* 55, no. 3:352-61.

Atkinson, Roland M.; Robert L. Tolson; and John A. Turner. 1993. "Factors Affecting Outpatient Treatment Compliance of Older Male Problem Drinkers." *Journal of Studies on Alcohol* 54, no. 1:102-106.

Baer, John S.; Helen M. Barr; Fred Bookstein; Paul D. Sampson; and Ann P. Streissguth. 1998. "Prenatal Alcohol Exposure and Family History of Alcoholism in the Etiology of Adolescent Alcohol Problems." *Journal of Studies on Alcohol* 59, no. 5:533-43.

Bagozzi, Richard P. 1992. "The Self-Regulation of Attitudes, Intentions, and Behavior." *Social Psychology Quarterly* 55, no. 2:178-204.

Bahr, Stephen J.; Auastasias C. Marcos; and Suzanne L. Maughan. 1995. "Family, Education and Peer Influences on the Alcohol Use of Female and Male Adolescents." *Journal of Studies on Alcohol* 56, no. 4:457-69.

Bailey, Margaret B. 1961. "Alcoholism and Marriage: A Review of Research and Professional Literature." Quarterly *Journal of Studies on Alcohol* 22, no. 1:81-97.

Baillie, Richard K. 1996. "Determining the Effects of Media Portrayals of Alcohol: Going beyond Short Term Influence." *Alcohol and Alcoholism* 31, no. 3:235-242.

Bales, Robert Freed. 1946. "Cultural Differences in Rates of Alcoholism." *Quarterly Studies of Journal on Alcohol* 6:480-99.

Bandura, Albert. 1969. *Principles of Behavior Modification*. New York: Holt, Rinehart and Winston.

Barnes, Grace M.; Ernst L. Abel; and A. S. Charles Ernst. 1980. *Alcohol and the Elderly. A Comprehensive Bibliography*. Connecticut: Greenwood Press.

Bates, Marsha E.; John Brick; and Helene R. White. 1993. "The Correspondence between Saliva and Breath Estimates of Blood Alcohol Concentration: Advantages and Limitations of the Saliva Method." *Journal of Studies on Alcohol* 54, no. 1:17-22.

Baumrind, D. 1985. In Howard B. Kaplan. 1987. "Substance Abuse Patterns and Their Relationship to Family Attitudes and Values." *Health Values* 11, no. 2: 40-46.

Beauchamp, Dan E. 1980. *Beyond Alcoholism*. Alcohol and Public Health Policy. Philadelphia: Temple University Press.

Beauvis, Fred; and Steve La Boueff. 1985. "Drug and Alcohol Abuse Intervention in American Indian Communities." *The International Journal of the Addictions* 20, no. 1:139-71.

Benjamin, Rommel; and Mary Benjamin. 1981. "Sociocultural Correlates of Black Drinking: Implications for Research and Treatment." *Journal of Studies on Alcohol*, Supplement no. 9:241-45.

Bennett, Gerald. 1983. "Alcohol Problems among the Young." In *Alcoholism*, edited by P. Golding. Boston: International Medical Publishers, MTP Press Limited.

Bennett, Joel B.; and Wayne E. K. Lehman. 1999. "Employee Exposure to Coworker Substance Use and Negative Consequences: The Moderating Effects of Work Group Membership." *Journal of Health and Social Behavior* 40: 307-22.

Bennett, Joel B.; and Wayne E. K. Lehman. 1998. "Workplace Drinking Climate, Stress, and Problem Indicators: Assessing the Influence of Teamwork." (Group Cohesion) *Journal of Studies on Alcohol* 59, no. 5:608-18.

Bergler, Edmund. 1946/1947. "Personality Traits of Alcohol Addicts." Quarterly *Journal of Studies on Alcohol*, no. 7:356-63.

Berkman, Lisa F. 1985. "Stress, Social Networks and Aging." In *The Combined Problems of Alcoholism, Drug Addiction and Aging*, edited by Edward Gottheil, Keith Druley and Howard Waxman. Illinois: Charles C. Thomas.

Beshai, Nabila N. 1990. "Providing Cost Efficient Detoxification Services to Alcoholic Patients." *Public Health Reports*. 105, no. 5:475-80.

Blum, Kenneth 1984. "Alcohol: the World's Most Devastating Drug" in Hand Book on Abusable Drugs. New York. Gardner Press.

Blumberg, Leonard U.; Thomas Shiply; and Joseph O. Moor 1971. "The Skid Row Man and the Skid Row Status Community. "*Quarterly Journal of Studies on Alcohol*, no. 32:909-41.

Bohman, M. 1978. "Some Genetic Aspects of Alcoholism and Criminality: A Population of Adoptees." *Archives of General Psychiatry* 35:269-76.

Bongers, I.M.B.; and J.A.M. Van Oers. 1998. "Mode Effects on Self-Reported Alcohol Use and Problem Drinking: Mail Questionnaires and Personal Interviewing Compared." *Journal of Studies on Alcohol* 59, no. 3:280-85.

Booth, Brenda; Joan Kirchner; John Fortney; Robin Ross and Kathryn Rost. 2000."Rural At-Risk Drinkers: Correlates and One-Year Use of Alcoholism Treatment Services." *Journal of Studies on Alcohol* 61, no. 2:267-77.

Bourne, Peter G.; and Ruth Fox, eds. 1973. *Progress in Research and Treatment*. New York: Academic Press.

Bowman, Richard S.; Leonard I. Stein; and Joseph R. Newton. 1975. "Measurement and Interpretation of Drinking Behavior (I), On Measuring Patterns of Alcohol Consumption (II), Relationships Between Drinking Behavior and Social

Adjustment in a Sample of Problem Drinkers." *Journal of Studies on Alcohol* 36, no. 9:1154-72.

Bradizza, Clara M.; Alan Reifman; and Grace M. Barnes. 1999. "Social and Coping Reasons for Drinking: Predicting Alcohol Misuse in Adolescents." *Journal of Studies on Alcohol* 60, no. 4:491-99.

Brecher, Edward M. 1985. *Licit and Illicit Drugs*. New York: Consumers Union.

Brody, Jacob A. 1985. "Alcohol and Aging—The Extent of the Problem from Limited Data." In *The Combined Problems of Alcoholism, Drug Addiction and Aging*, edited by Edward Gottheil, Skoloda, Thomas Keith A. Druley, and Howard Waxman. Illinois: Charles C. Thomas.

Broham. 1981. In *Alcoholism and Substance Abuse in Special Populations*, edited by Gary Lawson and Ann Lawson, 11-34. Maryland: Aspen Publishers.

Brown, B. 1990. In Keefe, Keunho; and Michael Newcomb. 1996. "Demographic and Psychosocial Risk for Alcohol Use: Ethnic Differences." *Journal of Studies on Alcohol* 57, no. 5:521-30.

Browne, Stephanie. 1983. "Children with an Alcoholic Parent." In *Alcoholism*, edited by P. Golding, 207-20. Boston: International Medical Publishers, MTP Press Limited.

Bruno, Leone; Brenda Stalcup; and Scott Barbour. 1998. *Alcohol: Opposing Viewpoints Series*. California: Greenhaven Press.

Bruun, Kettil. 1959. "Significance of Role and Norms in the Small Group for Individual Behavioral Changes while Drinking." Quarterly *Journal of Studies on Alcohol* 20, no. 1:53-64.

Brynum. 1984. In *Alcoholism, Etiology and Treatmen*t: Issues for Theory and Practice, edited by Bernard Segal, 69-87. New York: Haworth Press, Inc.

Bucholz, Kathleen; and Lee Robins. 1989. "Sociological Research on Alcohol Use, Problems and Policy." *Annual Review Sociology* 15 :163-86.

Budd, Richard J.; Richard J. Eiser; Michelle Morgan; and Philip Gammage. 1985. "The Personal Characteristics and Lifestyle of the Young Drinkers: The Results of a Survey of British Adolescents." *Drug and Alcohol Dependence* 16 :145-57.

Bufe, Charles. 1991. Alcoholics Anonymous: *Cult or Cure*. San Francisco: Sharp Press.

Butts, Stanley V.; and John Chotlos. 1973. "A Comparison of Alcoholics and Nonalcoholics on Perceived Locus of Control." Quarterly *Journal of Studies on Alcohol* 34:1327-32.

Byles, John A. 1978. "Violence, Alcohol Problems and Other Problems in Disintegrating Families." *Journal of Studies on Alcohol* 39, no. 3: 551-53.

Cadoret, R., and A. Gath 1978 "Inheritance of Alcoholism in Adoptees." In *Alcoholism Etiology and Treatment: Issues for Theory and Practice*, edited by Bernard Segal. New York: The Haworth Press.

Cadoret, Remi J.; Colleen A. Cain; and William M. Grove. 1980. "Development of Alcoholism in Adoptees Raised Apart from Alcoholic Biologic Relatives." *Archives of General Psychiatry* 37, no. 2 :561-63.

Caetano, Raul. 1984. "Ethnicity and Drinking in Northern California: A Comparison Among Whites, Blacks and Hispanics." *Alcohol and Alcoholism* 19, no. 1:31-44.

Cahalan, D.; and I.J. Cisin 1968. "American Drinking Practices: Summary of Findings from National Probability Sample." Quarterly *Journal of Studies on Alcohol* 29:130-51.

Callan, Victor J.; and Debra Jackson. 1985. "Children of Alcoholic Fathers and Recovered Alcoholic Fathers: Personal and Family Functioning." *Journal of Studies on Alcohol* 47,no. 2:180-82.

Cappell, Howard; and Peter C. Herman. 1972. "Alcohol and Tension Reduction: A Review." Quarterly *Journal of Studies on Alcohol* 33 : 33-64.

Carey, Kate B. 1995. "Heavy Drinking Contexts and Indices of Problem Drinking among College Students." *Journal of Studies on Alcohol* 56, no. 3:287-92.

Carey, Kate B.; and Christopher J. Correia, 1997. "Drinking Motives Predict Alcohol-Related Problems in College Students." *Journal of Studies on Alcohol* 58, no. 1:100-105.

Casswell, Sally. 1985. "The Organizational Politics of Alcohol Control Policy." *British Journal of Addiction* 80:357-62.

Casswell, Sally; Pat Brasch; Lynette Gilmore; and Phil Silva. 1985. "Children's Attitudes to Alcohol and Awareness of Alcohol-Related Problems." *British Journal of Addiction* :191-94.

Cherpitel, Cheryl J. 1998. "Differences in Performance of Screening Instruments for Problem Drinking among Blacks, Whites and Hispanics in an Emergency Room Population." *Journal of Studies on Alcohol* 59, no. 4:420-26.

_____. 1999. " Screening for Alcohol Problems in the U. S. General Population: A Comparison of the CAGE and TWEAK by Gender, Ethnicity, and Services Utilization." *Journal of Studies on Alcohol* 60, no. 5: 705-11.

Clair, David; and Myles Genest. 1987. "Variables Associated with the Adjustment of Offspring of Alcoholic Fathers." *Journal of Studies on Alcohol* 48, no. 4:345-54.

Clinard, Marshall B. 1974. Sociology of Deviant Behavior. New York: Holt, Rinehart and Winston.

Columbia Encyclopedia. 1993. Columbia University Press, 5th Edition.

Conger, John J. 1956. "Alcoholism: Theory, Problem and Challenge II: Reinforcement Theory and the Dynamics of Alcoholism." Quarterly *Journal of Studies on Alcohol* 17, no. 2 :296-305.

Connor, J. P.; R. J. Williams; and L. A. Ricciardelli. 1999. "Gender Differences in Drinking Restraint." *Journal of Studies on Alcohol* 60, no. 5:643-46.

Cooper, Stewart E. 1983. "Survey of Studies on Alcoholism." *International Journal of the Addictions* 18, no. 7:971-85.

Cornel, M.; R. A Knibbe; W. M. Van Zutphen; and M. J Drop. 1994. "Problem Drinking in a General Practice Population: The Construction of an Internal Scale for Severity of Problem Drinking." *Journal of Studies on Alcohol* 55, no. 4:466-70.

Cornel, Michiel; Ronald A Knibbe; André J. Knottnerus, Alex Volovics; and Maria J. Drop. 1996. "Predictors for Hidden Problem Drinkers in General Practice." *Alcohol and Alcoholism* 31, no. 3:287-96.

Cotton, Nancy S. 1979. "The Familial Incidence of Alcoholism: A Review." In *Why People Drink*, edited by W. Miles Cox. New York: Gardner Press.

Crowe, L. 1985. "Alcohol and Heredity: Theories about the Effects of Alcohol Use on Offspring." *Social Biology* 32, nos. 3-4:146-61.

Crum, Rosa M.; Margaret E. Ensminger; Marguerite J. Ro.; and Joan McCord. 1998. "The Association of Educational Achievement and School Dropout with Risk of Alcoholism: A Twenty-Five-Year Prospective Study of Inner-City Children." *Journal of Studies on Alcohol* 59, no. 3:318-26.

Cunningham, John A.; Donna Ansara; Cameron T. Wild; Tony Toneatto; and Anja Koski-Jännes. 1999. "What is the Price of Perfection? The Hidden Costs of Using Detailed Assessment Instruments to Measure Alcohol Consumption." *Journal of Studies on Alcohol* 6, no. 60:756-58.

Curran, Geoffrey M.; Scott F. Stoltenberg; Elizabeth M. Hill; Sharon A. Mudd; Frederic C. Blow; Robert A. Zucker. 1999. " Gender Differences in the Relationships among SES, Family History of Alcohol Disorders and Alcohol Dependence." *Journal of Studies on Alcohol* 60: 825-32.

Curran, Patrick J.; and L. Chassin. 1996. "A Longitudinal Study of Parenting as a Protective Factor for Children of Alcoholics." *Journal of Studies on Alcohol* 57, no. 3:305-13.

Curran, Patrick J.; Bengt O. Muthén; and Thomas C. Harford. 1998. "The Influence of Changes in Marital Status on Developmental Trajectories of Alcohol Use in Young Adults." *Journal of Studies on Alcohol* 59 : 647-58.

Demers, Andrée; Jocelyn Bisson; and Jézabelle Palluy. 1999. "Wives' Convergence with their Husbands' Alcohol Use: Social Conditions as Mediators." *Journal of Studies on Alcohol* 60, no. 3:368-77.

Dennison, Darwin; Thomas Prevent; and Michael Afflect. 1980. *Alcohol Behavior: An Activated Education Approach.* St. Louis: The C.V. Mosby Company.

de Vita, R. 1977. "Alcoholism as a Socio-Economic Problem." Presented at Seminar of the Medico-Social Risks of alcohol consumption, Nov. 17-18, Luxemburg. Published by Commission of European Communities, 1979.

Drake, Robert E.; and George E. Vaillant, 1988. "Predicting Alcoholism and Personality Disorder in a 33-year, Longitudinal Study of Children of Alcoholics." *British Journal of Addiction* 83:799-807.

Droller, H. 1964. "Some Aspects of Alcoholism in the Elderly." In *Drugs and the Elderly: Social and Pharmacological Issues*, edited by David Petersen, Frank Whittington and Barbara Payne. Illinois: Charles C. Thomas.

Dupree, Larry; Helen Broskowski; and Lawrence Schonfeld, 1984. "The Gerontology Alcohol Project: A Behavioral Treatment Program for Elderly Alcohol Abusers." *The Gerontologist* 24, no. 1-6:510-16.

Eastman, Clive. 1984. *Drink and Drinking Problems.* New York: Longman.

Edwards, G; A. Arif and R. Hodgson. 1982. Nomenclature and classification of Drug and Alcohol-related Problems: A shortened version of a WHO memorandum" *British Journal of Addiction. 77:3-20.*

Edwards, Griffith; Elspeth Kyle; and Peter Nicholls. 1973. "Alcoholics Admitted to Four Hospitals in England. I: Social Class and Interaction of Alcoholics with the Treatment System:" *Quarterly Journal of Studies on Alcohol* 35:499-522.

Edwards, Patricia; Cheryl Harvey; and Paul C. Whitehead. 1973. "Wives of Alcoholics: A Critical Review and Analysis." Quarterly *Journal of Studies on Alcohol* 34:112-32.

El-Guebaly, Nady; and David R. Offord, 1977. "The Offspring of Alcoholics: A Critical Review." *American Journal of Psychiatry* 134, no. 4:357-65.

Emrick, C.D. 1974. "A Review of Psychologically Oriented Treatment of Alcoholism I. The Use of Interrelationships of Outcome Criteria and Drinking Behavior following Treatment." In Richard S. Bowman; Leornard I. Stein; and Joseph R. Newton. 1975. Measurement and Interpretation of Drinking Behavior. *Journal of Studies on Alcohol* 36, no. 9:1154-72.

Ervin, C. Little; A. Streissguth; and D. Beck, 1988. "Alcoholic Fathering and a Relation to Child's Intellectual Development." *Alcoholism: Clinical and Experimental Research* 8:362-365. In *Psychological Factors Associated with the Risk for Alcoholism*, edited by Ralph E. Tarter and Kathleen Edwards.

Esser, P.H. 1968. "Conjoint Family Therapy for Alcoholics." *British Journal of Addiction* 63:177-82.

_____. 1971. "Evaluation of Family Therapy with Alcoholics." *British Journal of Addiction* 66:251-55.

Evenson, Richard C. 1986. "The Missouri Alcoholism Severity Scale: Relationship with Type of Alcohol Consumption." *Journal of Studies on Alcohol* 5, no. 47:381-83.

Feeney, Don J. 1981/1982. "Alcoholism." *American Journal of Drug and Alcohol Abuse* 8, no. 4:513-32.

Fellios, Peter G. 1989. "Alcoholism in Women: Causes, Treatment and Prevention." In *Alcoholism and Substance Abuse in Special Populations*, edited by Gary Lawson and Ann Lawson, 11-34. Maryland: Aspen Publishers.

_____. 1985. "The Social Victims of Drinking." *British Journal of Addiction* 80:307-314.

Fillmore, Kaye Middleton. 1988. "The 1980's Dominant Theory of Alcohol Problems—Genetic Predisposition to Alcoholism: Where Is It Leading Us?" In *Alcoholism Etiology and Treatment: Issues for Theory and Practice*, edited by Bernard Segal. New York: The Haworth Press.

Fillmore, Mark T.; and M. Vogel-Sprott. 2000. "Response Inhibition under Alcohol: Effects of Cognitive and Motivational Conflict." *Journal of Studies on Alcohol* 61, no. 2:239-46.

Fingarette, Herbert. 1988. *Heavy Drinking*. Los Angeles: University of California Press.

Finney, John; and Rudolph H. Moos, 1991. "The Long-Term Course of Treated Alcoholism: I. Mortality, Relapse and Remission Rates and Comparisons with Community Controls." *Journal of Studies on Alcohol* 52, no. 1:44-54.

Forney, Mary Ann; William K. Ripley; and Paul D. Forney. 1988. "A Profile and Prediction Study of Problem Drinking among First-Year Medical Students." *The International Journal of the Addictions* 23, no. 7:767-79.

Fox, K. 1968. In Gary Lawson; and Ann W. Lawson. 1989. *Alcoholism and Substance Abuse in Special Populations*. Maryland: Aspen Publishers.

Fox, K.; J.C Merrill; H.H. Chang; and J.A. Califano. 1995. "Estimating the Costs of Substance Abuse to the Medicaid Hospital Care Program." *American Journal of Public Health* 85, no. 1:48-54.

Frankel, Bhan; and John Murphy. 1974. "Physical Fitness and Personality in Alcoholism: Canonical Analysis of Measures Before and After Treatment." Quarterly *Journal of Studies on Alcohol* 35, no. 4: 1272-78.

Frankfort-Nachmias Chava; and David Nachmias. 1996. *Research Methods in the Social Sciences*. New York: St. Martin's Press.

Friedman, Jennifer; and John A Humphrey. 1985. "Antecedents of Collegiate Drinking." *Journal of Youth and Adolescence* 14, no. 1: 11-21.

Gerra, Gilberto; Amir Zaimovic; Roberto Sartori; Maria August Raggi; Carlotta Bocchi; Ursula Zanichelli; Mariamanuela Timpano; Valeria Zanichelli; Roberto Delsignore and Francesca Brambilla 1999. "Experimentally Induced Aggressiveness in Adult Children of Alcoholics (ACOAs): Preliminary Behavioral and Neuroendocrine Findings." *Journal of Studies on Alcohol* 60, no.6:776-83.

Glatt, Max. 1969. *Care and Welfare*. Alcoholism: A Social Disease. London: English Universities Press.

Glatt, Max; and D. R. Hills. 1968. "Alcohol Abuse and Alcoholism in the Young." *British Journal of Addiction* 63:183-91.

Gomberg, Edith L. 1985. "Alcoholism, Psychological and Psychosocial Aspects." In *Alcohol, Science and Society Revisited*, edited by E.L. Gomberg, H.R. White and J.A. Carpenter, 186-204. New Jersey: The Michigan Press.

Goode, Eric. 1984. *Deviant Behavior*. New Jersey: Prentice Hall.

Goodman, A. C.; E. Nishiura; and R. S. Humphreys. 1997. "Cost and Usage Impacts of Treatment Initiations: A Comparison of Alcoholism and Drug Abuse Treatments." *Alcoholism: Clinical and Experimental Research* 21, no. 5:931-38.

Goodwin, Donald W. 1971. "Is Alcoholism Hereditary? A Review and Critique." *Archives of General Psychiatry* 25:545-49.

_____. 1979. "Alcoholism and Heredity: A Review Hypothesis." *Archives of General Psychiatry* 36:57-61.

_____. 1981. "Family Studies of Alcoholism." *Journal of Studies on Alcohol* 42, no. 1:156-62.

_____. 1990. "Genetic Determinants of Reinforcement from Alcohol." In *Why People Drink*, edited by W. Miles Cox. New York: Gardner Press.

Goodwin, Donald W.; Fini Schulsinger; Leif Hermansen; George Winokur; and Samuel B. Guze. 1973. "Alcohol Problems in Adoptees Raised Apart from Alcoholic Biological Parents." *Archives of General Psychiatry* 28, no. 2:238-43.

Goodwin, Donald W.; Fini Schulsinger; Neils Møller; Leif Hermansen; George Winokur; and Samuel B. Guze. 1974. "Drinking Problems in Adopted and Non-Adopted Sons of Alcoholics." *Archives of General Psychiatry* 31, no. 2:164-69.

Goodwin, James S.; Clare Jeanne Sanchez; Paula Thomas; Curtis Hunt; Philip J Garry; and Jean M. Goodwin. 1987. "Alcohol Intake in a Healthy Elderly Population." *American Journal of Public Health*, 2:173-176.

Gordis, Enoch. 1988. "Alcohol and Aging." *Alcohol Alert*, no. 2:1-4. National Institute on Alcohol Abuse and Alcoholism: Department of Health and Human Services: no. 2:1-4.

_____. 1990. "Alcohol Use and Abuse: Where Do the Numbers Come From?" *Alcohol Alert*, National Institute on Alcohol Abuse and Alcoholism. Maryland: Department of Health and Human Services: no. 7:1-4.

Goss and Morosko. 1970. In Stanley V. Butts; and John Chotlos. 1973. "A Comparison of Alcoholics and Non-alcoholics on Perceived Locus of Control." Quarterly *Journal of Studies on Alcohol* 34:1327-32.

Graham, Kathryn; and Gail Schmidt. 1999. "Alcohol Use and Psychosocial Well-Being among Older Adults." *Journal of Studies on Alcohol* 60, no. 3:345-51.

Granovetter, M. 1973. "The Strength of Weak Ties In Ole-Jergen Skog. 1985. "The Collectivity of Drinking Cultures: A Theory of the Distribution of Alcohol Consumption." *British Journal of Addiction* 80:83-95.

Grant, Bridget F. 1997. "Barriers to Alcoholism Treatment: Reasons for Not Seeking Treatment in a General Population Sample." *Journal of Studies on Alcohol* 58, no. 4:365-71.

Gravitz, Herbert; Julie D. Bowden. 1985. Recovery: *A Guide for Adult Children of Alcoholics*. New York: Simon and Schuster.

Gurling, Hugh; and Robin Murray. 1984. "Alcoholism and Genetics: Old and New Evidence." In *Alcohol Related Problems*, edited by N. Krasner, J. S. Madden and R. J. Walker. New York: John Wiley and Sons.

Haglund, Robert M. J.; and Marc A. Schuckit. 1982. "The Epidemiology of *Alcoholism." In Alcoholism: Development, Consequences and Interventions*, edited by Nada J. Estes; and M. Edith Heinemann, 32-48. St. Louis: The C.V. Mosby Company.

Hanlon, John Joseph; and George E. Pickett, 1984. *Public Health Administration*. St. Louis: Times Mirror: Mosby College.

Hanson, David J. 1995. *Preventing Alcohol Abuse*. Alcohol, Culture and Control. Connecticut: Praeger.

Heath, Dwight B. 1995. "An Introduction to Alcohol and Culture in International Perspective." *In International Handbook on Alcohol and Culture*, edited by Dwight B. Heath. Connecticut: Greenwood Press.

Heather, Nick. 1995. "Interpreting the Evidence on Brief Interventions for Excessive Drinkers: The Need for Caution." *Alcohol and Alcoholism 30*, no. 3:287-96.

Heather, Nick; J. S. Tebbutt; R. P Mattick; and R. Zamir. 1993. "Development of a Scale for Measuring Impaired Control Over Alcohol Consumption: A Preliminary Report." *Journal of Studies on Alcohol* 54, no. 6:700-709.

Heck, Edward J.; and Michael D. Williams. 1995. "Using the CAGE to Screen for Drinking-Related Problems in College Students." *Journal of Studies on Alcohol* 56, no. 3:282-86.

Heien, Dale. 1996. "The Relationship between Alcohol Consumption and Earnings." *Journal of Studies on Alcohol* 57, no. 5:536-42.

Heien, Dale M.; and David J. Pittman. 1993. "The External Costs of Alcohol Abuse." *Journal of Studies on Alcohol* 54, no. 3:302-307.

Heien, Dale M.; and Greg Pompelli. 1987. "Stress, Ethnic and Distribution Factors in a Dichotomous Response Model of Alcohol Abuse." *Journal of Studies on Alcohol* 48, no. 5:450-55.

Hennessy, Michael; and Robert F Saltz. 1993. "Modeling Social Influences on Public Drinking." *Journal of Studies on Alcohol* 54, no. 2:139-45.

Herd, Denise. 1997. "Sex Ratios of Drinking Patterns and Problems among Blacks and Whites: Results from a National Survey." *Journal of Studies on Alcohol* 58, no. 1:75-82.

Hesselbrock, Victor M.; Michie N. Hesselbrock; and James R. Stabenau. 1985. "Alcoholism in Men Patients Subtyped by Family History and Anti-Social Personality." *Journal of Studies on Alcohol* 46, no. 1: 59-64.

Hilgard, Josephine R.; and Martha F. Newman. 1963. "Early Parental Deprivation as a Functional Factor in the Etiology of Schizophrenia and Alcoholism." *American Journal of Orthopsychiatry* 33, no. 1: 409-20.

Hodgins, D. C.; and L. Shimp. 1995. "Identifying Adult Children of Alcoholics: Methodological Review and a Comparison of the CAST-6 with Other Methods." *Addiction* 90, no. 2:255-67.

Horn, Thierry; Fred Paccaud; Marc Niquille; Veronique Koehn; Pierre Magnenat; and Bertrand Yersin. 1992. "Drinking Patterns among Medical In-Patients with Reference to MAST Categories: A Comparative Study." *Alcohol and Alcoholism* 27, no. 4: 439-47.

Humphreys, Keith; Rudolf H. Moos; and Caryn Cohen. 1997. "Social and Community Resources and Long-Term Recovery from Treated and Untreated Alcoholism." *Journal of Studies on Alcohol* 58, no. 3: 231-38.

Hussong, A. M.; and L. Chassin. 1977. "Substance Use Initiation among Adolescent Children of Alcoholics: Testing Protective Factors. *Journal of Studies on Alcohol* 58, no. 3:272-79.

Idleburg, Dorothy Ann. 1982. "An Exploratory Study of Treatment Outcomes in a 12-year Follow-up of Black and White Female Alcoholics." Ph.D. diss., p. 96.

Institute of Medicine. 1989. National Institute on Alcohol Abuse and Alcoholism. (US) 1990. In Thomas L. Burton and Deanna L. Williamson's "Harmful Effects of Drinking and the Use and Perceived Effectiveness of Treatment." *Journal of Studies on Alcohol* 56, no. 6:611-15. 1995.

Iwaarden, van M.J. 1985. "Public Health Aspects of the Marketing of Alcoholic Drinks." In *Alcohol Policies,* edited by Marcus Grant. Geneva: World Health Organization.

Jackson, Christine; Lisa Henriksen; and Denise Dickinson. 1999. "Alcohol-Specific Socialization, Parenting Behaviors and Alcohol Use by Children." *Journal of Studies on Alcohol* 60, no. 3:362-67.

Jackson, Joan K. 1954. "The Adjustment of the Family to the Crisis of Alcoholism." *Quarterly Journal of Studies on Alcohol* 15, no. 4: 562-86.

_____. 1959. "Family Structure and Alcoholism." *Mental Hygiene* 43, no. 3:403-10.

Jacob, Theodore; and Kenneth Leonard. 1986. "Psychosocial Functioning in Children of Alcoholic Fathers, Depressed Fathers and Control Fathers." *Journal of Studies on Alcohol* 47, no. 5:373-80.

Jacob, Theodore; Alison Favorini; Susan Miesel; and Carol M. Anderson, 1978. "The Alcoholic's Spouse, Children and Family Interactions." *Journal of Studies on Alcohol* 39, no. 7:1231-50.

Jellinek, E.M. 1960. *The Disease Concept of Alcoholism.* New Jersey: Hill House Press.

Jessor, R.; T. D. Graves; R. C. Hanson; and S. L. Jessor 1974. "Society, Personality and Deviant Behavior: A Study of a Tri-Ethnic Community." In L.V. Johnson and Marc Mâtre. "Anomie and Alcohol Use." *Journal of Studies on Alcohol* 39, no. 5:894-902.

Jin, Hua; Sean B. Rourke; Thomas L. Patterson; Michael J. Taylor; and Igor Grant. 1998. "Predictors of Relapse in Long-Term Abstinent Alcoholics." *Journal of Studies on Alcohol* 59:640-46.

Johnson, Eric O.; Amelia M. Arria; Guilherme Borges; Nicholas Ialongo; and James C Anthony. 1995. "The Growth of Conduct Problem Behaviors from Middle Childhood to Early Adolescence: Sex Differences and the Suspected Influence of Early Alcohol Use." *Journal of Studies on Alcohol* 56, no. 6:661-71.

Johnson, L.V.; and Marc Mâtre. 1974. "Anomie and Alcohol Use: Drinking Patterns in Mexican American and Anglo Neighborhoods." *Journal of Studies on Alcohol* 39, no. 5:894-902.

Johnson, Patrick B.; and Marc Glassman. 1999. "The Moderating Effects of Gender and Ethnicity on the Relationship between Effect Expectancies and Alcohol Problems." *Journal of Studies on Alcohol* 60, no. 1:64-69.

Jones, S.; S. Casswell; and J. R. Zhang. 1995. "The Economic Costs of Alcohol-Related Absenteeism and Reduced Productivity among the Working Population of New Zealand." *Addiction* 90, no. 11:1455-61.

Jung, John. 1994. *Under the Influence: Alcohol and Human Behavior.* California: Brooks/Cole Publishing Company.

Kaij, L.; J.Dock. 1975."Grandsons of Alcoholics: A Test of Sex-Linked Transmission of Alcohol Abuse." *Archives of General Psychiatry* 32:1379-81.

Kane, Geoffrey. 1981. *Inner City Alcoholism*. New York: Human Sciences Press.

Kaplan, Howard B. 1987. "Substance Abuse Patterns and Their Relationship to Family Attitudes and Values." *Health Values* 11, no. 2:40-46.

Kaskutas, Lee Ann; Constance Weisner; Mija Lee; and Keith Humphreys. 1999. "Alcoholics Anonymous Affiliation at Treatment Intake among White and Black Americans." *Journal of Studies on Alcohol* 60, no. 6:810-16.

Kastl, Albert J. 1969. "Changes in Ego Functioning Under Alcohol." *Quarterly Journal of Studies on Alcohol*, no. 2:20.

Katz, Renee S.; and Nicholas Hayes Ney. 1995. "Preventing Relapse." Ch.7. In *Treating Alcoholism*, edited by Stephanie Brown and Irvin D. Yalam. San Francisco: Jossey-Bass.

Keefe, Keunho. 1994. "Perceptions of Normative Social Pressure and Attitudes toward Alcohol Use: Changes during Adolescence." *Journal of Studies on Alcohol* 55, no. 1:46-54.

Keefe, Keunho; and Michael D. Newcomb. 1996. "Demographic and Psychosocial Risk for Alcohol Use: Ethnic Differences." *Journal of Studies on Alcohol* 57, no. 5:521-30.

Keil, Thomas J. 1978. "Sex Role Variations and Women's Drinking: Results from a Household Survey in Pennsylvania. *Journal of Studies on Alcohol* 39, no. 5:859-68.

Keller, Mark. 1975. "Multidisciplinary Perspectives on Alcoholism and the Need for Integration." *Journal of Studies on Alcohol* 36, no. 1: 133-47.

_____. 1976. "The Disease Concept of Alcoholism Revisited." *Journal of Studies on Alcohol* 37, no. 11:1694-1717.

Kenkel, Donald S. 1997. "Self-Insurance and Worksite Alcohol Programs: An Econometric Analysis." *Journal of Studies on Alcohol* 58, no. 2 : 211-19.

Kennedy, Robert S.; Janet J. Turnage; Gene G. Rugotzke; and William P. Dunlap. 1994. "Indexing Cognitive Tests to Alcohol Dosage and Comparison to

Standardized Field Sobriety Tests." *Journal of Studies on Alcohol* 55, no. 5:615-28.

Khavari, Khalil A.; and Philip D. Farber, 1978. "A Profile for the Quantification and Assessment of Alcohol Consumption: The Khavari Alcohol Test." *Journal of Studies on Alcohol* 39, no. 9: 1525-39.

Kingham, Richard J. 1958. "Alcoholism and the Reinforcement Theory of Learning." *Quarterly Journal of Studies on Alcohol* 19, no. 12:320-30.

Knibbe, R.A.; M.J. Drop; and Muytjens. 1987. "Correlates of Stages in the Progression from Everyday Drinking to Problem Drinking." *Social Science Medicine* 24, no. 5:463-73.

Knupfer, Genevieve. 1966. "Some Methodological Problems in the Epidemiology of Alcoholic Beverage Usage: Definition of Amount of Intake." *American Journal of Public Health and Nations Health* 56, no. 2:237-42.

Koch-Hattem, Alberta; and Debra Denman. 1987. "Factors Associated with Young Adult Alcohol Abuse." *Alcohol and Alcoholism* 22, no. 2 :181-92.

Kofoed, Lial; and James MacMillan,. 1986. "Alcoholism and Antisocial Personality: The Sociobiology of an Addiction." *The Journal of Nervous and Mental Disease* 174, no. 6:332-35.

Kofoed, Lial L; Robert L. Tolson; Roland M. Atkinson; Rodger L. Toth and John A. Turner. 1987. "Treatment Compliance of Older Alcoholics: An Elder-Specific Approach is 'Superior to Mainstreaming'" *Journal of Studies on Alcohol* 48, no. 1: 47-51.

Krasner, Neville; J.S. Madden; and Robin J. Walker. 1984. *Alcohol-Related Problems.* New York: John Wiley.

Kuhn, Thomas S. 1962. The Structure of Scientific Revolutions. Chicago: University of Chicago Press.

Kwapil, Thomas R. 1996. "A Longitudinal Study of Drug and Alcohol Use by Psychosis-Prone and Impulsive-Nonconforming Individuals." *Journal of Abnormal Psychology* 105, no. 1:114-123.

Lawson, Gary W.; and Ann W. Lawson. 1989. *Alcoholism and Substance Abuse in Special Populations*. Maryland: Aspen Publishers.

Leigh, Paul J. 1995. "Dangerous Jobs and Heavy Alcohol Use in Two National Probability Samples." *Alcohol and Alcoholism* 30, no. 1:71-86.

Levenson, Robert W.; Oliver N. Oyama; and Patricia S. Meek. 1987. "Greater Reinforcement From Alcohol for Those at Risk: Parental Risk, Personality Risk, and Sex." *Journal of Abnormal Psychology* 96, no. 3:242-53.

Levin, Jerome David. 1990. *Alcoholism: A Bio-Psycho-Social Approach*. New York: Hemisphere Publishing Corporation.

Levine, Harry Gene. 1978. "The Discovery of Addiction: Changing Conceptions of Habitual Drunkenness in America. *Journal of Studies on Alcohol* 19, no. 1:143-74.

Levy, R.J. 1958. "The Psychodynamic Functions of Alcohol." *Quarterly Journal Studies on Alcohol* 19:649-59.

Lindström, Lars. 1992. *Managing Alcoholism Matching Clients to Treatments*. New York: Oxford University Press.

Linsky, Arnolds 1987. "Social Stress, Normative Constraints and Alcohol Problems in American States." *Social Science and Medicine* 24, no. 10:875-83.

Linsky, Arnold S.; John P. Colby; and Murray A. Straus. 1986. "Drinking Norms and Alcohol-Related Problems in the United States." *Journal of Studies on Alcohol* 47, no. 3:384-93.

_____. Linsky, Arnold S.; Murray A. Straus; and John P. Colby. 1985. "Stressful Events, Stressful Conditions and Alcohol Problems in the United States: A Partial Test of Bales's Theory." *Journal of Studies on Alcohol* 46, no. 1:72-80.

Liskow, Barry; Jan Campbell; Elizabeth J. Nickel; and Barbara J. Powell, 1995. "Validity of the CAGE Questionnaire in Screening for Alcohol Dependence in a Walk-in (Triage) Clinic." *Journal of Studies on Alcohol* 56, no. 3:277-81.

Livingston, Ivor. 1985. "Alcohol Consumption and Hypertension. A Review with Suggested Implications." *Journal of the National Medical Association* 77, no. 2:129-35.

Mackey, Aurora. 1988. "New Treatment Programs Seek to Aid Recovery, Salvage Careers." In *Indianapolis Star*. 1988. "Alcohol, Other Drugs Impair Nurses, Doctors," April 24, : F-1+. Vol. 4, Article # 30.

Madden, J. S. 1984. *A Guide to Alcohol and Drug Dependence*. Bristol: Wright.

Maddox, George L. 1962. "Teenage Drinking in the United States." In *Society, Culture and Drinking Patterns*, edited by David Pittman, and Charles Snyder, 230-45. New York: John Wiley.

Maes, Hermine H.; Charlene E. Woodard; Lenn Murrelle; Joanne M. Meyer; Judy L. Silberg; John K.Hewitt, Michael Rutter; Emily Simonoff; Andrew Pickles; Rene Carbonneau; Michael C. Neale; and Lindon J. Eaves. 1999. "Tobacco, Alcohol and Drug Use in Eight-to Sixteen-Year-Old Twins: The Virginia Twin Study of Adolescent Behavioral Development." *Journal of Studies on Alcohol* 60:293-305.

Makela and Room. In Kathleen Bucholz; and Robins Lee. 1989. "Sociological Research on Alcohol Use, Problems and Policy." *Annual Review Sociology* 15:163-86.

Malouff, John; Nicola Schutte; Kimara Wiener; Christine Brancazio; and Darla Fish. 1993. "Important Characteristics of Warning Displays on Alcohol Containers." *Journal of Studies on Alcohol* 54, no. 4: 457-61.

Manis, Jerome G.; and Chester L. Hunt. 1957. "The Community Survey as a Measure of the Prevalence of Alcoholism." *Quarterly Journal of Studies on Alcohol* 18:212-16.

Mannis, Marty. 1958. *New Primer on Alcoholism*. New York: Holt, Rinehart and Winston.

Marlatt, G. A.; Demming, B. and Reid, J. B. "Loss of Control Drinking in Alcoholics: An Experimental Analogue." 1973. In Stanton Peele 1985. "The Implications and Limitations of Genetic Models of Alcoholism and Other Addictions." *Journal of Studies on Alcohol* vol. 47, no. 1:63-73.

Marshall, Ronald. 1992. "Family Composition and Alcohol Consumption: The Different Combinations of Family Units and Variations in Alcohol Consumption." Ph.D. dissertation, Howard University, Washington, D.C.

_____. 1999. "Sex Differences in Alcohol Consumption in Restaurants, Bars and Parties: Exploring the Impact and the Outcome: A Qualitative Approach" presented at the American Sociological Association 94th. Annual Meeting. August 6-9: Chicago.

Marshall, Ronald; and Anthony Tang. 1998. "The Correspondence between the Perception of Alcohol in the Workplace and Mental Health Problems: What are the Implications for Productivity?", University of the West Indies, St. Augustine. Mimeographed.

Marshall, Mac, ed. 1979. "Beliefs, Behaviors, and Alcoholic Beverages: A Cross-Cultural Survey." In David Hanson's 1995 *Preventing Alcohol Abuse: Alcohol, Culture and Control.* Connecticut: Praeger.

Masserman, Jules H.; and K. S. Yum. 1946. "An Analysis of the Influence of Alcohol on Experimental Neuroses in Cats." *Psychosomatic Medicine* 8, no. 1:36-52.

McCord, Joan. 1988. "Alcoholism: Toward Understanding Genetic and Social Factors." *Psychiatry* 51, no. 5:131-39.

McCormick, Robert. 1982. *Facing Alcoholism.* California: Oak Tree Publications.

McKenna, M.; J. Chick; M. Buxton; M. Howlett; D. Patience; and B. Ritson. 1996. "The SECCAT [Socio-Economic Costs and Consequences of Alcoholism Treatment] Survey: I. The Costs and Consequences of Alcoholism." *Alcohol and Alcoholism* 31, no. 6:565-76.

Mello, Nancy. 1972. "Behavioral Studies of Alcoholism." In *The Biology of Alcoholism.* Vol 2, edited by Benjamin Kissin and Henri Begleiter, 219-91. New York: Plenum.

Mendelson, Jack H.; and Nancy K. Mello. 1979. "One Unanswered Question about Alcoholism." *British Journal of Addiction* 74:11-14.

Michener, Andrew H.; John D. DeLamater; and Shalom H. Schwartz. 1986. *Social Psychology.* New York: Harcourt Brace Janovich.

Midanik, Lorraine T.; and Walter B. Clark, 1995. "Drinking-Related Problems in the United States: Description and Trends, 1984-1990." *Journal of Studies on Alcohol* 56, no. 4:395-402.

Miller, B.A.; W. R Downs; and M. Testa. 1993. "Interrelationships between Victimization Experiences and Women's Alcohol Use." In Sharon C. Wilsnack; Nancy D. Vogeltanz; Albert D. Klassen; Harris T. Robert. 1997. "Childhood Sexual Abuse and Women's Substance Abuse: National Survey Findings." *Journal of Studies on Alcohol* 58, no. 3:264-71.

Miller, Gary H.; and Neil Agnew. 1974. "The Ledermann Model of Alcohol Consumption: Description, Implications and Assessment." *Quarterly Journal of Studies on Alcohol,* vol. 35:877-98.

Miller-Tutzauer, Carol; Kenneth E. Leonard; and Michael Windle. 1991. "Marriage and Alcohol Use: A Longitudinal Study of 'Maturing Out.'" *Journal of Studies on Alcohol* 52, no. 5:434-40.

Milt, Harry. 1976. *Alcoholism: Its Causes and Cure—A New* Handbook. New York: Charles Scribner.

Mishara, Brian L.; and Robert Kastenbaum. 1980. *Alcohol and Old Age*. New York: Grune and Stratton, Inc.

Moos, Rudolph H.; and Bernice S. Moos. 1984. "The Process of Recovery from Alcoholism: III. Comparing Functioning in Families of Alcoholics and Matched Control Families." *Journal of Studies on Alcohol* 45, no. 2:111-18.

Moos, Rudolph H.; Becky Pettit; and Valerie Gruber. 1995. "Longer Episodes of Community Residential Care Reduce Substance Abuse Patients' Readmission Rates." *Journal of Studies on Alcohol* 56, no. 4:433-43.

Muhlin, Gregory. 1985. "Ethnic Differences in Alcoholic Misuse: A Striking Reaffirmation." *Journal of Studies on Alcohol* 46, no. 2: 172-73.

Mulford, Harold A.; and Donald E. Miller. 1960. "Drinking in Iowa: II. The Extent of Drinking and Selected Sociocultural Categories." *Quarterly Journal Studies on Alcohol* 21, no. 1:26-39.

_____. 1960. "Drinking in Iowa: III. A Scale of Definitions of Alcohol Related to drinking Behavior." *Quarterly Journal Studies in Alcohol* 21, no. 2:267-78.

Murray et al. 1983. In *Alcoholism Etiology and Treatment: Issues for Theory and Practice*, edited by Bernard Segal. New York: The Haworth Press.

Myers, Ted. 1984. "Alcohol and Violence: Self-Reported Alcohol Consumption among Violent and Non-violent Male Prisoners." In *Alcohol Related Problems*, edited by Neville Krasner; J.S. Madden and Robin J. Walker. New York: John Wiley.

a). National Institute of Mental Health (US). 1969 II. "Excessive Drinking: Nature of the Problem. Public Health Publication, No. 1640.: 5-28. Maryland: the Institute. :5-28.

b). National Institute on Alcohol Abuse and Alcoholism. (US) 1990. "Screening for Alcoholism." *Alcohol Alert*, Department of Health and Human Services: no. 8:1-4.

c). National Institute on Alcohol Abuse and Alcoholism. (US) 1990. "Children of Alcoholics: Are they Different?" *Alcohol Alert*, Department of Health and Human Services: no. 9:PH288:1-4.

d). National Institute on Alcohol Abuse and Alcoholism. (US) 1991. "Estimating the Economic Cost of Alcohol Abuse." *Alcohol Alert*, Department of Health and Human Services: no. 11:PH293:1-3.

Public Health Service Publication, no. 1640. 1969. "II. Excessive Drinking: Nature of the Problem." Maryland: National Institute of Mental Health,: 5-28.

Neff, James Alan. 1985. "Evaluating the Stress-Buffering Role of Alcohol Consumption: Variation by Type of Event and Type of Symptom." *Alcohol and Alcoholism* 20, no. 4:391-401.

Neff, James Alan; Sandra K. Burge. 1995. "Alcohol Use, Liberal/Conservative Orientations, and Ethnicity as Predictors of Sexual Behaviors." *Journal of Acquired Immune Deficiency Syndromes and Human Retrovirology* 8, no. 3:302-12.

Negrete, J.C. 1973. "Cultural Influences on Social Performance of Alcoholics: A Comparative Study." *Quarterly Journal of Studies on Alcohol* 34:905-16.

Neve, Rudie J. M.; Paul H. Lemmens; and Maria J. Drop. 1997. "Drinking Careers of Older Male Alcoholics in Treatment as Compared to Younger Alcoholics and to Older Social Drinkers. *Journal of Studies on Alcohol* 58, no. 3:303-11.

Newell, Nancy. 1950. "Alcoholism and the Father-Image." *Quarterly Journal of Studies on Alcohol* 11: 92-96.

Niven, R. 1983 In Stephanie Browne, "Children with an Alcoholic Parent." In *Alcoholism,* edited by P. Golding. 1983. Boston: MTP Press.

Nofz, Michael P. 1988. "Alcohol Abuse and Culturally Marginal American Indians." Social Casework: *The Journal of Contemporary Social* Work 69, no. 1:67-72.

O'Callaghan, Frances V.; David C. Chant; and Victor J. Callan, 1997. "Models of Alcohol Use by Young Adults: An Examination of Various Attitude Behavior Theories." *Journal of Studies on Alcohol* 58, no. 5:502-507.

O'Connor, Joyce. 1984. "Models of Drinking Behavior and Their Implications for Health Education of the Young." In *Alcohol Related Problems: Room for Maneuver*, edited by N. Krasner, J.S. Madden and R.J. Walker, 159-75. New York: John Wiley.

O'Connor Joyce 1975. In Lawson and Lawson 1989. *Alcoholism and Substance Abuse in Special Populations*. Maryland: Aspen Publishers.

O'Farrel, Timothy; Valerie Van Hutton; and Christopher M. Murphy, 1999. "Domestic Violence Before and After Alcoholism Treatment: A Two-Year Longitudinal Study." *Journal of Studies on Alcohol* 60, no. 3:317-21.

Olenick, Nancy Linn; and Douglas K. Chalmers. 1991. "Gender-Specific. Drinking Styles in Alcoholics and Non-alcoholics." *Journal of Studies on Alcohol* 52, no. 4:325-30.

Olson, Steve; and Dean R. Gerstein. 1985. *Alcohol in America: Taking Action to Prevent Abuse.* Washington, D.C.: National Academy Press.

Pandina, Robert J.; and Valerie Johnson. 1989. "Familial Drinking History as a Predictor of Alcohol and Drug Consumption among Adolescent Children." *Journal of Studies on Alcohol* 50, no. 3:245-52.

Parsons, Oscar A.; and Sara Jo Nixon. 1998. "Cognitive Functioning in Sober Social Drinkers: A Review of the Research Since 1986." *Journal of Studies on Alcohol.* Vol.59, 180-90.

Pearlin, Leonard I.; and Clarice W. Radabaugh. 1976. "Economic Strains and the Coping Functions of Alcohol." *American Journal of Sociology* 82, no. 3 :652-62.

Peele, Stanton. 1985. *The Meaning of Addiction.* Massachusetts: Lexington Books, D.C. Heath.

_____. 1986. "The Implications and Limitations of Genetic Models of Alcoholism and Other Addictions." *Journal of Studies on Alcohol* 47, no. 1:63-73.

Penick, Elizabeth C.; Elizabeth J. Nickel; Barbara J. Powell; Barry I. Liskow; Jan Campbell; Tamara M. Dale; Ruth E. Hassanein; and Elizabeth Nobel. 1999. "The Comparative Validity of Eleven Alcoholism Typologies." *Journal of Studies on Alcohol* 60, no. 2: 188-202.

Perkins, Wesley H. 1999. "Stress-Motivated Drinking in Collegiate and Postcollegiate Young Adulthood: Life Course and Gender Patterns." *Journal of Studies on Alcohol* 60, no. 2:219-27.

Phares, Richie and Davis. In Butts and Chotlos. 1973. "A Comparison of Alcoholics and Non-Alcoholics on Perceived Locus of Control." *Quarterly Journal of Studies on Alcohol* 34:1327-32.

Phillips, Lorne A. 1976. "An Application of Anomie Theory to the Study of Alcoholism." *Journal of Studies on Alcohol* 37, no. 1:78-84.

Pisani, Vincent D.; Jan Fawcett; David C. Clark; and Marcella McGuire. 1993. "The Relative Contributions of Medication Adherence and AA Meeting Attendance to Abstinent Outcome for Chronic Alcoholics." *Journal of Studies on Alcohol* 54, no. 1:115-19.

Pittman, David J.; and Charles Snyder, eds. 1962. *Society, Culture and Drinking Patterns.* New York: John Wiley.

Polich, Michael J.; David J. Amor; and Harriet B. Braiker. 1981. *The Course of Alcoholism Four Years After Treatment.* New York: John Wiley.

Potvin, Raymond H.; and Che-Fu. Lee. 1980. "Multistage Path Models of Adolescent Alcohol and Drug Use." *Journal of Studies on Alcohol* 41, no. 5:531-42.

Powers, Robert; and Irwin L. Kutash. 1985. "Stress and Alcohol." *The International Journal of the Addictions* 20, no. 3:461-82.

Reber, Arthur S. 1985. *The Penguin Dictionary of Psychology.* New York: Viking Penguin.

Rhea, Sally Ann; Craig T. Nagoshi; and James R. Wilson. 1993. "Reliability of Sibling Reports on Parental Drinking Behaviors." *Journal of Studies on Alcohol* 54, no. 1:80-84.

Riskin, Jules. 1963. "Methodology Studying Family Interaction." *Archives of General Psychiatry* 8, no. 4 :343-48.

Robinson, David, ed. 1979. *Alcohol Problems: Reviews, Research and Recommendations.* MacMillan: London.

Roe, A. 1944. "The Adult Adjustment of Children of Alcoholic Parents raised in Foster Homes." In W. Miles Cox *Why People Drink.* Gardner Press. :New York: Gardner Press.

Rogers, John D.; and Thomas K. Greenfield. 1999. "Beer Drinking Accounts for Most of the Hazardous Alcohol Consumption Reported in the United States." *Journal of Studies on Alcohol* 60, no. 6:732-39.

Roman, Paul M.; and H. M. Trice. 1967/1968. "The Sick Role, Labelling Theory and the Deviant Drinker." *International Journal of Social Psychiatry* 14, no. 4:245-51.

Room, Robin. 1979. "Priorities in Social Science Research on Alcohol." *Journal of Studies on Alcohol*, Supplement no. 8:248-68.

_____. 1985. "Dependence and Society." *British Journal of Addiction* 80:133-39.

_____. 1990. "Measuring Alcohol Consumption in the United States: Methods and Rationales." In *Research Advances in Alcohol and Drug Problems*. Vol. 10, edited by Lynn T. Kozlowski, Helen M. Annis, Howard D. Cappell, Frederick B. Glaser, Michael S. Goodstadt, Yedi Israel, Harold Kalant, Edward M. Sellers and Evelyn R. Vingilis. New York: Plenum Press.

Roosa, Mark W.; Irwin N. Sandler; Mary Gehring; Janette Beals; and Laurel Cappo. 1987. "The Children of Alcoholics Life-Events Schedule: A Stress Scale for Children of Alcohol-Abusing Parents." *Journal of Studies on Alcohol* 49:422-29.

Rose, Robert M.; and James Barrett. 1988. "Blaming the Patient." In *Alcoholism: Origin and Outcome*. New York: Raven Press.

Rubington, Earl. 1971. "The Changing Skid Row Scene." *Quarterly Journal of Studies on Alcohol* 32:123-35.

Rule, Brendan Gail; and Dorothy Phillips. 1973. "Responsibility Versus Illness Models of Alcoholism: Effects on Attitudes Toward an Alcoholic." *Quarterly Journal of Studies on Alcohol* 34:489-95.

Russell, James A.; and Albert Mehrabian. 1975. "The Mediating Role of Emotions in Alcohol Use." *Journal of Studies on Alcohol* 36, no. 11 :1508-36.

Rychtarik, Robert; G. Gerard J. Connors; Kurt H. Dermen; and Paul R. Stasiewicz. 2000. "Alcoholics Anonymous and the Use of Medications to Prevent Relapse: An Anonymous Survey of Members Attitudes." *Journal of Studies on Alcohol* 61, no. 1:134-38.

Sarantakos, Sotirios. 1998. Social Research. South Yarra: MacMillan Education Australia.

Schlesinger, Stephen E. and Lawrence K. Hoberg. 1988. *Taking Charge*. New York: Simon and Schuster.

Schuckit, Marc. 1980. "Self Rating of Alcohol Intoxication by Young Men With and Without Family Histories of Alcoholism." *Journal of Studies on Alcohol* 41, no. 3:242-49.

_____. 1982. "A Study of Young Men With Alcohol Close Relatives." *American Journal of Psychiatry* 139, no. 6:791-94.

_____. 1983. Alcoholic Men With No Alcoholic First-Degree Relatives." *American Journal of Psychiatry* 140, no. 4:439-43.

_____. 1984. "Subjective Responses to Alcohol in Sons of Alcoholics and Control Subjects." *Archives of General Psychiatry* 41, no. 9:879-84.

_____. 1985. "Studies of Populations at High Risk for Alcoholism." *Psychiatric Developments* 3: 31-63.

_____. 1987. Studies of Populations of High Risk for Future Development of Alcoholism. Genetics and Alcoholism: 83-96

_____. 1994. "A Clinical Model of Genetic Influences in Alcohol Dependence." *Journal of Studies on Alcohol* 55, no. 1:5-17.

Schuckit, Marc. 1998. "Biological, Psychological and Environmental Predictors of the Alcoholism Risk: A Longitudinal Study." *Journal of Studies on Alcohol* 59, no. 5:485-94.

_____. Schuckit, Marc; Donald A. Goodwin; and George Winokur. 1972. "A Study of Alcoholism in Half Siblings." *American Journal of Psychiatry* 128, no. 3:122-25.

Schuckit, Marc; Jeffrey L. Klein; and Geoffrey R. Twitchell. 1995. "The Misclassification of Family History Status in Studies of Children of Alcoholics." *Journal of Studies on Alcohol* 56, no. 1:47-50.

Schuckit, Marc; John W. Tsuang; Robert M. Anthenelli; Jayson Tipp; and John I. Nurnberger. 1996. "Alcohol Challenges in Young Men from Alcoholic Pedigrees and Control Families: A Report from the COGA Project." *Journal of Studies on Alcohol* 57, no. 4: 368-77.

Schuckit, Marc; Jayson E. Tipp; Tom L. Smith; Gerhard A. Wiesbeck; and Jelger Kalmijn. 1997. "The Relationship Between Self-Rating of the Effects of Alcohol and Alcohol Challenge Results in Ninety-Eight Young Men." *Journal of Studies on Alcohol* 58, no. 4: 397-404.

Schuckit, Marc; and Tom L. Smith. 1997. "Assessing the Risk for Alcoholism among Sons of Alcoholics." *Journal of Studies on Alcohol* 58, no. 2:141-45.

Searles, John S.; M. W. Perrine; James C. Mundt; and John E. Helzer, 1995. "Self Report of Drinking Using Touch-Tone Telephone: Extending the Limits of Reliable Daily Contact." *Journal of Studies on Alcohol* 56, no. 4:375-81.

Segrin, Chris; and Michelle Mize Menees. 1996. "The Impact of Coping Styles and Family Communication on the Social Skills of Children of Alcoholics." *Journal of Studies on Alcohol* 57, no. 1:29-33.

Seldin, Nathan E. 1972. "The Family of the Addict: A Review of the Literature." *International Journal of the Addictions* 7, no. 1:97-107.

Selzer, Melvin L. 1971. "The Michigan Alcoholism Screening Test: The Quest for a New Diagnostic Instrument." *American Journal of Psychiatry* 127, pt. 2:1653-58.

Selzer, Melvin; Vinokur, Amiram; and Rooijen Louis van. 1975. "A Self-Administered Short Michigan Alcoholism Screening Test (SMAST). *Journal of Studies on Alcohol* 36, no. 1 :117-26.

Senchak, Marilyn; Brian W. Greene; Ann Marie Carroll; and Kenneth E. Leonard. 1996. "Global, Behavioral and Self-Ratings of Interpersonal Skills among Adult Children of Alcoholic, Divorced and Control Parents." *Journal of Studies on Alcohol* 57, no. 6:638-45.

Seppa, Kaija; Timo Pitkäjärvi; and Pekka Sillanaukee. 1999. "Alcohol Consumption Profile by Time in Middle-Aged Men: A Longitudinal Study Based on Three Different Diagnostic Instruments." *Alcohol and Alcoholism* 34, no. 1:65-70.

Sher, Kenneth J.; Beth S. Gershuny; Lizette Peterson; and Gail Raskin. 1997. "The Role of Childhood Stressors in the Intergenerational Transmission of Alcohol Use Disorders." *Journal of Studies on Alcohol* 58, no. 4:414-27.

Shore, Elsie R. 1997. "The Relationship of Gender Balance at Work, Family Responsibilities and Workplace Characteristics to Drinking among Male and Female Attorneys." *Journal of Studies on Alcohol* 58, no. 3:297-302.

Silverman, David L. 1971. *The Theory of Organizations.* Heinemann New York: Basic Books.

Sitharthan, T.; D.J. Kavanagh; and G. Sayer. 1996. "Moderating Drinking by Correspondence: An Evaluation of a New Method of Intervention." *Addiction* 91, no. 3:345-55.

Sitomer, Curtis J. 1988. "Alcoholism as a Disease: A Bad Call?" *Christian Science Monitor*, July 18. 1+ California: The Christian Science Publishing Society.

Skog, Ole-Jørgen. 1985. "The Collectivity of Drinking Cultures: A Theory of the Distribution of Alcohol Consumption." *British Journal of Addiction* 80:83-95.

_____. 2000. "An Experimental Study of a Change from Over-the-Counter to Self-Service Sales of Alcohol Beverages in Monopoly Outlets." *Journal of Studies on Alcohol* 61, no. 1:95-100.

Skolnick, Jerome H. 1980. *The Stumbling Block: A Sociological Study of the Relationship Between Selected Religious Norms and Drinking Behavior*. New York: Arno Press.

Smith, Christopher J. 1986. "The Geography of Drinking." *Focus* 36, no. 4 :16-23.

Snyder, Charles. 1958. *Alcohol and the Jews*. Southern Illinois University Press, Feffer and Simons.

Sobell, Mark B.; and Linda C. Sobell. 1978. "The Nature of Alcohol Problems." Chapter 1 in *Behavioral Treatment of Alcoholic Problems*. New York: Plenum Press.

Sobell, Mark B.; Tony Toneatto; and Gloria I. Leo. 1993. Severely Dependent Alcohol Abusers May be Vulnerable to Alcohol Cues in Television Programs." *Journal of Studies on Alcohol* 54, no. 1:85-91.

Stanton, Duncan M. 1979. "Family Treatment Approaches to Drug Abuse Problems: A Review." *Family Process*: 251-79.

Stanton, Duncan M.; Thomas C. Todd; David B. Heard; Sam Kirschner; Jerry I. Kleiman; David T. Mowatt; Paul Riley; Samuel M. Scott; and John M. Van Deusen. 1978. "Heroin Addiction as a Family Phenomenon: A New Conceptual Model." *American Journal of Drug and Alcohol Abuse* 5, no. 2:125-50.

Steffen, John J.; Peter E. Nathan; and H. Augustus Taylor. 1974. "Tension- Reducing Effects of Alcohol: Further Evidence and Some Methodological Considerations." *Journal of Abnormal Psychology* 83, no. 5:542-47.

Steinglass, Peter. 1976. "Experimenting with Family Treatment Approaches to Alcoholism, 1950-1975: A Review." *Family Process* 15:97-117.

Steinglass, Peter; Linda A. Bennett; Steven J. Wolin; and David Reiss. 1987. *The Alcoholic Family*. New York: Basic Books.

Stockwell, Tim; Ray Hodgson; and Howard Rankin. 1982. "Tension Reduction and the Effects of Prolonged Alcohol Consumption." *British Journal of Addiction* 77: 65-73.

Stoduto, Gina; Edward M. Adlaf; and Robert E. Mann. 1998. "Adolescents, Bush parties and Drinking-Driving." *Journal of Studies on Alcohol* 59, no. 5: 544-48.

Strauss, Robert. 1988. "Interdisciplinary Biobehavioral Research on Alcohol Problems: A Concept Whose Time Has Come." In *Alcoholism Etiology and Treatment: Issues for Theory and Practice,* edited by Bernard Segal, 33-46. New York: Haworth Press.

Strauss, In Segrin, Chris; and Michelle Mize Menees. 1996. "The Impact of Coping Styles and Family Communication on the Social Skills of Children of Alcoholics." *Journal of Studies on Alcohol* 57, no.1:29-33.

Susser, Mervyn. 1985. "Separating Heredity and Environment." *American Journal of Preventive Medicine* 1, no. 2:5-22.

Talashek, Marie L. 1987. "Parental Alcoholism and Adolescent Ego Identity." *Journal of Community Health Nursing* 4, no. 4:211-22.

Tarter, Ralph E.; and Dorothea U. Schneider. 1976. "Models and Theories of Alcoholism." In *Alcoholism*, edited by Ralph E. Tarter and Arthur A. Sugarman. New York: Addison-Wesley Publishing.

Tarter, Ralph E.; and Kathleen Edwards. 1988. "Psychological Factors Associated with the Risk for Alcoholism." *Alcoholism: Clinical and Experimental Research* 12, no. 4:471-80.

Tarter, Ralph E. 1976. "Empirical Investigations of Psychological Deficit." In *Alcoholism: Interdisciplinary Approaches to an Enduring Problem*, edited by Ralph E. Tarter and A. Arthur Sugarman, 359-93. Massachusetts: Addison-Wesley Publishing.

Teitelbaum, Lesley; and Brian Mullen. 2000. "The Validity of the MAST in Psychiatric Settings: A Meta-Analytic Integration." *Journal of Studies on Alcohol* 61, no. 2:254-61.

Terhune, William B. 1968. *The Safe Way to Drink: How to Prevent Alcohol Problems Before they Start.* New York: William Morrow.

Tracy, Joseph I.; and Marsha E. Bates, 1994. "Models of Functional Organization as a Method for Detecting Cognitive Deficits: Data from a Sample of Social Drinkers." *Journal of Studies on Alcohol* 55, no. 6:726-38.

Trice, Harrison M.; and Michael Paul Roman. 1969-70. "Delabeling, Relabeling, and Alcoholics Anonymous." *Social Problems* 17:538-46.

Tweed, Sandra H.; and Carol D. Ryff, 1991. "Adult Children of Alcoholics: Profiles of Wellness amidst Distress." *Journal of Studies on Alcohol* 52, no. 2:133-41.

Vannicelli, Marsha-Lee. 1972. "Mood and Self-Perception of Alcoholics when Sober and Intoxicated: I. Mood Change. II. Accuracy of Self-Prediction." *Quarterly Journal of Studies on Alcohol* 33:341-57.

Vogel-Sprott, Muriel. 1997. "Is Behavioral Tolerance Learned? *Alcohol Health and Research World* 21, no. 2:161-68.

Volk, Robert J.; Jeffrey R. Steinbauer; and Scott B. Cantor. 1996. "Patient Factors Influencing Variation in the Use of Preventive Interventions for Alcohol Abuse by Primary Care Physicians." *Journal of Studies on Alcohol* 57, no. 2:203-209.

Wall, Anne-Marie; Riley E. Hinson; and Sherry A. McKee. 1998. "Alcohol Outcome Expectancies, Attitudes toward Drinking and the Theory of Planned Behavior." *Journal of Studies on Alcohol* 59, no. 4: 409-19.

Walsh, B.M. 1985. "Production of and International Trade in Alcoholic Drinks: Possible Public Health Implications." In *Alcohol Policies,* edited by Marcus Grant. Geneva: World Health Organization.

Walsh, Diana Chapman. 1989. "Social Responses to Substance Abuse." In *Handbook of Medical Sociology,* edited by Howard E. Freeman, Sol Levine and Leo G. Reeder, 128-42. New Jersey: Prentice Hall.

_____. 1990. "The Shifting Boundaries of Alcohol Policy." *Health Affairs.* Summer: 47-62.

Walsh, Diana Chapman; Philip J. Cook; Karen Davis; Marcus Grant; Pekka Sulkunen; George E. Vaillant; and Thomas L. Delbanco, 1989. "The Cultural Dimensions of Alcohol Policy Worldwide." *Health Affairs,* : 48-61.

Ward, David. 1980. *Alcoholism: Introduction to Theory and Treatment.* Iowa: Kendall/Hunt Publishing Company.

Wechsler, Henry; Barbara Moeykens; Andrea Davenport; Sonia Castillo; and Jeffrey Hansen. 1995. "The Adverse Impact of Heavy Episodic Drinkers on Other College Students." *Journal of Studies on Alcohol* 56, no. 6:628-34.

Weed, Nathan C.; James N. Butcher; and Carolyn L. Williams. 1994. "Development of MMPI-A Alcohol/Drug Problem Scales." *Journal of Studies in Alcohol* 55, no. 3:296-302.

Weiner, Carolyn L. 1981. *The Politics of Alcoholism*. New Jersey: Transaction Books.

Wekesser, Carol. 1994. *Alcohol–Current Controversies*. California: Greenhaven Press.

Westermeyer, Joseph. 1974. "Alcoholism from the Cross-Cultural Perspective: A Review and Critique of Clinical Studies." *American Journal of Drug and Alcohol Abuse* 1, no. 1:89-105.

White, Helene Raskin. 1985. "Sociological Theories of the Etiology of Alcoholism." In *Alcohol, Science and Society Revisited,* edited by Edith Gomberg, Helene White and John Carpenter, 205-29. New Jersey: University of Michigan Press.

Widom, Cathy, Timothy Ireland; and Patricia J. Glynn, 1995. "Alcohol Abuse in Abused and Neglected Children Followed-up: Are They at Increased Risk? *Journal of Studies of Alcohol* 56, no. 2:207-17.

Wilkins, R.H. 1974. *The Hidden Alcoholic in General Practice*. London: Eleck Science.

Williams, E.Y. 1950. The Anxiety Syndrome in Alcoholism." *Psychiatric Quarterly* 24, no. 1:782-87.

Williams, Roger J. 1947. "The Etiology of Alcoholism: A Working Hypothesis Involving the Interplay of Hereditary and Environmental Factors." *Quarterly Journal of Studies on Alcohol* 7, no. 4:567-87.

Williams, Timothy P; and Robert P. Lillis. 1986. "Changes in Alcohol Consumption by 18-year-Olds Following an Increase in New York State's Purchase Age to 19." *Journal of Studies on Alcohol.* 47, no. 4:290-96.

Wilsnack, Sharon C.; Nancy D. Vogeltanz; Albert D. Klassen; and Harris T. Robert. 1997. "Childhood Sexual Abuse and Women's Substance Abuse: National Survey Findings." *Journal of Studies on Alcohol* 58, no. 3:264-71.

Wilson, Terrence G. 1978. In *Alcoholism: New Directions in Behavioral Research and Treatment*, edited by Peter E. Nathan, G. Alan Marlatt and Tor LØberg. New York: Plenum Press.

Wilson, Terence G.; David B. Abrams; and Thomas R. Lipscomb. 1980. "Effects of Intoxification Levels and Drinking Pattern on Social Anxiety in Men." *Journal of Studies on Alcohol* 41, no. 3: 250-64.

Windle, Michael. 1994. "Characteristics of Alcoholics who Attempted Suicide: Co-Occurring Disorders and Personality Differences with a Sample of Male Vietnam Era Veterans." *Journal of Studies on Alcohol* 55, no. 5:571-77.

_____. 1996. "An Alcohol Involvement Typology for Adolescents: Convergent Validity and Longitudinal Stability." *Journal of Studies on Alcohol* 57, no. 6:627-37.

_____. 1999. "Psychopathy and Antisocial Personality Disorder among Alcoholic Inpatients." *Journal of Studies on Alcohol* 60, no. 3:330-36.

Wolfgang, Lori A., ed. 1997. "Charting Recent Progress: Advances in Alcoholic Research." *Alcohol Health and Research World* 21, no. 4: 277-86.

Wood, Phillip K.; Kenneth J. Sher; Darin J. Erickson; and Kurt A. Debord. 1997. "Predicting Academic Problems in College from Freshman Alcohol Involvement." *Journal of Studies on Alcohol* 58, no. 2:200-210.

Yalisove, Daniel. 1998. "The Origins and Evolution of the Disease Concept of Treatment." *Journal of Studies on Alcohol* 59, no. 4 : 469-76.

Yamazaki, S. 1996. "Children of Alcoholics Screening Test (CAST) and Influence of Parents' Drinking on Their Children." Nippon Kashu Eisei Zasshi – *Japanese Journal of Public Health* 43, no. 2:45-54.

Yersin, Bertrand; Yves Trisconi; Fred Paccaud; Felix Gutzwiller; and Pierre Magnenat. 1989. "Accuracy of the Michigan Alcoholism Screening Test for Screening of Alcoholism in Patients of a Medical Department." *Archive of Internal Medicine* 149:2071-74.

Zucker, Robert A. 1979. "Developmental Aspects of Drinking Through the Young Adult Years." In *Youth, Alcohol and Social Policy*, edited by Howard T. Blane and Morris E. Chafetz, 91-146. New York: Plenum Press.

AUTHOR INDEX

SUBJECT INDEX